THE KNOWLEDGE OF GOD

THE KNOWLEDGE OF GOD

Essays on God, Christ, and Church

Michael Allen

t&tclark
LONDON • NEW YORK • OXFORD • NEW DELHI • SYDNEY

T&T CLARK
Bloomsbury Publishing Plc
50 Bedford Square, London, WC1B 3DP, UK
1385 Broadway, New York, NY 10018, USA
29 Earlsfort Terrace, Dublin 2, Ireland

BLOOMSBURY, T&T CLARK and the T&T Clark logo are
trademarks of Bloomsbury Publishing Plc

First published in Great Britain 2022
Paperback edition published 2023

A catalogue record for this book is available from the British Library.

Library of Congress Cataloging-in-Publication Data
Names: Allen, Michael, 1981-author.
Title: The knowledge of God : essays on God, Christ and church / Michael Allen.
Description: London ; New York : T&T Clark, 2022. | Includes bibliographical references
and index. | Identifiers: LCCN 2021029029 (print) | LCCN 2021029030 (ebook) |
ISBN 9780567699374 (hb) | ISBN 9780567699411 (paperback) | ISBN 9780567699381
(epdf) | ISBN 9780567699404 (epub)
Subjects: LCSH: God (Christianity) | Jesus Christ–Person and
offices. | Church. | LCGFT: Essays.
Classification: LCC BT103 .A425 2022 (print) | LCC BT103 (ebook) | DDC 231–dc23
LC record available at https://lccn.loc.gov/2021029029
LC ebook record available at https://lccn.loc.gov/2021029030

ISBN: HB: 978-0-5676-9937-4
        PB: 978-0-5676-9941-1
        ePDF: 978-0-5676-9938-1
        ePUB: 978-0-5676-9940-4

Typeset by Integra Software Services Pvt. Ltd.

To find out more about our authors and books visit www.bloomsbury.com
and sign up for our newsletters.

CONTENTS

PREFACE: GOD, GOSPEL, AND THE CATHOLIC CHURCH

This collection serves as a non-identical twin volume alongside *The Fear of the Lord: Essays on Theological Method*. Whereas that book addresses matters of theological prolegomena, the present text turns to material topics of theological concern: God, Christ, and the character of human communion found with God and one another. While one book turns methodological and the other foregrounds the material, it is hoped that readers who happen to consider them alongside one another will observe commonalities: the material judgments actually shape the purportedly prolegomenal postures, whereas the methodological missives help clarify the sort of analysis being offered in these topical studies. It is in knowing God that one learns more of how one best may know God.

Both volumes take their titles from Solomon's guidance: "My son, if you receive my words and treasure up my commandments with you, making your ear attentive to wisdom and inclining your heart to understanding; yes, if you call out for insight and raise your voice for understanding, if you seek it like silver and search for it as for hidden treasures, then you will understand the fear of the LORD and find the knowledge of God" (Prov. 2.1-5). This volume explores that knowledge of God found by the son who treasures the wisdom of his posterity, attends to scriptural wisdom, inclines virtuously unto the Lord's self-presentation, and prayerfully pursues the triune God as for hidden treasure. In so doing, these chapters truly seek to know God and to convey something of that knowledge more fully. These chapters focus largely on several thematic clusters: God, Christ, and church. In each case, however, they are about God. When describing incarnation or *ekklesia*, they are just as theological in attention as when they consider Trinity directly.

Their mode of argument varies somewhat, with some essays focusing on historical retrieval and others tilting in the direction of sustained exegetical commentary. It should be obvious that they do not purport to cover the full range of topics needed to provide a dogmatic account of the triune God or of Jesus Christ or of the doctrine of the church. They are preparatory and exploratory. I have sought to avoid repeating arguments offered in my monographs.[1] And yet, they do evince an overlapping set of concerns regarding the nature of Christian systematic theology and its need to attend patiently to tasks of interpretive, historical, and

---

1. Of closest pertinence on matters theological, Christological, and ecclesiological, see Michael Allen, *Justification and the Gospel: Understanding the Contexts and Its Controversies* (Grand Rapids, MI: Baker Academic, 2013), esp. chs. 3 and 6; Michael Allen, *Sanctification* (New Studies in Dogmatics; Grand Rapids, MI: Zondervan Academic, 2017), esp. chs. 2 and 5; Michael Allen, *Grounded in Heaven: Re-centering Christian Life and Hope in God* (Grand Rapids, MI: Eerdmans, 2018), esp. ch. 2.

analytical work. Systematic questions regarding the breadth, priorities, and coherence of biblical teaching appear repeatedly throughout them. In that regard, I do offer them as practiced examples of the methodological approach sketched in the varied chapters found in *The Fear of the Lord*.

The first five chapters consider the nature of the triune God. "The Central Dogma" explores the concept of theocentrism, reflecting on how it might be that Reformed theology simultaneously holds a catholic doctrine of God and yet is most distinguished by its doctrine of God. In so doing it turns to the significance of contemplating God (a doctrine of the Trinity) and also viewing other realities—all of them—in a theocentric manner (a Trinitarian theology of *x*, *y*, or *z*). The fifth chapter on "Trinity: Contemplative and Practical Wisdom" returns to that duality of theological tasks, reading various theological trends in the last century through their engagement of the scriptural economy of the triune God's works and the explanatory power found in offering a Trinitarian reading of other realities. Two chapters offer historical and exegetical analysis of Exod. 3:14, seeking to perceive how it prompts engagement of scripture and metaphysics together. Surely no other biblical passage has so arrested my attention as this one. A chapter on divine fullness presents an occasion for reflecting on an attribute of God that seems formally to share much with wider Greek thought, albeit expressed in a distinctively Christian and Trinitarian manner. I have discovered in this process of research that the so-called theism of the Christian tradition (oft termed "classical theism" or "classical Trinitarianism") has underappreciated exegetical roots, significantly textured engagement with non-Christian philosophy, and functions hand in glove with the full range of Christian teaching. By contrast, revisions to that approach of Trinitarian theism invariably gain a smaller exegetical footing, a more homogenous approach to extra-biblical resources (either contrastively or correlatively), and a widespread modification of many more *loci* than would be initially gauged. Orthodox or creedal theology actually alerts one to the mystery of the faith, whereas revisions to that approach tend to smooth off those challenging edges in search of a more pacific approach.

The next five chapters turn to Christology, attending to the mystery of the incarnation from various vantage points. My first book, *The Christ's Faith*, considered Christology, taking a debate localized to Pauline studies (the *pistis christou* debate) and exploring its theological entailments more broadly. In particular, I sought to consider the reality of the Christ's faith by ranging more widely to attend to the humanity of Christ, by taking in anthropological, metaphysical, and soteriological matters. I have since felt impelled to follow up, sometimes expanding that argument further and sometimes modifying elements therein.[2] I remain convinced that perceiving Christ well means no less than exploring his life as God, his full human experience, his covenantal context, and

2. See also "'From the Time He Took the Form of a Servant': The Christ's Pilgrimage of Faith," *International Journal of Systematic Theology* 16, no. 2 (2014): 4–24; repr. in *Justification and the Gospel*, ch. 3.

his soteriological action on behalf of his people. Chapters here span the inner life of the triune God, the nature of the Son of God's humanity as assumed in the incarnation, and the way in which covenant and the fourfold state of humanity serve as registers within which to make sense of human need and Christ's grace. In each of these explorations, systematic reflection summons us to more, affirming certain truths and working hard to coordinate them with other significant biblical teachings. Breadth, proportion, and integration cannot be ignored, and they don't get noticed intuitively apart from disciplined formation in the practice of Christian doctrine. My goal in each of these explorations is to help tend more attentively and patiently to this mystery of the faith.

Chapter 6 considers the Son's personal relation to the Father within the triune life, considering "Eternal Generation after Barth." In so doing, I assess the influence of Karl Barth on the way in which the doctrine of the triune relations has been approached via the economy of the gospel of the electing God. The chapter addresses how the incarnate Son's relation to his heavenly Father does and does not relate to the Son's generation eternally of his Father. The next chapter turns to expand and to modify my earlier argument (initially in chapter 4 of *The Christ's Faith*) regarding the contemporary debate about the fallen or unfallen flesh assumed by Christ; "Christ's Humanity" adds nuance to that debate by injecting not one but two affirmations into those discussions. Chapter 8, written with my colleague Scott R. Swain, also explores how the Son's earthly obedience reveals something (though not everything) of his eternal life with God the Father.[3] Recent years have seen concern over contemporary subordination, an important correction though one which always threatens to prompt overreactions. Polemical theology can quickly turn parasitic if proportionality and breadth are not kept close to hand as systematic principles. Chapter 9 explores covenant language and how it serves to provide categories for understanding humanity and, by extension, the incarnate human redeemer named Jesus of Nazareth. Chapter 10 surveys four ways in which Scripture depicts humans (in creation, fall, grace, and glory), seeking to push against foreshortened accounts that wrongly homogenize language of "identity" for supposedly Augustinian or Christological reasons. These last two chapters explore Christology by way of its covenantal and anthropological settings, in both cases pushing back against foreshortened analyses that fail to take in the full register of biblical and theological teaching.

Finally, three chapters begin to sketch a doctrine of the church. Here theology proper and Christology are not left behind; a catholic and Reformed approach to ecclesiology will remain vigilant in seeing that Trinitarian and Christological teaching functions in an operative way. An analysis of the invisibility of the church begins and grounds its argument by tending to the singular holiness of the God of the church. In so doing, Chapter 10 seeks to recover the invisibility of the church as a matter of Trinitarian perception that has been frequently maligned or

---

3. It is worth noting that the title is "The Obedience of the Eternal Son" rather than "The Eternal Obedience of the Son." Let the reader understand.

eclipsed in the empirically and ethnographically dominated turn in more recent ecclesiology. Next, a chapter on the catholicity of the church roots that theme in the work of Christ and the promise of his gospel. In both cases, different theological programs (whether of more historicist Trinitarianisms or of Anglo-Catholicism, respectively) result in distinct ecclesiologies. Reformed theology has only recently begun to address the foment of modern ecclesiological debates (especially in the impressive works of John Webster, Gary Badcock, Michael Horton, and Robert J. Sherman), but it remains yet to be explored still more broadly and, in so doing, to offer a more fulsome alternative to the impressively articulated Anglo-Catholic schematics offered decades ago by Michael Ramsey or E. L. Mascall. These chapters help identify areas of overlapping concern as well as directions for more focused Reformed construction in future work. Finally, I seek to deploy Augustine's teaching on the *totus Christus* as a way of doing two things: first, viewing the church in light of Christology and theology proper; and, second, exploring ways in which one's ecclesiology manifests itself in the prayer life of a resurrected community. The way Christ's people pray his Psalms says much about what sort of people they in fact are and even more about what sort of Head he is for his Body.

These studies are testimonies on the way. A fuller account of each of these (and other) topics remains to be offered in a multivolume systematic theology. These chapters do present an integrated approach that is being put to work toward that larger project. So these are studies along the path. Here too it is instructive that Proverbs 2 not only speaks of finding God's knowledge but also of "walk[ing] in the way of the good and keep[ing] to the paths of the righteous" (2.20), reminding readers that wisdom demands a pilgrimage and, therefore, calls for patient persistence in following the path.

*****

This collection of essays and its sibling (*The Fear of the Lord: Essays on Theological Method*) gather studies prepared over the course of the last fifteen years. I have resisted the urge to rewrite and refashion, modifying only by updating bibliographic references and correcting formatting or typos. My teaching assistant, Angel Roman-Diaz, helped with preparing the essays for production. My colleague, John Muether, prepared the index. I thank a host of publications for permission to republish material here: *International Journal of Systematic Theology*, *European Journal of Theology*, *Trinity Journal*, *Reformed Faith & Practice*, *Journal of Theological Interpretation*, *Pro Ecclesia*, and Zondervan Academic. Various friends and colleagues read chapters on different occasions, and I have noted them where I can. I should especially highlight three people in particular: Wesley Hill, Jonathan Linebaugh, and Scott Swain, who contribute to my ongoing research and writing in all manner of ways. I conclude by saying that it remains a pleasure to work with Anna Turton and the Bloomsbury team and an honor to publish again with T&T Clark, now in their 200th year of publishing Christian theology.

Ascension Day 2021
Oviedo

Chapter 1

THE CENTRAL DOGMA: ORDER AND PRINCIPLES OF REFORMED CATHOLICITY

Reformed catholicity can easily appear aesthetic, regarding one's preference for the antique or the exotic. Perhaps a bit more substantively, reformed catholicity can be identified as a methodological or formal program, a modus operandi for doing theology today. I want to explore its material grounds, however, by reflecting on how Reformed theology relates to the catholic faith. An orienting question might be: What is most distinctive about Reformed theology? The most formatively unique facet of Reformed theology is its doctrine of God, and yet the Reformed doctrine of God must be defined as a non-innovative catholic doctrine of God. How can both statements be true? To crack this nut, I will explore the idea of central dogmas and their recent demise as well as analyze a path toward making sense of the root of Reformed theology in its deeper catholic commitment. The Reformed tradition has taken a catholic doctrine of God and reformed Christian doctrine by applying it more synthetically, that is, more broadly and consistently. By analyzing the center of Reformed theology in the doctrine of God, the principled roots of reformed catholic theological practice can be better appreciated.

The Demise of the Central Dogma

First, we ought to acknowledge the oddity of a Reformed theologian commending the notion of a central dogma today. It was not always an odd claim. Historians of doctrine long spoke of the significance of central dogmas from the nineteenth to the mid-twentieth century. Sometimes Lutheranism was identified as a theological movement rooted in the principle of justification by faith alone, and even today analyses of Lutheranism that follow the early-twentieth-century Luther renaissance or the more recent Radical Lutheran tilt will regularly describe justification by faith alone as a *discrimen* for all theology or of the law-gospel distinction as an epistemic rule for all theologizing.[1] By contrast, modern historians have suggested different central dogmas at the heart of the Reformed tradition. Many in the nineteenth century identified predestination/election as the heart of the Reformed system.

---

1. Mark Mattes, *The Role of Justification in Contemporary Theology* (Grand Rapids, MI: Eerdmans, 2004), 177–90.

Alexander Schweizer was pivotal in this trend, arguing that predestination was a speculative element of the doctrine of God from which the Reformed speculatively deduced other doctrinal claims.[2] Weber followed suit, and later interpreters in the mid-twentieth century would pair these earlier historiographic approaches with a propensity to identify central dogmas by means of literary placement (e.g., judging the movement of predestination from book 1 to book 3 of Calvin's *Institutes* to have architectonic significance).[3] In the twentieth century, others turned to union with Christ as a purported central dogma at least of Calvin's theology, if not of later declensions.[4]

In recent years Richard Muller has challenged this methodology. He has challenged the historiographic claims about early Reformed theological systems and later Reformed Orthodox dogmatics more broadly. He differentiates between deductive derivation of doctrines from some central dogma and causal connections of various topics to God.

> Whereas many of the theologies of the seventeenth century follow an *a priori* or "synthetic" model of exposition, this pattern of discourse does not represent a series of logical deductions of doctrinal topics or arguments one from the other: neither predestination nor any other doctrine serves as a central pivot of system or overarching motif controlling other doctrines. Both in the descriptions of method found in the Reformed orthodox prolegomena and in the subsequent presentation of the topics of theology, what is evident is not a model of deduction from controlling principles but a model in which the topics traditionally elicited in the course of exegesis are lined out in a suitable order or teaching and the doctrine developed by means of the application of a large-scale hermeneutic involving, for the most part the collation and comparison of biblical texts in the light of theological concerns and the use of ancillary tools, including logic and philosophy.[5]

Muller does not herein rebut all such language about centrality or prioritization, but he pushes back strongly upon the notion of a synthetic system which has been deduced from an epistemic principle. He regularly references the existence of a material principle, but he points to the exegetical art as leading where logical deduction might otherwise be purported to play a generative role. His study of the

---

2. Alexander Schweizer, *Centraldogma*, vol. 1, 40; on "deductive" language, see esp. Schweizer, *Glaubenslehre*, vol. 1, 96–101.

3. Hans Emil Weber, *Reformation, Orthodoxie, and Rationalismus*, vol. 2 (Gütersloh: C. Bertelsmann, 1951), 63–73, 98–128.

4. See, e.g., Charles Partee, "Calvin's Central Dogma Again," *The Sixteenth Century Journal* 18, no. 2 (Summer 1987): 191–200.

5. Richard A. Muller, *Post-Reformation Reformed Dogmatics: The Rise and Development of Reformed Orthodoxy, ca. 1520 to ca. 1725*, vol. 1: *Prolegomena to Theology* (2nd ed.; Grand Rapids, MI: Baker Academic, 2003), 125.

formation of Calvin's *Institutes* and its order of teaching (*ordo docendi*) is no small part of his revision to scholarship in as much as he shows the way in which Romans helped provide a common places (*loci communes*) guide to the major topics of theology (a lesson learned from his friend Melanchthon).[6] Far more might be said regarding the details here, but suffice it to say that those engaging early and high Reformed scholastic theology do so with our antennae up regarding the dangers of speculative central dogmas.

Herman Bavinck on the Root of Calvinism

Amidst the decades of scholars searching for the center, in Paul and the canon and, yes, also in Reformed dogmatics, we find the theological witness of Herman Bavinck. In 1894 Bavinck contributed an essay entitled "The Future of Calvinism" to the *Presbyterian & Reformed Review*. To address what future might await this tradition, he was impelled to define and to root that tradition in something deeper than religious ephemera and more substantive than even its most superstar luminaries. So he said this:

> The root principle of this Calvinism is the confession of God's absolute sovereignty.
> Not one special attribute of God, for instance His love or justice, His holiness or
> equity, but God Himself as such in the unity of all His attributes and perfection
> of His entire Being is the point of departure for the thinking and acting of the
> Calvinist. From this root principle everything that is specifically Reformed may
> be derived and explained. It was this that led to the sharp distinction between
> what is God's and creature's, to belief in the sole authority of the Holy Scriptures,
> in the all-sufficiency of Christ and His word, in the omnipotence of the work of
> grace. Hence also the sharp distinction between the divine and human in the
> Person and the two natures of Christ, between the external internal call, between
> the sign and the matter signified in the sacrament. From this source likewise
> sprang the doctrine of the absolute dependence of the creature, as it is expressed
> in the Calvinistic confessions in regard to providence, foreordination, election,
> the inability of man. By this principle also the Calvinist was led to the use of that
> through-going consistent theological method, which distinguishes him from
> Romanist and other Protestant theologians.

Bavinck speaks here of "God Himself as such" as a "point of departure for the thinking and acting of the Calvinist." He speaks "not [of] one special attribute of

---

6. Richard A. Muller, "*Ordo docendi*: Melanchthon and the Organization of Calvin's Institutes, 1536–1543," in *Melanchthon in Europe: His Work and Influence beyond Wittenberg* (ed. Karin Maag; Grand Rapids: Baker Book House, 1999), 123–40; repr. in *The Unaccommodated Calvin: Studies in the Foundation of a Theological Tradition* (Oxford Studies in Historical Theology; New York: Oxford University Press, 2000), 118–39.

God, for instance His love or justice, His holiness or equity, but [of] God Himself as such in the unity of all His attributes and perfection of His entire Being [a]s the point of departure for the thinking and acting of the Calvinist." The simple fullness of the triune God is the root of Calvinist or Reformed faith and practice. He terms this a "point of departure" and says also that "from this root principle everything that is specifically Reformed may be derived and explained." God as such is the ontological principle of all Reformed faith and practice.

Lest we think it wrong-footed enough to search for a center to one's theology, we may be alarmed to hear Bavinck pressing still farther. He relates this "root principle" to more than merely a doctrinal system:

> Not only in the whole range of his theology, but also outside of this, in every sphere of life and science, his effort aims at the recognition and maintenance of God as God over against all creatures. In the work of creation and regeneration, in sin and grace, in Adam and Christ, in the Church and the sacraments, it is in each case God who reveals and upholds His sovereignty and leads it to triumph notwithstanding all disregard and resistance. There is something heroic and grand and imposing in this Calvinistic conception. Viewed in its light the whole course of history becomes a gigantic contest, in which God carries through His sovereignty, and makes it, like a mountain stream, overcome all resistance in the end, bringing the creature to a willing or unwilling, but in either case unqualified, recognition of His divine glory. From all things are, and accordingly they all return to Him. He is God and remains God now and forever; Jehovah, the Being, the one that was and is and that is to come.

Observe that "every sphere" functions as space and time for recognizing and maintaining "God as God over against all creatures." The fullness of the Creator–creature distinction echoes into each sphere.

A skeptic might understandably ask if this kind of God-centered focus does not fall short of giving a vibrant account of humanity and creation more broadly in its integrity, much less as bearing dignity and agential responsibility. Bavinck imagines such an objection and seeks to cut it off at its knees.

> For this reason the Calvinist in all things recurs upon God, and does not rest satisfied before he has traced back everything to the sovereign good-pleasure of God as its ultimate and deepest cause. He never loses himself in the appearance of things, but penetrates to their realities. Behind the phenomena he searches for the noumena, the things that are not seen, from which the things visible have been born. He does not take his stand in the midst of history, but out of time ascends into the heights of eternity. History is naught but the gradual unfolding of what to God is an eternal present. For his heart, his thinking, his life, the Calvinist cannot find rest in these terrestrial things, the sphere of what is becoming, changing, forever passing by. From the process of salvation he

therefore recurs upon the decree of salvation, from history to the idea. He does not remain in the outer court of the temple, but seeks to enter into the innermost sanctuary.[7]

The crucial sentence notes that "He never loses himself in the appearance of things, but penetrates to their realities." By "recurring upon God" in all things, he grants them dignity and integrity rather than relativizing them into irrelevance.[8] And what image will encapsulate this approach to thinking all things in light of God? Bavinck turns to the temple, telling us that the Calvinist "does not remain in the outer court ... but seeks to enter into the innermost sanctuary." The holy of holies is no less earthy, though it is all the more so for its heavenly significance. Here the image of the temple courts does highlight creaturely integrity: just as the Old Testament recounts the nature of the stores which will be put toward this cultic construction (1 Kgs. 5-6 and 7:13-51), so this metaphor points us toward attending not merely to the glory of God present here but also the human frame within which that glory finds its abode. Bavinck's suggestion seeks to honor the courts and furnishings of the temple apparatus in its variety and range—noting that there are a number of distinctives to Reformed faith and practice, confession and piety, mission and vocation—while also noting that it is the glory of God that alone makes it the "Most Holy Place."

7. Herman Bavinck, "The Future of Calvinism" (published 1894 in The Presbyterian & Reformed Review): http://scdc.library.ptsem.edu/mets/mets.aspx?src=BR1894517&div=1 (accessed February 26, 2018). While the essay identifies the doctrine of God as the "central dogma," a recent volume has argued that Christ actually serves as the center for Bavinck's theology: see Bruce R. Pass, *The Heart of Dogmatics: Christology and Christocentrism in Herman Bavinck* (Forschungen Zur Systematischen Und Okumenischen Theologie 169; Göttingen: Vandenhoeck & Ruprecht, 2020).

8. Yet Bavinck need not go the route of, for instance, Jacques Marie Pohier, who suggests that Thomas Aquinas's account of charity (*ST* 2a2ae.25-26) tilts toward the claim that "God does not want to be everything" or to be that for the sake of which we love everything (*God—In Fragments* [trans. John Bowden; New York: Crossroad, 1986], 266–78). Pohier reads Thomas against Augustine here and suggests that this Thomistic reading of charity better fits with Gen. 2:18ff. (a text which deems life lived alongside only God as being "alone"). Yet his exegesis of Gen. 2 need not segregate communion across sexual, creaturely lines, and his account of Thomas on charity fails to attend to ways in which he also not merely prioritizes but also integrally yokes love for God and love for others (see *ST* 2a2ae.27.5, reply on loving God "wholly" [*totaliter*] in light of Deut. 6:4-5). Pohier wrongly severs the two facets of Jesus's claim about the great commandment (Mt. 22:36-40; Mk 12:28-33; see also Lk. 10:25-28), failing to propose a way of loving the neighbor that in so doing does not fail to love God with one's all.

Theological Order: Analyzing and Exegeting the Catholic Root and the Reformed Fruit

What more can be said regarding Bavinck's proposal? I want to consider it analytically and exegetically and then to ask what explanatory power it may have in keeping us alert to the formative significance of not simply catholic theology, but of a distinctively Reformed mode of practicing catholic theology. In the time that remains then, I will analyze his terms, locate them exegetically, and consider the implications his sketch has for construing the posture of reformed catholicity.[9]

First, the terms of his construction merit analysis. Bavinck's sketch begins with what he calls a "root principle" of Calvinism. I prefer generally to use the term "Reformed" rather than Calvinism, Calvinist, or Calvinian, but we can leave that terminological point to the side for the sake of argument.[10] His language of root is the key facet here. He seems to suggest that "God Himself as such in the unity of all His attributes and perfection of His entire Being is the point of departure for the thinking and acting of the Calvinist."

While this may well be the root of uniquely Reformed claims, this doctrinal prism is generically catholic. The Reformed have no unique purchase on "the sharp distinction between what is God's and creature's." Calvin did not invent "belief in the sole authority of the Holy Scriptures." Zwingli was not the sole witness to "the all-sufficiency of Christ and His word." Dordt was not the lone prophetic cry regarding "the omnipotence of the work of grace." These claims were prizes of the catholic past, admittedly refracted and developed further in the context of sixteenth- and seventeenth-century debates but catholic affirmations nonetheless.

What more can be said about this root, that is, about "God Himself as such"? Bavinck turns to the term "Sovereignty" here to develop it, and that trades on the creedal language of God as "Almighty" (as in "I believe in God the Father Almighty"). Others have used different categories to attest this singularity. Thomas Aquinas would distinguish between uncreated and created being and, thus, between the Creator and all such creatures. He would also employ the language of the term "aseity" to mark out God alone as the one who possesses "life in himself" or, as other biblical and classical texts put it, divine fullness, self-sufficiency, or (especially in a modern register) independence. August Lecerfe calls "the doctrine of the infinity of God the foundation of Calvinism."[11] In recent years, the philosopher Robert Sokolowski sums up such affirmations with his language

9. For further description, see Michael Allen and Scott R. Swain, *Reformed Catholicity: The Promise of Retrieval for Theology and Biblical Interpretation* (Grand Rapids, MI: Baker Academic, 2015); and Michael Allen, "Reformed Retrieval," in *Theologies of Retrieval: An Exploration and Appraisal* (ed. Darren Sarisky; London: T&T Clark, 2017), 67–80.

10. Michael Allen, *Reformed Theology* (London: T&T Clark, 2010), 3–4; see also Scott R. Swain, "Introduction," in *The Oxford Handbook of Reformed Theology* (ed. Michael Allen and Scott R. Swain; Oxford: Oxford University Press, 2020), 2–3.

11. Auguste Lecerfe, *An Introduction to Reformed Dogmatics* (London: Lutterworth, 1949), 379.

of "the Christian distinction."[12] Bavinck will take up the jargon of independence as a more modern rendition of aseity or self-sufficiency in his *Reformed Dogmatics*. There he acknowledges, first, that "in this regard the Reformation introduced no change," but also that "among the Reformed this perfection of God comes more emphatically to the fore." And why a preference for independence over aseity? "While aseity only expresses God's self-sufficiency in his existence, independence has a broader sense and implies that God is independent in everything: in his existence, in his perfections, in his decrees, and in his works."[13]

> Whatever the conceptual register, the Reformed root regards God's categorical singularity.
> "I am the first and the last; besides me there is no god.
> Who is like me? Let him proclaim it …
> Is there a God besides me? There is no Rock; I know not any"
>
> (Isa. 44:6-8).

The prophet's attestation recalls Israel to revelation given earlier in the mysterious naming of the burning bush episode: "I AM who I AM" (Exod. 3:14). This tetragrammaton depicts first and last, beginning and end (cf. Rev. 22:13) and the one "who is and who was and who is to come" (cf. Rev. 1:8). Bounding the sets of creaturely experience, of our experience of time and all its meaning, the LORD is denoted as surpassing them and of not being bound by them just as much as we learn elsewhere that this one alone is not bound by space (see 1 Kgs. 8:27). While the tense of the tetragrammaton remains ambiguous—whether past ("I have been whom I have been"), present ("I am who I am"), or future ("I will be who I will be")—the self-referential character of this name impels the judgment that this God of our fathers cannot be likened to or compared with any other, brokers no competitors or peers, and ultimately exists and lives in a class of his own.[14]

So God is "King of Kings" and "Lord of Lords" in such a way that he stands alone. "I am the LORD, that is my name; my glory I give to no other, nor my

---

12. Robert Sokolowski, *The God of Faith and Reason: Foundations of Christian Theology* (Notre Dame, IN: University of Notre Dame Press, 1982), 23.

13. Herman Bavinck, *Reformed Dogmatics*, vol. 2: *God and Creation* (ed. John Bolt; trans. John Vriend; Grand Rapids, MI: Baker Academic, 2004), 152.

14. On the significance of Exodus 3 in catholic and Reformed theology, see Michael Allen, "Exodus 3 after the Hellenization Thesis," *Journal of Theological Interpretation* 3, no. 2 (2009): 179–96, reprinted as Chapter 2 in the present volume; "Exodus 3," in *Theological Commentary: Evangelical Perspectives* (ed. Michael Allen; London: T&T Clark, 2011), 25–40, reprinted as Chapter 3 in the present volume; "Divine Attributes," in *Christian Dogmatics: Reformed Theology for the Church Catholic* (ed. Michael Allen and Scott R. Swain; Grand Rapids, MI: Baker Academic, 2016), 68–77. See also now the fine-grained analysis of Andrea Saner, *"Too Much to Grasp": Exodus 3:13-15 and the Reality of God* (Journal of Theological Interpretation Supplements; Winona Lake, IN: Eisenbrauns, 2015).

praise to carved idols" (Isa. 42:8). Relatedly, his singularity is bound up with his self-sufficiency, whether as revealed in Jesus's words ("as the Father has life in himself, so he has granted the Son also to have life in himself," Jn 5:26) or in Paul's sermonic affirmation ("The God who made the world and everything in it, being Lord of heaven and earth, does not live in temples made by man, nor is he served by human hands, as though he needed anything," Acts 17:24-25). We may and should confess divine aseity or self-sufficiency or self-existence or, yes, also divine independence. Perhaps a related term of greater biblical import would be to speak herein of divine "fullness," drawing on the ways in which Ephesians takes up the language of the *pleroma* in its commendation of God's own life which will be shared with his redeemed in Christ (Eph. 1:23; 3:19). In summing up the root of Reformed theology, I want to briefly describe the value of speaking first of divine fullness relative to related terms such as independence, self-existence or self-sufficiency, and especially aseity.[15]

Aseity gestures toward fullness, though it does not comprehend the doctrine. Aseity specifically signals the fullness or self-sufficiency of God's existence.[16] Fullness moves beyond that claim to make a still further one. God has "life in himself" (Jn 5:26), but he is also blessed "from everlasting unto everlasting" (Neh. 9:5). God not only possesses mercy but is "rich in mercy" (Eph. 2:4) and has "riches of his glory" (Rom. 9:24). Whereas aseity is necessary to fullness, touting the self-possession of God's existence, aseity is not itself sufficient to signal the overflow that is the divine fullness. God is not only without beginning or end as *a se*, that is, the "first and the last," but also the "living one" who is replete and filled to overflowing with vitality (Rev. 1:17-18). Indeed, he is not only "Alpha and Omega," but also the one "who is and who was and who is to come, the Almighty" (Rev. 1:8; see also Rev. 4:8).[17] This fullness marks God out to be the one known by the high priest as "the Blessed One" (Mk 14:61),[18] the "blessed God" (1 Tim. 1:11), and "God, the blessed and only ruler, the king of kings and lord of lords" (1 Tim. 6:15). When we attest the blessedness and richness of God in and of himself, we indicate his reality as the one who possesses all fullness and whose own character is rich. He not only has what he has by himself—rather than from another—but he has it excessively.

15. See broader analysis in Michael Allen, "Divine Fullness: A Dogmatic Sketch," *Reformed Faith & Practice* 1, no. 1 (2015), reprinted as Chapter 4 in the present volume.

16. On a positive account of aseity, see John Webster, "Life In and Of Himself," in *God without Measure: Working Papers in Christian Theology*, vol. 1: *God and the Works of God* (London: T&T Clark, 2015), 13–28; and especially Augustine, *Tractates on the Gospel of John 11-27* (Fathers of the Church 79; Washington, DC: Catholic University of America Press, 1988), tract. 22.

17. Rev. 1:17 and 4:8 surely seek to render an amplification of Exod. 3:14, expanding on that text's temporal under-determination and amplifying it in all three tenses.

18. Some translations (e.g., ESV) simply render "the Blessed" here.

If this is my slight tweaking of Bavinck's Reformed root—namely, the way in which God is uniquely or singularly perfect not only in existence but in action, and not only in action but in excess—then we can look backward historically and observe that this is not remotely unique to the Reformed but sits snugly alongside catholic affirmations of aseity and fullness, and we are now in a position to glance forward and analyze how the Reformed might distinctively apply or extend this tenet across the range of theological topics.[19] Bavinck here depicts other ideas flowing from this catholic root. I think it is accurate to use the language of Reformed fruit here to express the organic growth from the catholic root.

Because the claim is that these other doctrines relate to divine sovereignty or fullness as fruit to a root, then we can and should ask: How does this proposal sit alongside the historiographic criticism of central dogmas? And here a distinction has already been made between what Richard Muller himself calls "causal and logical necessity." The historian puts it just so: "An early modern Reformed theologian could, in other words, argue on biblical grounds the causal interconnection of such doctrinal topics as predestination, calling, faith, union with Christ, justification, sanctification, and glorification, and at the same time recognize that no one of these topics could be deduced logically from another."[20] Various works of God manifest the imprint of God's own character in all its sovereignty, self-sufficiency, and fullness. God being this way means that God will act so as to accord with this way. And yet the order of being and causality need not line up exactly with the order of knowing. Our access to these other topics occurs not by way of logical necessity, that is, by deductive reasoning but by exegetical tracing of divine instruction to its intellectual and spiritual ends. Indeed, this exegetically, non-poietic character of the Christian intellect itself derives causally from our relation to a perfect God who shares his intellectual riches—what Ephesians will call wisdom (1:17-18; 3:18-19)—with his people in Christ's power. Precisely because of his rich beneficence and directly owing to our intellectual dependency, we exist always in a posture of receivership and exegesis marks the intellectual practice fitting to the covenantal-metaphysical entailments of this gracious economy.

John Webster has helpfully related the ontological and the epistemological principles of theology by building on the claims of Bavinck in speaking of not only an ontological principle but also its concomitant cognitive principles.

The Holy Trinity is the ontological principle (*principium essendi*) of Christian theology; its external cognitive principle (*principium cognoscendi externum*) is

---

19. For help in this regard, see especially the working papers in John Webster, *God without Measure*: Working Papers in Christian Theology, vol. 1: *God and the Works of God* (London: T&T Clark, 2015).

20. Richard Muller, "From Reformation to Orthodoxy: The Reformed Tradition in the Early Modern Era," in *Calvin and the Reformed Tradition* (Grand Rapids: Baker Academic, 2012), 30.

the Word of God presented through the embassy of the prophets and apostles; its internal or subjective cognitive principle (*principium cognoscendi internum*) is the redeemed intelligence of the saints.[21]

Webster distinguishes the ontological and cognitive principles, such that God's metaphysical causality of all theological reflection cannot be converted into direct deduction or immediate revelation of all theological truths. Rather, God's causal action works through the external signs of Scripture and the internal illumination of redeemed reason. While God provides the metaphysical basis of all other truths and realities, that claim is not the same as saying that their reality might be deduced from knowledge of God. No, exegetical induction functions as the cognitive principle under pneumatological illumination. In Webster's language, God may be the ontological warrant, but there is still need for the "embassy of the prophets and apostles" in announcing that ontological link.

Far from a tracing out of the catholic root toward varied Reformed fruits leading to a deductive analysis of epistemic central dogmas, then, Bavinck's sketch should be received as an exegetical prompt to alert us to the deep metaphysical logic of Scripture itself. Analytically, then, we ought to acknowledge that theology does have what might be called an ontological principle or central object, the triune God in all his fullness, and that other topics relate as objects for theological examination only in as much as they participate in that divine fullness whether in nature, grace, or glory. That said, affirmation of the Trinity as an ontological principle or central dogma does not thereby fall foul of Muller's historiographic concerns about central dogma theory unless its ontological centrality funds a deductive rather than exegetical process of theological argument.[22] Might we even say, further, that the centrality of God and of his fullness points us or gestures

---

21. John Webster, "Principles of Systematic Theology," *International Journal of Systematic Theology* 11, no. 1 (2009): 58; repr. in *Domain of the Word: Scripture and Theological Reason* (London: T&T Clark, 2012), 135. See also Franciscus Junius, *A Treatise on True Theology* (trans. David Noe; Grand Rapids, MI: Reformation Heritage, 2014), 196–203; Johannes Polyander, "Disputation 1: Concerning the Most Sacred Theology," in *Synopsis Purioris Theologiae*, vol. 1: *Disputations 1-23* (ed. Dolf te Velde; trans. Riemer A. Faber; Leiden: Brill, 2015), 39–41; and Herman Bavinck, *Reformed Dogmatics*, vol. 1: *Prolegomena* (ed. John Bolt; trans. John Vriend; Grand Rapids, MI: Baker Academic, 2003), 213–14. Analysis of Junius, Polyander, and other post-Reformation Reformed theologians on the causes of theology may be found in Richard A. Muller, *PRRD*, 1:238-245.

22. See especially the subtle claims made contrary to central dogma proposals which fund an epistemological rather than metaphysical account in Muller, *PRRD*, 1:125-132. "Since, moreover, the actual topics of theological system are understood as arising from revelation and not from reason, the synthetic arrangement of those topics does not and cannot indicate their logical deduction from a single central doctrine. The contrary opinion, that dependence indicates both determinism and the deductive character of theological system, is the fundamental error in Schweizer's conception of Reformed theology" (131).

unto the radically inductive character of theological construction as based on the thoroughly non-poietic character of Christian doctrine? Because God is God and we are not, we receive and hear rather than construct and deduce the lineaments of faith and practice.[23] Schweizer and others who take a preponderant fixation on God's sovereignty or his fullness to serve as a deductive prompt for Reformed theology fail therein to appreciate the creaturely posture of living as creatures of the eternally full and fully generous God of the illumining gospel.

Second, we might ask whether the Scriptures themselves point or gesture toward such a center. Different pathways might show such a central hub of wisdom's revelation. Holy Scripture does not itemize a thematic hub but that does not mean that the shape of scripture is bereft of any guidance regarding priorities or principles of integration. Texts such as 1 Corinthians do remind us that there are degrees of significance when we consider Christian doctrine. Whereas Paul would address matters regarding knowledge, parties and schisms, sexual morality, financial generosity, liturgical practice, and spiritual gifts, he nonetheless identifies certain evangelical convictions as being matters of "first importance" (ἐν πρώτοις) in 1 Cor. 15:3. We see that just as Paul does not shirk from commending the "whole counsel of God" (Acts 20:28), so he also prompts us to begin the work of theological triage by identifying matters of primary, secondary, and tertiary significance.

We might observe a parallel in a cognate discipline, whether it be Pauline studies or biblical theology more broadly. What is the center of Paul's theology or of the Bible as a whole? Does Paul focus on justification or participation or apocalyptic? Does the Bible fix upon kingdom or covenant or temple? We look to Pauline studies and see massive debates regarding the center of Paul's thought, whether of the mystical sort (Schweitzer), the existential sort (Bultmann), the apocalyptic form (Käsemann), the participationist union (Sanders, now Campbell and Gorman), or otherwise. But what is a center in such discussions? Rarely is an effort made at defining the term. Daniel Brendsel has considered potential objections to this quest for a center and has sought to provide a plausible pathway forward.[24] Priorities are not necessarily central, however, in as much as centrality not only speaks of emphasis but also of integration. A high priority may not necessarily play a formative, integrated role in matters of secondary significance. Debates about Pauline of biblical centers too rarely get at metaphysical or ordered webs of interactivity and stay at the surface level of superficial literary construction

---

23. See especially John Webster, "The Holiness of Theology," in *Holiness* (Grand Rapids, MI: Eerdmans, 2003), 16–17. Webster pushes against *poiesis* rather than speculation (as occurs in the tradition following Vos: Murray, Gaffin, and the like) given that speculation can be positively prompted or poietically deduced, which are two notably different postures of contemplation.

24. Daniel J. Brendsel, "Plots, Themes, and Responsibilities: The Search for a Center of Biblical Theology Reexamined," *Themelios* 35, no. 3 (2010): 400–12.

(which is not uninteresting, but is simply more a matter of what Bavinck would call the "outer courts").[25]

Perhaps what may be glazed over as pedestrian biblical literary features might prompt us to a better exegetical alertness. We can observe that Paul not infrequently yokes together divine works that might seem rather distant. "For what we proclaim is not ourselves, but Jesus Christ as Lord, with ourselves as your servants for Jesus' sake. For God, who said, 'Let light shine out of darkness,' has shone in our hearts to give the light of the knowledge of the glory of God in the face of Jesus Christ" (2 Cor. 4:5-6). Paul herein commends his proclamation of the Lordship of Christ and of our posture as his subjects or servants, and he grounds that apostolic kerygma in three realities: (1) God's creative act of summoning light out of darkness, (2) God's illumination of the knowledge of God, and (3) the glory of God present in the face of Jesus Christ. Creation—illumination—incarnation; most analyses of doctrine would locate these at rather disjunctive or at least distant plots on the thematic map of the Christian faith. But each is tethered together in that they attest the divinely powerful and altogether interruptive action that brings life, blessing, and divine glory where none could rightly be expected. The darkness promised no burgeoning sublime. The Corinthians' opacity gave no reason for expecting wisdom. And the generational advance of Jesus's forebears did not mark the upward march of human progress such that we would expect the next one, this Jesus, surely to be "full of grace and truth." Yet God acted in each instance decisively and graciously with power out of his fullness to bring grace and truth.

Or consider Romans 4 where Paul will say:

> That is why it depends on faith, in order that the promise may rest on grace and be guaranteed to all his offspring—not only to the adherent of the law but also to the one who shares the faith of Abraham, who is the father of us all, as it is written, "I have made you the father of many nations"—in the presence of the God in whom he believed, who gives life to the dead and calls into existence the things that do not exist. In hope he believed against hope.
>
> (Rom. 4:16-18)

Explaining Father Abraham takes Paul to resurrection and to creation itself. In creation, God "calls into existence the things that do not exist." In resurrection, "the God in whom he believed gives life to the dead." And so Paul is not surprised that God's justification of Father Abraham "depends on faith."

Such doctrinal integralism is not uniquely Pauline, as some feature of an overly cranial mind, nor is it even specifically apostolic, as a product of the New Testament era. We see such connections repeatedly in the Old Testament witness, wherein

---

25. Such contemporary debates would be helpfully pressed ahead by engaging with earlier Protestant discussions of "fundamental articles" as, e.g., in Herman Witsius, "Dissertation II: Fundamental Articles," in *Sacred Dissertations on the Apostles' Creed* (Phillipsburg, NJ: Presbyterian & Reformed, 1993), 16–33.

the redemption of Israel is yoked again and again to God's creative agency and lordship. Gerhard von Rad wrote "The Theological Problem of the Old Testament Doctrine of Creation" in 1936 to address the way in which the Hebrew Scriptures connect teaching on God's creative act with Israel's experience of redemption.[26] Many texts relate the two themes: Psalm 104 acclaims the one who "stretches out the heavens like a tent" (104:4) and declares "May the Lord rejoice in his works" (104:31), alluding to his work of creative power. Psalm 105 begins with a call for his people to "tell of all his wondrous works" and to "remember the wondrous works that he has done" (105:2, 5), though it specifies his works as "his miracles, and the judgments he uttered" (105:5) and goes on to recount patriarchal and Israelite covenant history. Both Psalms attest his "glory" (104:31; 105:3), though they locate that glory in different engagements or missions of God's action which cannot be praised apart from each other.

Von Rad claimed that creation was always mentioned after the fact as a later and subordinate concern meant to shore up Israelite confidence in covenant redemption. While such may read the yoked attestations of creation and redemption in an unhelpful manner historically and theologically, it would be equally problematic to miss the tethered nature of the truths altogether. Creation and redemption do attest God's glory together; the Psalms and other portions of the OT witness to this connection. Indeed, Walter Moberly has shown that the Book of Genesis serves as "the old testament of the Old Testament" in illumining that creational and then electing backdrop to the account of Israel's redemption from Egypt and subsequent life with God.[27] Surely Genesis 1-11 serve as a creational context and theological prompt for the calling of Abram and its unfolding implications in Genesis 12-50. The universal and particular are connected ultimately because one and the same God—a God whose fullness is such that he fills all in all without thereby ceasing to be full—creates and redeems. The Gospel according to John patterns after this kind of scriptural rhythm in that it attests the Word as life-giver in creation (Jn 1:1-4) before attending to his redemptive beneficence (1:5-18).

These integralist webs do not function deductively, but they time and again point to the divine character behind the divine works and further yoke those works together by means of their common expression of that divine fullness. They are

---

26. Gerhard Von Rad, "The Theological Problem of the Old Testament Doctrine of Creation," in *The Problem of the Hexateuch and Other Essays* (London: SCM, 1984), 131–42. More recent extensions and corrections can be found in Christopher R. Seitz, "The Old Testament as Abiding Theological Witness," in *Word Without End: The Old Testament as Abiding Theological Witness* (Grand Rapids, MI: Eerdmans, 1998), 3–12; idem, "Our Help Is in the Name of the Lord, the Maker of Heaven and Earth," in *Figured Out: Typology and Providence in Christian Scripture* (Louisville, KY: Westminster John Knox, 2001), 180–3; and Neil MacDonald, *Metaphysics and the God of Israel: Systematic Theology of the Old and New Testaments* (Grand Rapids, MI: Baker Academic, 2006), viii–xi.

27. R. W. L. Moberly, *The Old Testament of the Old Testament: Patriarchal Narratives and Mosaic Yahwism* (Overtures to Biblical Theology; Minneapolis, MN: Fortress, 1992).

not epistemological derivations of divine action but inductive meditations upon how the gospel of the full God wholly manifests God's own being. In so doing we have prophetic and apostolic prompts for thinking not merely the canonical range of Christian doctrine but also the theological center of that confession. We have no gesture toward a deductive central dogma, but we do have the first fruits of a metaphysical and covenantal scope and sequence that is not satisfied with the "outer courts" but regularly recurs to the "Most Holy Place."

The Practice of Reformed Catholicity: Synthetic, Not Deductive Connections

Hopefully my analysis and exegetical sketch of Bavinck's account leaves you thinking it meaningful and also scripturally impelled. We ought not only ask *where does it come from?* but also ask *what does it imply?* and *how might it be teased out?* Time will not allow exploring particular instances, but we do well to remember that Bavinck offered quite the extensive list of Reformed fruit which blossom forth from the catholic root. He itemizes as follows:

Divine initiative
Unconditional predestination
Creation from nothing (*ex nihilo*)
Unilateral institution of the covenant
Election of Israel
Virgin Birth
Miracles
Resurrection from the dead
Pentecost
Effectual Calling and Regeneration
Justification of the ungodly
Sacramental institution
Scriptural authority—sole final authority
Ecclesiastical polity: Jesus as Lord of the church

From his list of many such topics, we could turn to various particulars to see that Reformed distinctives do not arise by way of random judgments but instead flow forth from a central commitment to triune fullness, aseity, and lordship, that is, to what Bavinck called God's sovereignty which is him in all his glorious attributes. If he is right, Reformed distinctives do not draw us away from the catholic faith but closer and further into that catholic center. To pursue the posture of reformed catholicity then downplays neither the specific and definitive markers of Reformed theology (relative to other catholic theologies) nor its ontological roots in the doctrine of the triune God as attested in the catholic creeds and the witness of the doctors of the church.

We do well to discuss and to celebrate the varied fruit, not only doctrinally but across Reformed practice as well. I will conclude, however, by simply summing up that these are not random or disparate topics even if they are discrete loci that appear in varied places across the biblical canon and the scope and sequence of Christian divinity. Each of them manifests the fullness of the triune God in some distinct manner, and the scriptures regularly yoke or integrally link them by means of their common display of God's sovereign and beneficent fullness in all and over and through all things. As Antonius Thysius stated in the sixth disputation of the *Synopsis Purioris Theologiae* at Leiden, "God is treated not only as the principle upon which it is constructed and the source of our knowledge of it but also as the subject and the foremost primary locus of theology from which all others flow forth, by which they are held together, and to which they should be directed."[28] This doctrine has synthetic, system-wide implications which are ontological but are not deductively epistemological in form. But this doctrine does advance the glory of Reformed theology and draw us from the outer courts into the Most Holy Place, for the most distinctive thing about Reformed theology is how its thoroughly catholic doctrine of God is applied consistently to the other topics of theology, just as the kingdoms of our thought become the kingdoms of our Lord and of his Christ.

---

28. "Disputation 6: About the Nature of God and His Divine Attributes," in *Synopsis purioris theologiae*, 1:151.

Chapter 2

EXODUS 3 AFTER THE HELLENIZATION THESIS

Exodus 3 describes an epic encounter between the God of Israel and the servant of the LORD.[1] Moses stumbles upon the burning bush, which is fiery yet unconsumed. Redemption is promised, even as a summon is given. God here enters world affairs in a new way, thus this ground is holy. We might deem this imagery prophetic, foretelling even, for interpretation of this passage has proven also to be fiery yet unconsumed, full of promise yet altogether difficult, on an intellectual terrain all its own. A *locus classicus* for the doctrine of God and the notion of theological language, it has shaped texts from Gregory's *Life of Moses* to Thomas's *Summa Theologiae* down to the present day. Yet its interpretation has been much contested in the twentieth century, as part of the modern project of dethroning metaphysics climaxed in the philosophy of Martin Heidegger. Exodus 3 in the guise of what some Thomists termed "the metaphysics of Exodus" (E. Gilson) was mere "ontotheology" and, thus, sub-Christian.[2] Any positive account of the divine naming given at the burning bush was taken as a capitulation to the natural theology of the Hellenists. In place of such speculation, narratival analysis has focused on the literary and textual contours of this mysterious encounter and the elusive God portrayed therein. If there is anything like a consensus among contemporary exegetes regarding this text, it is that very little is revealed about the divine identity or character.

Two things will be argued in this chapter: first, the so-called Hellenization thesis will be described and located within its modern cultural context; second, the inaccuracy and insufficiency of this thesis as an explanatory hypothesis for what went on when the early church engaged Bible and cultural capital in the context of doctrinal exposition will be teased out, by way of analyzing Augustine's interpretation of Exodus 3 and his development of the doctrine of divine simplicity;

---

1. My thanks to Prof. Jean-Luc Marion for his help with this chapter. The Postgraduate Systematic Theology Seminar at Wheaton College as well as a gracious audience at the 2008 Annual Meeting of the Society of Biblical Literature also offered constructive feedback.

2. For analysis of modern neo-Scholasticism and its effects on reading Exodus 3, see Fergus Kerr, "Stories of Being," in *After Aquinas: Versions of Thomism* (Oxford: Blackwell, 2003), 73–96. Neo-scholastic Thomism or Neo-Thomism can be understood well by reference to Romanus Cessario, *A Short History of Thomism* (Washington, DC: Catholic University of America Press, 2005), 24–8.

furthermore, his account of the divine naming in Exodus 3 will be shown to also capitalize on the narratival revelation of God. In short, I will show that, according to Augustine the Hellenist theologian par excellence, both metaphysics and narrative analysis are requisite for properly naming God in as much as YHWH names himself in these two ways here in Exodus 3. Hopefully, this exegetical and contextual argument shores up claims made by others and further dethrones the "Hellenization thesis" as a helpful historical framework.

I

First, we must describe the "Hellenization thesis" if we are to move beyond it. Its apt critic, Paul Gavrilyuk, has dubbed it "the theory of theology's fall into Hellenistic philosophy."[3] The theory has dominated theology and the history of Christianity within the past century, largely following its forceful articulation in the *Dogmengeschichte* of Adolf von Harnack. Harnack's major concern was the supposed turn from ethics to dogma, the shift away from history to ontology. More recently, Jürgen Moltmann has asserted that these early fathers (and the classical tradition which followed them) baptized Aristotle in their teaching on the identity and character of God.[4] In Moltmann and others, this historical take on the classical tradition serves particular ethical and political ends.[5] A distinctly Christian ethic, with all the prophetic entailments that Moltmann teases out, morphed into a Constantinian *apologia* for the establishment.

To grasp the theory, we do well to focus on one component rather than this pastiche. Gavrilyuk outlines five tenets of this theory, related to the doctrine of divine immutability. We should note that he is describing the "Hellenization thesis" as applied to divine impassibility, and we will later see how his summary describes the thesis more broadly applied. Here are his five observations:

(1) divine impassibility is an attribute of God in Greek and Hellenistic philosophy;

(2) divine impassibility was adopted by the early Fathers uncritically from the philosophers;

(3) divine impassibility does not leave room for any sound account of divine emotions and divine involvement in history, as attested in the Bible;

---

3. Paul Gavrilyuk, *The Suffering of the Impassible God: The Dialectics of Patristic Thought* (Oxford Early Christian Studies; New York: Oxford University Press, 2004).

4. Jürgen Moltmann, *The Trinity and the Kingdom* (trans. Margaret Kohl; San Francisco, CA: Harper, 1991), 20–2.

5. For astute analysis of the cultural factors playing into this debate (focused on the doctrine of impassibility within the broader host of attributes affirmed by classical theism), see Ronald Goetz, "The Suffering God: The Rise of a New Orthodoxy," *The Christian Century* 103 (April 16, 1986): 385–9.

(4) divine impassibility is incompatible with the revelation of the suffering God in Jesus Christ;

(5) the latter fact was recognized by a minority group of theologians who affirmed that God is passible, going against the majority opinion.[6]

While Gavrilyuk focuses on the doctrine of divine impassibility, his analysis does serve as a paradigm for grasping this "Hellenization thesis." Several points should be drawn out of Gavrilyuk's sketch and deserve emphasis. First, the "Hellenization thesis" typically involves (though it does not logically require) a belief in a monolithic Greek philosophy, from which theologians cull certain tenets and concerns. Second, the "Hellenization thesis" stands or falls with the claim that the fathers of the early church borrowed from Greek philosophy *uncritically* or, as we might say, on its own terms and with respect to its own questions. Third, the "Hellenization thesis" insists that such borrowing is inherently antithetical to the material content of the gospel; in this vein, a contrast is typically employed between Greek and Hebraic modes of thought.[7] For example, the contrast can be viewed in microcosm by considering eschatology and the blessed hope: for the Hebrew gospel, the kingdom of God; for the metaphysicians, the beatific vision or intellectual apprehension of God's essence. Whereas the hopes of the Old Testament prophets centered on new creation, what is later called "the new heavens and new earth," the philosophically intoxicated fathers began to ponder eternal bliss in the guise of a never-ending sophist colloquium, on par with a mix of mystical experience and a session of the Society of Biblical Literature. In a virtual reversal of Rom. 12:2, the early fathers were conformed to the thinking of the age, deformed by the paganizing of their minds, thereby lessening their ability to discern what was the will of God, what is good, acceptable, and perfect.

This "Hellenization thesis" has suggested that metaphysical accounts of the character of God heap various divine attributes upon dogmatics from thoroughly secular and, worse, overly speculative intellectual indulgence. God becomes the most perfect being, best known by maximally construing whatever traits and characteristics are highly valued in culture at large. For Stoics, so the theory goes, *apatheia* would be valued; thus, God is altogether impassible.[8] God is viewed as the maximal projection of human ambition, quantitatively but not qualitatively transcendent. Take an admirable trait, maximize it, and deem it a divine attribute; in this, the classical tradition is seen as a precursor to Ludwig Feuerbach. Of course, in so doing, the classical tradition moved upward in its theology (applying human traits to God) for the sake of validating downward (stamping human authority and power with divine fiat). Because eternal bliss was like a perfect knowing of God (mimicking the action of the *Word*), the philosophically minded fathers were the

---

6. Gavrilyuk, *The Suffering of the Impassible God*, 176.

7. See the famous criticism of such reductionisms in James Barr, *The Semantics of Biblical Language* (Oxford: Oxford University Press, 1961).

8. Gavrilyuk, *The Suffering of the Impassible God*, ch. 1.

most spiritual; or, later, because the spiritual life was quite detached from physical embodiment, the religious (monastics) were the most holy; or, most crass of all, because the one true God was lord of all, the political powers are most like God and represent God in an unquestionable and, if need be, wrathfully decisive way. Metaphysical theology leads to human oppression. Both Harnack and Moltmann have (admittedly different) sociopolitical and ethical reasons for opposing classical theism, judged deficient as a grounds for human flourishing, enriching freedom, and sustaining life on this planet. Indeed, the "Hellenization thesis" describes the metaphysical basis for the Constantinian status quo and, eventually, multitudes of religious wars in the modern era.

How does this account of the "Hellenization thesis" relate to Exodus 3? Étienne Gilson claimed: "Of course we do not maintain that the text of Exodus is a revealed metaphysical definition of God; but if there is no metaphysic *in* Exodus there is nevertheless a metaphysic *of* Exodus."[9] Not only its supporters, but also detractors of classical theism have focused on the burning bush. According to Franz Rosenzweig, "all those who find here notions of 'being,' of 'the-one-who-is,' of 'the eternal,' are all Platonizing … God calls himself not 'the-one-who-is' but 'the one-who-is-there,' i.e. there for you, there for you at this place, present to you, with you or rather coming toward you, toward you to help you."[10] Augustine and Aquinas, to name two chief exponents of the classical Western tradition, employ Exodus 3 as a foundational text for the metaphysics of Scripture. If the "Hellenization thesis" rightly depicts the logic of a developing Christian metaphysics, as Rozenweig and others suggest, then it must accurately describe how exegesis of Exodus 3 works itself out in their writings.

II

We will consider the accuracy and sufficiency of this theory as an explanatory hypothesis for the negotiation between Bible and cultural, intellectual capital in the dogmatic debates of the early church. Was the divine identity and character construed according to pagan philosophical tenets, or were these secular terms and categories made subservient to deeper exegetical impulses? Nowhere has this question proven more intractable than with regard to the text of Exodus 3, a classic text for metaphysics and theology in both the Jewish and Christian traditions. That the Septuagint translated Exod. 3:14 as *ego eimi ho on* ("I am the one who is") led to the introduction of "Being" as an inference from this text and, thus, involved its interpretation with metaphysics. Again, Gilson makes the point clearly: "From

---

9. Étienne Gilson, *The Spirit of Medieval Philosophy* (New York: Charles Scribner's Sons, 1940), 433.

10. Franz Rosenzweig, "A Letter to Martin Goldner," in Martin Buber and Franz Rosenzweig, *Scripture and Translation* (trans. Lawrence Rosenwald with Everett Fox; Bloomington: Indiana University Press, 1994), 191.

this moment it is understood that the proper name of God is Being and that ... this name denotes his very essence."[11]

Modern critical readers of Exod. 3:14 have attempted to distance the Hebrew text (and its historical antecedents[12]) from the metaphysical dogmatism of traditional Christian exegesis.[13] Finding the statement *ehyeh asher ehyeh* ("I am who I am" or "I will be what I will be") to be somewhat vague, elusive, or perplexing, modern exegetes find YHWH to be denying Moses any knowledge or characterization of the divine identity.[14] That textual point made, they then frequently juxtapose their account with the dogmatic, metaphysical, and essentialist readings they find present throughout the Christian tradition.[15] Many lace their criticism with some disparaging typology—distinguishing their "contextual" reading from the "Greek," "Aristotelian," or "onto-theological" readings of the church fathers.[16] Modern exegetes did not invent this idea of patristic "Hellenizing" exegesis, however; they have learned from a whole host of theologians to view the Western theological tradition as one long history of degeneration.[17] Augustine has come under fire as the chief metaphysical *eisegete*, in the critiques of Colin Gunton and other contemporary theologians.[18] Indeed, along with Thomas Aquinas, he has been

11. Gilson, *The Spirit of Medieval Philosophy*, 51.

12. On the source-critical debates see R. W. L. Moberly, *The Old Testament of the Old Testament: Patriarchal Narratives and Mosaic Yahwism* (Overtures to Biblical Theology; Minneapolis, MN: Fortress, 1992).

13. Similar questions apply to Jewish and Muslim interpretations, on which see Paul Vignaux (ed.), *Dieu et l'être: Exégèses d'Exode 3,14 et de Coran 20,11-24* (Paris: Etudes Augustiniennes, 1978); Alain De Libera and Emilie Zum Brunn (eds.), *Celui qui est: interpretations juives et chrétiennes d'Exode 3.14* (Paris: Cerf, 1986); David Ford and C. C. Pecknold (ed.), *The Promise of Scriptural Reasoning* (Directions in Modern Theology; Oxford: Blackwell, 2007), 77-104.

14. Martin Noth takes Exodus 3 to be a delay of real naming [*Exodus: A Commentary* (trans. J. S. Bowden; OTL; Philadelphia: Westminster, 1962), 44-5]. For a sharp reply, see Dennis J. McCarthy, "Exod. 3:14: History, Philosophy, and Theology," *CBQ* 40 (1978): 311-22.

15. See, e.g., Christopher R. Seitz, *Figured Out: Typology and Providence in Christian Scripture* (Louisville, KY: Westminster John Knox, 2001), 140.

16. Richard Bauckham, *God Crucified: Monotheism and Christology in the New Testament* (Grand Rapids, MI: Eerdmans, 1998), 78-9; George A. F. Knight, *Theology as Narration: A Commentary on the Book of Exodus* (Grand Rapids, MI: Eerdmans, 1976), 23.

17. See, e.g., Robert W. Jenson, *Systematic Theology*, vol. 1: *The Triune God* (New York: Oxford University Press, 1997), 48 fn. 47; for references to others who chart such a narrative, see Lewis Ayres, *Nicaea and Its Legacy: An Approach to Fourth-Century Trinitarian Theology* (New York: Oxford University Press, 2004), 384 fn. 3, 388 fn. 8. Ayres' book is a large-scale rebuttal of this portrait.

18. Colin Gunton, "Augustine, the Trinity, and the Theological Crisis of the West," *SJT* 43 (1990): 33-58; *pace* Lewis Ayres, "Augustine, the Trinity, and Modernity," *AugSt* 26 (1995): 127-33; as well as the earlier work of Endre von Ivánka, *Plato christianus: Ubernehme und Umgestaltung des Platonismus durch die Väter* (Einsiedeln: Johannes, 1964).

greatly maligned as the worst of the Hellenizing theologians, a Christian Platonist even.[19] Whereas Janet Martin Soskice has recently offered three essays that largely remove Aquinas from any sensible criticism along these lines, I will now argue a parallel case for Augustine.[20] Indeed, I will suggest that the Bishop of Hippo managed to uphold the major emphases which mark contemporary exegesis of this episode, affirming the incomprehensibility of God, the importance of narrative, etc. Yet he did so in explicitly metaphysical terms, suggesting that narratival and apophatic theology can also take the form of theological ontology. Again, the argumentative force of this should be highlighted: by tackling the supposed worst case of Hellenization, I will be going to the heart of the theory. To that end, I will focus on the way in which Augustine, the Bishop of Hippo, interpreted the famed account of the burning bush in Exodus 3.

> But Moses said to God, "If I come to the Israelites and say to them, 'The God of your ancestors has sent me to you,' and they ask me, 'What is his name?' what shall I say to them?" God said to Moses, "I AM WHO I AM." He said further, "Thus you shall say to the Israelites, 'I AM has sent me to you.'"
>
> Exod. 3:13-14 (NRSV)

Augustine references Exod. 3:14 in several works. His references to it are not frequent, though they are formative.[21] That is, Augustine refers to this text at critical places in his theological argument. While this can be seen by investigation of the explicit references to the divine name, the pervasive function of the theological notion found in Exod. 3:14 by Augustine can only be demonstrated by noting its contextual, polemical, and structural role in his works.[22]

19. Most recently, see Philip Cary, *Inner Grace: Augustine in the Traditions of Plato and Paul* (New York: Oxford University Press, 2008), 127–30.

20. Janet Martin Soskice, "Athens and Jerusalem, Alexandria and Edessa: Is there a Metaphysics of Scripture?" *IJST* 8, no. 2 (April 2006): 149–62; idem, "Naming God: A Study in Faith and Reason," in *Reason and the Reasons of Faith* (Theology for the Twenty-First Century; ed. Paul J. Griffiths and Reinhard Hütter; London: Continuum, 2005), 241–54; idem, "The Gift of the Name: Moses and the Burning Bush," in *Silence and the Word: Negative Theology and the Incarnation* (ed. Oliver Davies and Denys Turner; Cambridge: Cambridge University Press, 2002), 61–75.

21. Scott MacDonald, "The Divine Nature," in *The Cambridge Companion to Augustine* (Cambridge Companions to Philosophy; ed. Norman Kretzmann and Eleonore Stump; New York: Cambridge University Press, 2001), 89 fn.31. MacDonald also mentions peripheral references to Exod. 3:14 in Augustine's corpus (which, due to their brevity, will not be discussed in our text): *De doct. Christ.* 1.32,35; *De nat.boni c.Man.* 19 and *De cru. Dei* 12.2, 8.11.

22. For an older account of Augustine's reading of Exodus 3, see Emilie Zum Brunn, *St. Augustine: Being and Nothingness* (New York: Paragon House, 1988).

1. Confessions[23]

Augustine's biographical account recorded in his *Confessions* comes to its turning point in book VII, where Augustine notes his encounter with the Platonist and Scriptural traditions. Having earlier noted his pre-conversion adherence to Aristotle's "Categories" in thinking about divinity and corporeality (IV.16), Augustine here notes that his encounter with the Platonist texts led him to "return to my own self" (VII.10). Augustine's interiority does not provide for knowledge of self or God. Rather, Augustine's search within demonstrates the distance between self and God. Section 10 contains numerous references to the difficulty in knowing God: God is a different type of light, above the human mind, Maker instead of that made, eternal, far away, and in a distant land; humanity is not yet able to see, possessing "weak eyes," in need of food, and of a lower order. In face of such distance between himself and God, Augustine can only "sigh by night and day." Augustine then wonders, "Is truth then nothing at all, simply because it has no extension in space, with or without limits?" At that moment, Augustine is comforted by the divine name given to Moses as recorded in Exod. 3:14, "I am the God who IS" (VII.10).

Augustine finds great comfort in reception of this divine revelation, noting that he "might more easily have doubted that I was alive than that Truth had being."[24] He then looks to the world around him, in light of this new name of God, and notices the contingent nature of created things—things "of a lower order" that "have no absolute being in themselves, nor are they entirely without being" (VII.11). "Only that which remains in being without change" exists absolutely. Augustine has used Exod. 3:14 to distinguish God from creation, to note creation's analogical relationship to God (existing, but not in the same way as God), and, therefore, to articulate the basis for a strong dose of negative theology.

2. City of God[25]

Augustine's great political treatise ought to be treated as a theological work tied to Scriptural interpretation.[26] Augustine twice refers to Exod. 3:14, with different purposes in each discussion.

Augustine discusses the role of Platonisms in relation to Christianity in book VIII, noting that Plato is the best philosopher (VIII.9). While Augustine notes several tenets of Plato's philosophy which are quite amenable (if not identical)

---

23. Saint Augustine, *Confessions* (trans. R. S. Pine-Coffin; New York: Penguin, 1961). Parenthetical references in main text refer to book and subsection.

24. Note that his epistemic priority is quite distinct from Descartes's famed *cogito ergo sum*. Cf. Michael Hanby, *Augustine and Modernity* (Radical Orthodoxy; London: Routledge, 2003).

25. Saint Augustine, *City of God* (trans. Henry Bettenson; New York: Penguin, 1972). Parenthetical references in main text refer to book and subsection.

26. On his sources, see J. Van Oort, *Jerusalem and Babylon: A Study into Augustine's City of God and the Sources of his Doctrine of Two Cities* (Leiden: E. J. Brill, 1991).

to Christianity, the idea of God's simplicity is primary. Augustine's exposition of Christian understandings of simplicity and immutability is reduced to a quotation of Exod. 3:14 (VIII.11).

The divine name "implies that in comparison with him who really *is*, because he is unchangeable, the things created changeable have no real existence." Critical to this statement is the qualifier "real"—creatures' existence is accidental and, therefore, not real or intrinsic, but given or suspended from elsewhere. But God's existence is essential and inherent to God's own nature. Augustine then states that "this truth Plato vigorously maintained and diligently taught" (VII.11). He then notes that Plato may have attained this knowledge from creation itself, or from the Scriptures (but see his earlier doubts about the historical possibility of Plato's encountering the Scriptures—VIII.11). Augustine then criticizes the Platonists (following Plato himself) for worshiping many gods (VIII.12-13), a polemic that is the whole purpose of the book (VIII.1). Important for our purposes is Augustine's use of Exod. 3:14 to note a distinction between God and creation—real existence versus accidental existence.

Augustine later discusses the role of angels in the construction of the "two cities" (XII.1), as their agency precedes that of humans. Augustine desires to debunk metaphysical dualism to "prevent anyone from thinking, when we are talking of the apostate angels, that they could have had another kind of nature derived from some other First Principle, and that God was not the author of their nature" (XII.2). Obviously, such a metaphysical dualism would remove the place of hope and eschatological expectancy for those suffering amidst the ruins of the "earthly city" and, therefore, presents a sharp pastoral concern. Augustine notes that the fastest way to debunk dualism is "to understand clearly what God said by the mouth of his angel when sending Moses to the children of Israel: God said, 'I am HE WHO IS.'" Augustine intends to note that God alone exists eternally and, therefore, alone qualifies as creator of any nature(s), be they good or bad. It is the way that Augustine elucidates this uniqueness that is of interest.

"For God is existence in a supreme degree—he supremely *is*—and he is therefore immutable" (XII.2). While Augustine initially seems to make the Creator–creature distinction quantitative (God's existence is of a *supreme degree* compared to ours), his explanation of the quantitative difference pushes the distinction in a qualitative direction. God "supremely *is*" such that he is immutable. If this were merely quantitative, then humans' progression up the scale of being would end in immutability. But acquired immutability is an oxymoron. One cannot attain to immutability or essential existence. Therefore, God's existence—worth talking about because it is (as Augustine says elsewhere) *peculiar*—must be qualitatively different from that of creatures. God cannot change, thereby necessitating talk of God's simplicity. God cannot change; no accidents can be ascribed to God; therefore, God is simply substantial. Even God's existence is essential. Augustine has utilized Greek terms (from Aristotle's "Categories") and subverted them by bringing God's existence into the substantial realm and, therefore, denying the necessity of accidents being potentially ascribed to a substance.

Augustine's discussions of Exod. 3:14 in *Civitatis Dei* articulate the doctrine of divine simplicity, the analogical nature of language about God, and the nuanced use of Platonic (and Aristotelian) philosophy. His use of the term "immutable" as a necessary result of God's simplicity can also be noted: to be simple is to be un-changeable.[27]

3. Sermons[28]

Only one sermon explicitly mentions Exod. 3:14. As it is situated in a collection of homilies, rather than a coordinated theological work, its importance to Augustine's pulpit ministry cannot be ascertained apart from detailed cross-referencing of thematic structures and a chronology of Augustine's preaching schedule. Such examination is beyond the scope of this paper; however, a brief look at *Sermon 7* will confirm other observations about Augustine's use of Exod. 3:14 and deserves our attention.

Sermon 7 is Augustine's only exposition of the account of the burning bush as recorded in Exodus 3. Augustine notes various ways of explaining "I am who I am": "I am eternal" or "who cannot change" (7.7). Augustine does not find this to provide information about God so much as to limit knowledge of God: "This is no creature—not sky, not earth, not angel, not power, not thrones, not dominions, not authorities." Moses, Augustine, and the listener are not left in a state of unknowing, however, given that this divine name is followed by a "name of mercy": "I am the God of Abraham, the God of Isaac, and the God of Jacob" (Exod 3:15). Augustine notes that God gives a negative name, followed by an historical name. He distinguishes between the two names by a contrast between "that name in himself, this one for us" (7.7).[29]

---

27. For Augustine "immutability" is a linguistic qualifier: God does not change as we do. Likewise, though not explicated in this paper, "impassibility" is a linguistic qualifier: God does not suffer passion as we do. Taking impassibility as a linguistic qualifier or grammatical rule for God-talk makes interpretive sense of patristic claims that the "impassible suffered." The "suffering of God" is interesting only to the degree that one discusses *how* God suffers. See Gavrilyuk, *The Suffering of the Impassible God*, as well as David B. Hart, "No Shadow of Turning: On Divine Impassibility," *ProEcc* 11 (2002): 184–206. The tie between divine simplicity and other divine names (eternal, impassible, immutable, etc.) is further discussed (though not explained) in *Sermon 7.7*; on the relation between the attributes (though unrelated to Augustine), see Michael S. Horton, *Lord and Servant: A Covenant Christology* (Louisville, KY: Westminster John Knox, 2005), 40–1.

28. Saint Augustine, *Sermons*, vol. I: *On the Old Testament* (Works of Saint Augustine; trans. Edmund Hill; New York: New City, 1990). Parenthetical references in the main text refer to the sermon and subsection.

29. Augustine's contrast here is the type of statement that has led to modern criticisms regarding his distancing God's triune life in himself from God's life for us in the economy of salvation, as in William Placher, *Narratives of a Vulnerable God: Christ, Theology, and Scripture* (Louisville, KY: Westminster-John Knox, 1994), 80 fn.54; Catherine Mowry LaCugna, *God for Us: The Trinity and Christian Life* (San Francisco, CA: Harper, 1991), 7–8. While Augustine's phrasing here can be misleading, contextual reading demonstrates his affirmation of the economy as entailing true (albeit partial) knowledge of God's life *in se*. Cf. F. Bourassa, "Theologie trinitaire chez saint Augustin," *Greg* 58 (1977): 675–725.

God's naming of himself provides an epistemic check on human efforts to know God—God is not an item in the universe (sky, earth, angel, etc.). Moses "believes this meant a lot for men" in that it showed our limitations. Again, images of distance and limitation are mentioned: "vast difference between this and men," "slightest ray of light," "how far, far below he is," "how far, far removed," and "ever so unlike it he is" (7.7). Moses is driven to understand "that he was far, far from being equal to what was said to him, not to what he was shown, and practically incapable of attaining it on his own." But "God encourages the desperate man" with a second name, identifying himself historically with Moses's ancestors. The negative qualification given in the first divine name limits even the historical identification of God given in the second divine name, providing a narrative clue for how to read these Scriptural narratives for divine identity.

Augustine's pastoral motivation for expositing this text comes in the concluding paragraph to *Sermon 7*. "Let us then praise, though we cannot find words for it, his being and love his mercy" (7.7). Adoration and liturgy are the mode of theological speech appropriate to this unique God. His being must be praised, even though words cannot be found to characterize God perfectly. Imperfect speech must make do: being must be praised, even though God cannot properly be spoken of in the category of being. Augustine addressed the need for negative theology to limit our theological speech and for God's historical acts to give content to our speech about God. He also based analogical speech in the giving of the divine name in Exod. 3:14. Augustine has used the traditional interpretation of Exod. 3.14 as a narrative clue to qualify God-talk and reading of Scripture.

4. Exposition of the Psalms[30]

Twice in his commentary on the Psalms Augustine references the giving of the divine name in Exod. 3:14. Each entails an extended discussion of God's name, and both introduce a new element into our study of Augustine's use of Exodus 3.

Augustine discusses the contemplative gaze in his comments on Ps. 121, noting the ascent of the mind to Being-Itself (*idipsum*).[31] Being-Itself exists eternally and truly "in the highest sense" (121.5). Augustine notes this to bring attention to God's incomprehensibility. But, as with the second divine name given in the episode of the burning bush, a word of encouragement follows this negative qualifier: Christ shows forth Being-Itself. Rather than dwell in self-pity, "hold on instead to what he whom you cannot understand became for you. Hold onto the flesh of Christ …

30. Saint Augustine, *Exposition of the Psalms*, vol. III: *121–50* (Works of Saint Augustine; trans. Maria Boulding, O. S. B.; New York: New City, 2004). Parenthetical references within the main text will refer to the psalm and subsection.

31. For helpful orientation to Augustine's emphasis on contemplation as inherent in theology, see A. N. Williams, "Contemplation: Knowledge of God in Augustine's *De Trinitate*," in *Knowing the Triune God: The Work of the Spirit in the Practices of the Church* (ed. James J. Buckley and David S. Cunningham; Grand Rapids, MI: Eerdmans, 2001), 121–46.

because Christ himself, even Christ, is rightly understood by this name, *I AM WHO I AM*, inasmuch as he is in the form of God."

This revelation of God in Christ is not apart from that attested in Exod. 3:15 by the soothing giving of a second divine name—"the God of Abraham, Isaac, and Jacob." Rather, Augustine then ties Christ's exegesis of God (Jn 1:18) to the Abrahamic promises to bless all nations as fulfilled in Jesus of Nazareth and his church. The second divine name includes God's presence in Christ.

The negative qualifier to speech about God—God, Being-Itself, is different from all else—is not meant to lead to despair. Rather, "I [God] am coming down to you, because you cannot come up to me" (121.5). Though humans cannot analogously work upward to knowledge of God, God's revelation in the Scriptural stories can be analogously received.[32] Augustine wants to buttress faith, noting the faltering nature of human existence as contrasted to the ever-faithful life of Being-Itself, and declares that "the city that *shares in the Selfsame* shares in that stability" (121.6). Contemplation is the mode by which this sharing occurs. Here Augustine traces out a path of ascent: beyond the body, the heavenly bodies, the human soul, the human mind, to Being-Itself (121.6). "No one of himself has absolute being," and the devil's efforts to attain such led to death and pain which has extended even to humans. "But now at last, … let the humbled soul turn back to him who is Absolute Being and find its place in the city that *shares in the Selfsame*" (121.6).

Augustine also discusses Exod. 3:14 in his exposition of Ps. 134 where he discusses the way in which God is good—essentially (134.3). Augustine extends this account to explain analogical language for God: "The things he has made do exist; yet, when we compare them with him, we know that he alone is true being" (121.4). Further, "when not compared with him they do exist, for they derive their being from him, but compared with him they do not exist, because he is true being, unchangeable being, and this can be said of him alone" (121.4). Creation requires a metaphysical distinction be made between absolute being and contingent (or accidental) being.[33] Being and goodness can be spoken of God only analogously to such speech about creatures.

Again Augustine notes the soothing balm given to Moses and Christians in the revelation of God in Christ. Though the first divine name given to Moses implies an inability to truly know God, God does not remain aloof. Rather, God identifies himself in Christ (121.5). Eventually, God's identification in Christ fulfills the prior identification with God's history amidst Israel (121.6). As in his comments on Ps.

---

32. Language of "reception" is not meant to minimize human agency. Rather, it is meant to acknowledge the asymmetrical nature of agency (divine preceding and providing for human). Cf. Kathryn Tanner, *God and Creation in Christian Theology: Tyranny or Empowerment?* (Minneapolis, MN: Fortress, 1988); David S. Cunningham, "Interpretation: Toward a Rehabilitation of the Vestigia Tradition," in *Knowing the Triune God*, 193.

33. For a masterly exposition of the metaphysically subversive character of *creatio ex nihilo*, see Janet Martin Soskice, "Athens and Jerusalem, Alexandria and Edessa: Is There a Metaphysics of Scripture?" 149–62.

121, Augustine here notes that God's activity in redemptive history provides the contours for an analogical knowledge of God as negatively qualified by the first divine name given in Exod. 3:14.

Augustine discusses Exod. 3:14 in numerous contexts. In every case the divine name function to negatively qualify human speech about God, by noting God's qualitative distinction from creation. Augustine notes that God does not remain unknown, because God reveals himself amidst Israel and Christ. The first divine name given in Exod. 3:14 is not the final word, granted that it is quickly followed by the comforting words of divine identification given to Moses in Exod. 3:15 (and eventually with their extension in the apostolic witness to Christ's self-presentation). But the divine name in Exod. 3:14 does limit all speech about God, even the narrative accounts given later in Exodus (3:15, as well as chs.33–34) and throughout the Scriptures, by serving as a "narrative clue" for right reading and God-talk.

5. The Trinity[34]

Augustine's use of Exod. 3:14 in *De Trinitate* demonstrates the systematic shape this text fashions upon his broader theological method. While Augustine only references the text four times (I.2, 17; V.3; VII.10), the occurrences come at crucial points in his argument. Attention to his polemical context also clarifies the fundamental role of Exod. 3:14 for his Trinitarian theology.

Augustine introduces *De Trinitate* as an account of the "reasons they [the Arians] clamor for, and to account for the one and only and true God being a trinity, and for the rightness of saying, believing, understanding that the Father and the Son and the Holy Spirit are of one and the same substance or essence" (I.4). By this point, Augustine has already mentioned Exod. 3:14, noting that God peculiarly *is*. Augustine notes that this attestation is only mentioned once in Scripture precisely because it is so distinct from human existence. On the contrary, many creaturely terms are used frequently to attest some truth about God (e.g., God as shelter, jealous spouse, or regretful creator). Augustine worries about those who take these attestations wrongly in any of three ways: (1) use of sensible experience to directly speak about God; (2) use of psychology to directly speak about God; or (3) those who haughtily profess that which they know to be foolish (I.1). All three types "conceive of God in bodily terms"—as corporeal and composite. Augustine then marshals Exod. 3:14 to refute the notion of divine corporeality (I.2). Exod. 3:14 makes God "difficult to contemplate" (I.3). Divine simplicity—signified by this first divine name—serves as a narrative clue for how to read the Scriptures rightly, by noting the metaphysical distance and analogical relation of this divine character from all creatures toward whom God elects to be present. Again, the difficulty of understanding the divine substance makes revelation in Christ necessary, that we might thereby "be endowed with the necessary purification" for seeing the divine

---

34. Saint Augustine, *The Trinity* (Works of Saint Augustine; trans. Edmund Hill; New York: New City, 1991). Parenthetical references in the main text refer to book and subsection.

essence. The brevity of the exposition testifies to either theological hubris or a shared assumption among the Christian community who would read this text.

Throughout Augustine's interaction with the Arians in *De Trinitate*, the doctrine of divine simplicity is always assumed as a common starting-point.[35] In fact, it will be shown to frame the theological core found in books V-VII. Therefore, Augustine's brevity in explaining Exod. 3:14 here must not be attributed to exegetical sloppiness or interpretative hubris. Rather, Augustine can assume that Exod. 3:14 will be read this way, his way, as a testimony to divine simplicity and as a negative qualifier on theological speech.

Augustine references Exod. 3:14 again in book I. Augustine has traced the narrative of redemptive history in brief, from Christ's coming through the church's existence to the final contemplation of Father, Son, and Holy Spirit as one God in consummation (I.14-17). The final contemplation of God views God's triunity as metaphysically simple, though this awaits the removal of darkness and sin (I.17).[36] God's simplicity is then shown to be a hermeneutical ground for occasional focus upon one divine person (e.g., "Spirit of Truth"). Not all need be mentioned because they are essentially simple. Augustine has laid the groundwork for his investigation of Scripture, analytical study of doctrine, and interpretation of creation.[37]

Augustine next mentions Exod. 3:14 in book V, where he begins his extended analysis of Arian doctrine.[38] Here he references the Divine Name to denote the common ground between the Arians and his pro-Nicene doctrine.[39] Exodus 3 buttresses discussion of God as "substance" (*ousia*) which is unchangeable (V.3). This is a unique substance, as typically the term "substance" is matched by its modifying predicate term "accident." God, being simple and inherently existent, may not be modified; thereby, accidents are disallowed from theological speech.

---

35. On the fundamental nature of divine simplicity in Augustine's theology, see Lewis Ayres, "The Fundamental Grammar of Augustine's Trinitarian Theology," in *Augustine and His Critics* (Christian Origins; ed. Robert Dodaro and George Lawless; London: Routledge, 2000), 51–76; idem, "'Remember that you are Catholic' (*serm* 52, 2): Augustine on the Unity of the Triune God," *JECS* 8 (2000): 39–82; T. J. Van Bavel, "God in between Affirmation and Negation According to Augustine," in *Augustine Presbyter Factus Sum* (*Collectanea Augustiniana*; ed. Joseph T. Lienhard, Earl C. Muller, and Roland Teske; New York: Peter Lang, 1998), 73–97.

36. Williams, "Contemplation," 126–7. Williams also notes the importance of the doctrine of simplicity for Augustine's spirituality (Cf. XV.29).

37. On reading Augustine's development of certain "analogies" to the Trinity as "interpretation" of the divine image in creation, see Cunningham, "Interpretation: Toward a Rehabilitation of the Vestigia Tradition," 183–7. Cunningham helpfully debunks the critique of Augustine's "analogies" offered by (among others) Colin Gunton, *The One, the Three, and the Many* (Cambridge: Cambridge University Press, 1993), 144.

38. On the polemical context see Michel R. Barnes, "The Arians of Book V and the Genre of *De Trinitate*," *JThS* 44 (1993): 185–95.

39. On the term "pro-Nicene," see Lewis Ayres, *Nicaea and Its Legacy*, 6, 167–8, 236–40.

Any predicate spoken of God cannot be accidental. The entire Arian objection—that a divine Son would make birthing inherent to the divine substance and, therefore, disallow the divinity of the Father—falters without this assumed doctrine of divine simplicity. Augustine begins books V-VII with a re-affirmation of the doctrine as commonly understood by anti-Nicene and pro-Nicene parties. Differences only come into play when discussing the existence of a linguistic category which Augustine will term "relational"—predicates which may be affixed to God neither accidentally, nor by way of substance.

In book VII Augustine is nearing the conclusion of his doctrinal comments in the core of *De Trinitate* (books V-VII). He is commenting on linguistic rules for speaking about God, noting the inadequacy of the terms "person" and "substance" when speaking of the trinity (VII.7-11). Augustine notes that God is "called being truly and properly in such a way that perhaps only God ought to be called being" (VII.10). God is also frequently called "substance," though Augustine notes the danger that this might distance God's existence from his being good, wise, loving, just, etc. Augustine's argument depends upon the etymological tie between "substance" and the verbal form "to subsist," which requires complexity. Upon noting this limitation, Augustine does not solve the issue so much as conclude it by reference to Exod. 3:14, then saying that "whether he is called being, which he is called properly, or substance which he is called improperly, either word is predicated with reference to self, not by way of relationship with reference to something else. So for God to be is the same as to subsist, and therefore if the trinity is one being, it is also one substance" (VII.10). Augustine then goes on to consider the linguistic problems inherent in use of the term "person" to answer the question, "Three what?"

Augustine does not reference Exod. 3:14 frequently in *De Trinitate*, but it shapes the structure of the book in two ways: (1) it is inherent to the polemical context which necessitates the work: the shared doctrine of divine simplicity derived from Exod. 3:14 is what necessitates and allows dialogue between Arians and pro-Nicenes; and (2) Exod. 3:14 provides a negative qualifier to theological language which shapes the way Augustine addresses the Nicene terminology in usage ("person" and "substance")—terminology which he finds lacking, but adequate if qualified rightly. The narrative clue provided in the first divine name demonstrates the functional adequacy and analogous nature of all God-talk, even those identifications of God provided in the Scriptures. Augustine offers a humble admission of the graced nature of creedal language drawn from the Scriptures and divine speech, yet limited by finitude and eschatological indeterminacy. Christians may speak of God only adequately as God has so granted, never assuming that words work perfectly but knowing that God has granted everything necessary for salvation.

III

Karl Barth described the perennial dilemma of God-talk in 1921: "As ministers we ought to speak of God. We are human, however, and so cannot speak of God. We ought therefore to recognize both our obligation and our inability and by that very recognition give God the glory."[40] Classical theism has appeared to many to deny the mystery and thus the grace which mark human thought and speech about God; the "Hellenization thesis" has for a century now provided a way to correct this supposed hubris, largely by shirking metaphysics in favor of narrative.[41]

Though God's elusiveness may appear to exclude anything like metaphysical theology, investigation of Augustine's reading of Exod. 3:14 has demonstrated that Christian metaphysics can (and has) avoid(ed) univocal language, linguistic hubris in speaking of God, and many of the errors of later metaphysics which have only more recently infiltrated Christian theology.[42] Indeed, this chapter has argued that Augustine's metaphysical theology and his ontological reading of Exodus 3 avoids "Hellenization" and actually coheres well with the consensus of modern exegetical scholarship in emphasizing elusiveness and incomprehensibility, as well as the importance of narrative in identifying and naming the divine one. Metaphysical analysis may well help bring mystery into relief, rather than negate its very existence.

Indeed, one can now point to something of a growing interdisciplinary acknowledgment of the co-inherence of narrative theology and theological metaphysics, which avoids "onto-theology," the eclipse of the history of redemption as found in the contours of Scripture, and minimization of the doctrine of the Trinity.[43] Likewise, theologians and exegetes have begun to engage the text of

40. Karl Barth, "The Word of God and the Task of the Ministry," in *The Word of God and the Word of Man* (trans. Douglas Horton; London: Hodder and Stoughton, 1928), 186.

41. For a delightful exception in the literature of dogmatics from the late nineteenth and early twentieth centuries, see Herman Bavinck, *Reformed Dogmatics*, vol. 1: *Prolegomena* (ed. John Bolt; trans. John Vriend; Grand Rapids, MI: Baker Academic, 2003), 607–10.

42. The move toward univocity in speaking of God and humans certainly plays some causal role in making metaphysics a way toward knowledge of God, as opposed to a negative qualifier for linguistic practice. Cf. David Burrell, "Analogy, Creation, and Theological Language," in *The Theology of Thomas Aquinas* (ed. Rik Van Nieuwenhove and Joseph Wawrykow; South Bend, IN: University of Notre Dame Press, 2005), 77–98; idem, "From Analogy of 'Being' to the Analogy of Being," in *Recovering Nature: Essays in Natural Philosophy, Ethics, and Metaphysics in Honor of Ralph McInerny* (ed. John P. O'Callaghan and Thomas S. Hibbs; South Bend, IN: University of Notre Dame Press, 1999), 253–66; John Milbank, "Intensities," *ModTheo* 15 (1999): 445–97; Soskice, "Naming God: A Study in Faith and Reason."

43. Jean-Luc Marion, *God without Being* (Religion and Postmodernism; trans. Thomas A. Carlson; Chicago, IL: University of Chicago Press, 1991); John Milbank, "Only Theology Overcomes Metaphysics," in *The Word Made Strange: Theology, Language, Culture* (Oxford: Blackwell, 1997), 36–52; David Bentley Hart, *The Beauty of the Infinite: The Aesthetics of Christian Truth* (Grand Rapids, MI: Eerdmans, 2003), 212–49, 300–18; William Placher, *The Domestication of Transcendence: How Modern Thinking about God Went Wrong* (Louisville, KY: Westminster John Knox, 1996), a book intended to reconceive the relationship between narrative and metaphysics as suggested by Placher's earlier work, *Narratives of a Vulnerable God*.

Exodus in a distinctly theological manner, open to the subversion of pagan
metaphysics and its attainment of certain divine attributes by divine revelation of
divine names.[44] With these trends in mind, Augustine's exegesis, when viewed by
the eyes of faith and attuned to the Christian subversion of Plato and metaphysics,
does not seem full of hubris, much less *eisegesis*.[45] Textual scholars as diverse as
Donald Gowan, Brevard Childs, and Michael Fishbane read Exod. 3:14 in much
the same way that Augustine and the classical Christian tradition has: God's
naming demonstrates God's transcendence, necessitates analogical discussion
of God, qualifies any claim to speak of God, and requires attention to God's
particular presence amidst Israel and in Christ to provide adequate identification
of this elusive God.[46]

44. Soskice, "The Gift of the Name: Moses and the Burning Bush"; idem, "Athens and
Jerusalem, Alexandria and Edessa: Is there a Metaphysics of Scripture?"; Matthew Levering,
"Participation and Exegesis: Response to Catherine Pickstock," *ModTheo* 21 (2005): 587–601;
Herbert McCabe, "The Involvement of God," in *God Matters* (Springfield, IL: Templegate,
1987), 39–51; David Burrell, "Distinguishing God from the World," in *Language, Meaning,
and God: Studies in Honor of Herbert McCabe* (ed. Brian Davies; London: Geoffrey Chapman,
1987), 75–91; Brian Davies, "Classical Theism and the Doctrine of Divine Simplicity," in
Language, Meaning, and God, 51–74; Christopher A. Franks, "The Simplicity of the Living
God: Aquinas, Barth, and Some Philosophers," *ModTheo* 21 (2005): 275–300; Richard A.
Muller, "Incarnation, Immutability, and the Case for Classical Theism," *WTJ* 45 (1983):
22–40; Jean-Luc Marion, "In the Name: How to Avoid Speaking of 'Negative Theology,'" in
God, the Gift, and Postmodernism (Indiana Series in the Philosophy of Religion; ed. John
D. Caputo and Michael J. Scanlon; Bloomington: Indiana University Press, 1999), 20–41;
Thomas. A Carlson, *Indiscretion: Finitude and the Naming of God* (Chicago, IL: University of
Chicago Press, 1999); Thomas A. Carlson, "Postmetaphysical Theology," in *The Cambridge
Companion to Postmodern Theology* (Cambridge Companions to Religion; ed. Kevin J.
Vanhoozer; Cambridge: Cambridge University Press, 2003), 58–75; Peter Ochs, "Scriptural
Logic: Diagrams for a Postcritical Metaphysics," in *Rethinking Metaphysics* (Directions in
Modern Theology; ed. L. Gregory Jones and Stephen E. Fowl; Oxford: Blackwell, 1995),
65–92.
45. On Augustine's theological exegesis, see Jaroslav Pelikan, "Canonica Regula: The
Trinitarian Hermeneutics of Augustine," in *Augustine: "Second Founder of the Faith"*
(*Collectanea Augustiniana*; ed. Joseph C. Schnaubelt and Frederick Van Fleteren; New York:
Peter Lang, 1990), 329–43; Bryan M. Litfin, "The Rule of Faith in Augustine," *ProEcc* 14
(2005): 85–101.
46. Donald Gowan, *Theology in Exodus: Biblical Theology in the Form of a Commentary*
(Louisville, KY: Westminster John Knox, 1994), 76–97; Brevard S. Childs, *Exodus: A
Critical and Theological Commentary* (Old Testament Library; Louisville, KY: Westminster,
1974), 46–89; Michael Fishbane, *Text and Texture: Close Readings of Selected Biblical
Texts* (New York: Schocken Books, 1979), 67; Terence Fretheim, *Exodus: A Commentary*
(Interpretation; Louisville, KY: Westminster John Knox, 1991): 62–7. Fretheim is a
complicated case when it comes to characterizing the divine as presented in Exodus and

I have certainly not demonstrated that Augustine's exegesis of Exod. 3:14 led him to a doctrine of divine simplicity and insistence upon the role of negative theology distinct from his reliance upon Platonisms. Yet the analysis of Augustine's metaphysical exegesis of the divine naming has shown great similarities to contemporary exegetical concerns and, in so doing, has demonstrated once more the insufficient nature of broad-brush critiques of "Hellenizing" exegesis or metaphysical theology. Augustine read Exodus 3 and subverted metaphysical traditions by means of his attention to the Scriptural narratives of creation and election (of Israel, Christ, and the church), emphasizing the Creator--creature distinction, the doctrine of simplicity, the analogical nature of theological language, and the free identification of God with the economy of salvation. The divine name ("I will be what I will be") serves as a narrative clue and a metaphysical qualification for rightly reading the narrative of this God of Israel. At least with regard to this text, the "Hellenization thesis" does not explain what Augustine is doing; rather, we must provide a less reductionistic account of his metaphysics of narrative.

the OT, though his commentary hints at something quite like the traditional interpretation (of course, he shows no sign of acknowledging this given his broader polemics against "metaphysics"—see his *Exodus*, 2-3). Cf. Terence Fretheim, *The Suffering of God: An Old Testament Perspective* (Overtures to Biblical Theology; Philadelphia, PA: Fortress, 1984); idem, "Some Reflections on Brueggemann's God," in *God in the Fray: A Tribute to Walter Brueggemann* (ed. Timothy K. Beal and Tod Linafelt; Minneapolis, MN: Fortress, 1998), 24-37; idem, "Exodus 3: A Theological Interpretation," in *The Theological Interpretation of Scripture: Classic and Contemporary Readings* (Blackwell Readings in Modern Theology; ed. Stephen Fowl; Oxford: Blackwell, 1997), 143-54. Fretheim's reserve and brevity in his *Exodus* commentary allow for the traditional reading (even if it does not necessitate it), whereas he elsewhere (and quite forcefully in *The Suffering of God*) explicitly distances his account from the transcendent God of the classical tradition.

Chapter 3

THE BURNING BUSH

Theological commentary seeks to make plain and accessible the breadth and emphases of the biblical text, with special concern to show its canonical and confessional implications. Certain texts are packed densely with doctrinal content. Exodus 3 must rank at the forefront of such a list. In his magisterial commentary, Brevard Childs observed that "the amazing fact is how seminal this one passage continues to be for each generation." Thus, he thought that both biblical and dogmatic theologians must partner together in a quest to glean the truths of this text. To that end, he claimed that "it lies in the nature of dogmatic theology to go beyond the biblical witness and to draw out the critical implications of its testimony for the modern church in the language of its culture. Perhaps the biblical theologian can best serve in this case by attempting to sketch some of the parameters of the two testaments."[1] As an exercise in theological commentary, this chapter seeks to engage exegesis, biblical theology, the history of interpretation, and contemporary dogmatic formulation. These disciplines may be usefully distinguished, though here they will not be separated. Due to the constraints of space, some areas will be given less attention than others—those interested in the nest of issues related to source criticism and the history of interpretation will have to look elsewhere for satisfaction (even if some of these issues are briefly considered here).[2]

I will examine three major areas of concern: the setting of the text (in Exodus as well as in the biblical canon), the naming of God in the text, and the implications of this revelation. Thus, this chapter focuses especially on the material found in

---

1. Brevard S. Childs, *The Book of Exodus: A Critical, Theological Commentary* (Old Testament Library; Louisville, KY: Westminster, 1974), 88.
2. For engagement of source-critical issues see R. W. L. Moberly, *The Old Testament of the Old Testament: Patriarchal Narratives and Mosaic Yahwism* (Overtures to Biblical Theology; Minneapolis, MN: Fortress, 1992), ch. 1. In addition, development of the history of interpretation will be piecemeal and minimal. For such considerations, see my "Exodus 3 after the Hellenization Thesis," *JTI* 3, no. 2 (2009): 179–96, now reprinted as Chapter 2 in this volume. For the history of interpretation in not only Christian, but also Jewish and Muslim traditions, see Paul Vignaux (ed.), *Dieu et l'être: Exégèses d'Exode 3,14 et de Coran 20,11-24* (Paris: Etudes Augustiniennes, 1978); Alain De Libera and Emilie Zum Brunn (eds.), *Celui qui est: interpretations juives et chrétiennes d'Exode 3.14* (Paris: Cerf, 1986).

verses 13-15, though it seeks to locate these verses within its wider settings.[3] There are contextual reasons for focusing on these verses, in as much as the identity of God is most fully revealed here. It is this revelation that seems to add gravity to Moses's calling and to make sense of the miracles soon to come Israel's way. Only the presence of the sovereign creator in her midst can account for the defeat of Pharaoh and the freedom of the Jews.

The Setting

Understanding the text requires grasping its context. As part of God's Word, we can and must think of contexts near and far. Exodus 3 resides within a particular book: the Exodus. This book makes up a sizable chunk of the larger cadre of texts within the canon known as the Pentateuch or the Law. The Law is one of three major parts of the Old Testament, and thus an early entry into the Christian Bible. With this elementary survey in mind, we can quickly see that context can be multilayered. In doing theological commentary, we are reading this account within a whole economy of God's revelatory work. For the sake of brevity, we will focus on two basic contexts, within which Exodus 3 must be viewed: in Exodus and in the whole Bible.

In Exodus

The book of Exodus portrays the freedom given to the Israelites. The first chapter recounts the struggles of Israel under the reign of a new Pharaoh: the workload is increased and the innocents are to be killed. Moses is introduced in chapter two, kept from slaughter by the cunning of his mother and the ironic generosity of Pharaoh's daughter. There are conflicting realities here in these first chapters. On the one hand, Israel has flourished: they "were fruitful and increased greatly; they multiplied and grew exceedingly strong, so that the land was filled with them" (1:7). In other words, they were fulfilling the mandate originally given to Adam and reiterated time and again throughout the Pentateuch (see Gen. 1:26ff. *et al*). They were multiplying and spreading out as far as possible. On the other hand, little movement was possible. They were slaves. Not only that, but they quickly became oppressed slaves, just as soon as the influence of Joseph in the royal court died out (1:8). With the loss of this sway, the Israelites were seen as a threat and a curse (1:9), and the Egyptians began to constrict their freedoms.

The entry of Moses into the story suggests a remedy or divine response to the guile and ruthlessness of this new Pharaoh. Just as soon as Hebrew sons are ordered dead, we are told that a son is born. His very name alludes to the fact that he was "drawn out" from the mass killings (2:10). The miraculous birth sets the

---

3. For textual argument for the distinctiveness of these verses within the wider account see Moberly, *The Old Testament of the Old Testament*, 17–21.

stage for an Israelite triumph, and Stephen's sermon in Acts 7 accentuates the sense of hope that pervades this early phase of Exodus. He refers to Moses as "beautiful in God's sight" (Acts 7:20) and as "mighty in his words and deeds" (7:22). Yet such optimism is tempered immediately. The boy, Moses, is born, saved from death, and eventually grows up to be a man, yet he kills an Egyptian in defense of an Israelite. He must flee the scene, leaving for Midian and anonymity (Exod. 2:15). By the time he meets the first Midianites, they identify him not as a miraculous survivor of the murder of the Hebrew sons, but as an Egyptian (2:19). When his Midianite wife bears a son, Moses names him Gershon, "for he said, 'I have been a sojourner in a foreign land'" (2:22).[4] Moses—and, through him, the readers of Exodus—are aware that this hero is far from home. It is this story that provides a preface to Exodus 3.

What does Exodus 3 do within the book of Exodus? In this immediate context, its point is to explain the call of Moses to serve as God's ambassador to the Egyptian Pharaoh. Though his birth was miraculous, and his deeds would be mighty, it is only when he encounters God that he becomes useful and effective. Exod. 3:2 offers a superscription: "And the angel of the LORD appeared to him in a flame of fire out of the midst of the bush." Exodus 3-4 recounts a lengthy conversation between the angel (identified as the LORD himself from 3:4 onward) and Moses, when this sojourner is called and commissioned for prophetic service. Not only that, but Moses is given instructions as to his modus operandi. He is to perform miracles, pass along the LORD's demand that Pharaoh free the Hebrews, and persevere through the slow process of a hardened ruler only gradually succumbing to the divine summons (4:21-23). This encounter makes all the difference, for Moses has experienced the presence of God and learned much about the character of God. Indeed, the people of Israel immediately accept Moses as a truth-telling ruler when he returns to their fold (4:31). Previously, the Hebrews doubted Moses's capacity to adjudicate their own internal disputes (2:14; cf. Acts 7:35), but now they seem to encourage his representation of them on the stage of foreign affairs—in Pharaoh's court.

Not only does the call of Moses occur here, but it happens at "Horeb, the mountain of Go" (v. 1). Thus, this passage must be viewed as continuous with the later events at Horeb (Exod. 19-40). In both Exodus 3-4 and 19-40, the nearness and dwelling of God provides authority: now, to the ministry of Moses; later, to the book of the covenant. There are verbal links as well, in both cases God "calls out" of a bush or a mountain (3:4; 19:3). The main character of Exodus 3, then, is actually the LORD. At every point, the wherewithal of Moses is minimized: he

---

4. Jon D. Levenson believes the Exodus is really a response to exile, not slavery, in as much as it changed the status of Israelites but not of Egypt itself ("Exodus and Liberation," in *The Hebrew Bible, the Old Testament, and Historical Criticism: Jews and Christians in Biblical Studies* [Louisville, KY: Westminster John Knox, 1993], 138). In this case, Gershon would be a microcosm for the whole of Israel, though this is not altogether obvious in the text.

doubts, he makes excuses, he eventually needs a spokesperson to articulate his own thoughts and words (cf. the commissioning of Aaron in 4:14-16). As Childs comments, "Grounds for his being sent do not rest on Moses' ability, but on his being a vehicle for God's plan."[5] It must be clarified, though, that the notable factor here is that talent or ability or even exceptional character is not required to be a vehicle for God's plan. Moses is remarkably underwhelming.[6] Yet God promises: "I will be with your mouth and with his mouth and will teach you both what to do" (4:15). So this chapter speaks of God's commitment to reveal, to commission, to redeem the Israelites from captivity.

In the Canon

The burning bush incident recurs throughout the canon. In other words, it proves to be a crucial segment of Scripture, as evident by later references and allusions to its terminology and, more pervasively though less explicitly, by its formative influence upon the thought-forms of other biblical texts. As mentioned earlier, Stephen's sermon in Acts 7 shows that this was a turning point in the Moses narrative: "This Moses, whom they rejected, saying, 'Who made you a ruler and a judge?'—this man God sent as both ruler and redeemer by the hand of the angel who appeared to him in the bush" (Acts 7:35). Note that Stephen sees the burning bush encounter as the means by which Moses is transformed from joke to judge, from ruthless to redemptive. Stephen clearly articulates the historical and narrative function of the text as part of the broader history of God's redemption of Israel.

How does Exodus 3 function within the wider canon? "At different levels and in various ways" must be our first reply. Whereas the immediate focus of Exodus 3-4 is upon the call and authority of Moses as spokesperson for Israel (and texts like Acts 7 pick up on this), the text's wider resonance involves concern for speech about God. That is, the way in which its immediate concern occurs sheds light on a greater issue—deep knowledge of God's character. Israel needs a spokesperson and a savior. Moses was introduced on the scene earlier, yet it is only when he gains profound knowledge of the name of the LORD that things begin to move forward.

Huldrych Zwingli took the whole of Isaiah 40 to be commentary upon the divine name found in Exod. 3:14-15. Isaiah 40, and the whole of Isaiah 40-48, offers vivid description of God's transcendence and sovereign rule over the nations. Because

---

5. Childs, *The Book of Exodus*, 74.

6. Moses raises four objections or questions to his calling by God. Whether or not these are legitimate questions, signs of unbelief or improper fear, or some combination thereof, is not very clear. We do know that Moses had an appropriate fear of God at the inception of the encounter (3:6), though it is evident that by the conclusion of the narrative he has taxed God's patience (4:14). Whether or not Moses sins in questioning, he surely proves unexceptional and unremarkable. While he also says "Here I am" when addressed by God (3:4), he fails to show the immediate courage and commitment displayed by Isaiah (Isa. 6:1-8) and Joshua (Josh. 1) in their commissioning accounts.

he rules over and above all nations, God can employ various political powers for his purposes and then judge them for their sins. At every point, however, God's transcendent rule is linked to the course of human history and tangible experience. While God is not to be identified with history or anything therein (*a la* G. F. W. Hegel's *Geist*), God governs and guides history to his purposes. As has been shown by a number of biblical scholars, there are numerous lexical allusions to the exodus in Isaiah, where the deliverance of Israel is construed as an anticipated "new exodus."[7] Even more telling are thematic parallels that clearly exist: in both texts, the message is that God reigns over all threats, so God's people must trust him to provide.[8] The character of God instills the confidence of salvation to come and the credence of God's prophet (see repeated reference to YHWH in Isa. 45:14, 21-24).

Rev. 1:8 alludes also to the revelation of the name YHWH. The Apocalypse of Jesus Christ given to John first identifies God: "'I am the Alpha and the Omega,' says the Lord God, 'who is and who was and who is to come, the Almighty.'" The emphasis here is on the constancy and everlastingness of this God, signaled by comparing him to the first and last letters of the Greek alphabet. Indeed, at every point in history, he is "the Almighty," the "Lord God." Commentators throughout the centuries have observed consistently that this seems to restate the name from Exodus: "I AM who I AM" (3:14).[9] Not only are there lexical ties between Rev. 1:8 and the LXX rendering of Exod. 3:14, but both texts show a concern to emphasize that God does not change.[10] Taken with the intertextuality evident in Isaiah's use of Exodus, we see that the God who provided for the patriarchs can supply the needs of enslaved Israelites a half millennium later, and the God who raised Jesus from the dead can ensure the future of his disciples struggling after his ascension.

Here we have an instance of background moving to foreground at the canonical and synthetic level. This means that we need to observe the distinction between exegesis and systematic theology, even as we maintain their organic unity. The immediate narrative focus of Exodus 3 is the call of Moses and its role in the redemption of Israel. The way this happens—the manner in which Moses is shown

---

7. Brevard S. Childs, *Isaiah: A Commentary* (Old Testament Library; Louisville, KY: Westminster John Knox, 2000), 110–11; as well as a host of studies on the intertextual use of the Exodus imagery in Isaiah and then in the NT: Joel Marcus, *The Way of the Lord: Christological Exegesis of the Old Testament in the Gospel of Mark* (Studies of the New Testament and Its World; Edinburgh: T&T Clark, 1992), ch. 2; Rikki E. Watts, *Isaiah's New Exodus in Mark* (Wissentschaftliche Untersuchungen zum Neuen Testament 2:88; Tübingen: Mohr-Siebeck, 1997); David W. Pao, *Acts and the Isaianic New Exodus* (Wissentschaftliche Untersuchungen zum Neuen Testament 2:130; Tübingen: Mohr-Siebeck, 2002).

8. Indeed, Levenson argues that the first message of the Exodus is "a story of the enthronement of YHWH and the glad acceptance of his endless reign by his redeemed, the whole House of Israel" ("Exodus and Liberation," 142).

9. For a classic instance see Philo's comments in his *Vita Mos*, I.75.

10. Childs argues that Rev. 1:8 moves as a natural development from Exodus 3 and Isa. 44:6 (*The Book of Exodus, 83*).

something new and powerful and by which his reputation is transformed from presumptive judge to authentic ruler—reveals great truths of God's character, and this proves to have enduring doctrinal implications. By seeing how Moses is called, we see much of the one who calls him.[11] Here we see a remarkable example of how revelation accomplishes things: growth in theological maturity seems to have a noticeable impact upon the character and comportment of Moses.

Intertextuality may run the other way also. The Jewish rabbi Rashi noted the similarity between Gen. 1:1-2 and Exod. 12:1-2.[12] He said that the latter was the real inception of what we call the Old Testament: the birth of Israel. While his focus on Exod. 12:2 may be a bit too narrow (though it is not without lexical links to Gen. 1:1-2), there are important conceptual ties to be seen between Exodus and Genesis. Genesis provides the wider angle lens to the focused concentration found in the rest of the Old Testament; whereas Genesis (especially chs. 1-11) considers God's gracious gift of the whole world, this is but background to the later consideration of God's election of Israel. If Gen. 1:1 accentuates the transcendence of God over creation, forming and making it, then Exodus 3 functions within this later section to remind us of God's transcendence.

We can view this pictorially:

God of the World	God of Israel
Genesis 1	Exodus 3
God creates and, thus, precedes creation.	God transcends both Israel and Egypt and, indeed, the whole world.
God dwells in creation, especially in Eden.	God identified in history, especially the history of Israel.

Both Genesis 1 and Exodus 3 reveal much about God, even as the narratives focus on others (creation *writ large* or Moses, respectively).[13] More pointedly, both reveal that God is other than and exceeds creation, even as God dwells within and can be known amidst creation. To understand these two emphases, we must focus on the divine naming found in Exod. 3:13-15.

11. It would be well worth making comparison between this call of Moses and the experience of Saul on the Damascus Road, in as much as both callings seem to involve new knowledge of God's identity and character. For helpful analysis of the latter event, see Seyoon Kim, *The Origin of Paul's Gospel* (Wissentschaftliche Untersuchungen zum Neuen Testament 2:4; Tübingen: Mohr Siebeck, 1984). In an excursus, Kim notes the antithetical link between the Damascus Road and the Sinai theophany (Exod. 19ff.), leaving examination of the earlier events at Horeb still to be considered (see 233–68).

12. M. Rosenbaum and A. M. Silbermann (eds.), *The Pentateuch with the Commentary of Rashi: Genesis* (Jerusalem: Silbermann, 1972), 2.

13. For further reflection on debates regarding the theological link between Genesis and Exodus, how Genesis is the "Old Testament of the Old Testament," see R. W. L. Moberly, "On Reading Genesis 12–50," in *The Theology of the Book of Genesis* (Old Testament Theology; Cambridge: Cambridge University Press, 2009), 121–40.

The Naming

While the call of Moses is the immediate contextual point of Exodus 3, the naming of God is its wider doctrinal focus. This new knowledge tips the scales narratively, such that a story gone wrong is sharply reversed from this point onward. Because later canonical occurrences fix upon this aspect of Exodus 3, we have biblical reasons for focusing our commentary here as well.

> 13 Then Moses said to God, "If I come to the people of Israel and say to them, 'The God of your fathers has sent me to you,' and they ask me, 'What is his name?' what shall I say to them?" 14 God said to Moses, "I am who I am." And he said, "Say this to the people of Israel, 'I am has sent me to you.'" 15 God also said to Moses, "Say this to the people of Israel, 'The Lord, the God of your fathers, the God of Abraham, the God of Isaac, and the God of Jacob, has sent me to you.' This is my name forever, and thus I am to be remembered throughout all generations"
>
> (ESV).

Before investigating the naming, we must reflect on the question being asked. As mentioned earlier, Moses offers four questions in response to God's commission. The second question—"If I come to the people of Israel and say to them, 'The God of your fathers has sent me to you', and they ask me, 'What is his name?' what shall I say to them?"—arises in verse 13. It is not obvious what Moses envisions here, and it seems that the Israelites never ask anything quite like this when he returns to them. What lies behind this question? Most likely, Moses is not asking for a new name. If so, and if he passed this new name along to the Israelites, how would they verify its rightful application to their God? More likely, Moses is asking about the meaning and significance of God's name or identity: What has God revealed to him that inspires such confidence in him amidst this dreadful circumstance of slavery?[14] What has Moses learned of God that instills a new boldness and confidence, even leading him to return from the wilderness to the land of Egypt? Moses asks for a name—he seeks a character or an identity—ultimately, he wants reasons for hope of success.

We will consider the naming in two parts: the name of mystery and the name of mercy.

---

14. The commentary offered by Exod. 6:2-9 upon the giving of the name in Exod. 3:13-15 suggests this, as God expounds the meaning of the name YHWH as his promised presence and their imminent deliverance, which ought to be trusted based on his prior faithfulness to their ancestors (6:3ff.). On the relationship of Exodus 3 and 6, see Moberly, *The Old Testament of the Old Testament*, 5-35; Christopher R. Seitz, "The Call of Moses and the 'Revelation' of the Divine Name," in *Word without End: The Old Testament as Abiding Theological Witness* (Grand Rapids, MI: Eerdmans, 1998), 229–47.

The Name of Mystery

"I AM WHO I AM" (v. 14). Few statements have provided grist for the mill quite like this enigmatic name. First, we must note the translational difficulty. It might be rendered in past, present, or future tense: "I have been whom I have been," "I am who I am," or "I will be whom I will be." Exegetes have made much hay over the varying shades of meaning implicit in one or more of these renderings. Nonetheless, the basic import of the text is the same in any case, for all three translations maintain the self-referential nature of the name. Because of this self-referentiality, it makes sense to abbreviate the name (as is frequent in the Bible) to "I AM." That is the key: strictly speaking, God can only be understood by reference to God. Perhaps it is best to compare this situation to that of other beings. An interested observer could come to identify me by making comparisons and contrasts with other beings, be they human or animal. Look at a crowd, point out differences in various ways, and eventually you can identify me in that crowd. I am taller than some, shorter than others, etc. Identification works by way of comparing those within a given species or group.

Yet Exod. 3:14 jolts us by saying that God is not grouped with others. God can only be known by comparison to himself. The name seems tautologous at first glance. It humbles the reader. Martin Noth even took Exod. 3:14 to be a delay of real naming.[15]

We must note, however, that this is a name given. The enigmatic is not altogether impenetrable. We must honor the *revealed* importance of the elusive.[16] I have elsewhere offered a historical analysis of Augustine's exegesis of this passage, and a few remarks made by the great Bishop of Hippo prove instructive at just this point.[17] Augustine notes various ways of explaining "I am who I am": "I am eternal" or the one "who cannot change."[18] Augustine does not find this to provide information about God so much as to limit knowledge of God: "This is no creature—not sky, not earth, not angel, not power, not thrones, not dominions, not authorities." God's naming of himself provides an epistemic check on human efforts to know God—God is not an item in the universe (sky, earth, angel, etc.). Moses "believes this meant a lot for men" in that it showed our limitations. Again, images of distance and limitation are mentioned: "vast difference between this and men," "slightest ray of light," "how far, far below he is," "how far, far removed," and "ever so unlike it he is." Moses is driven to understand "that he was far, far from being equal to what was said to him, not to what he was shown, and practically incapable of attaining

---

15. *Exodus: A Commentary* (Old Testament Library; trans. J. S. Bowden; Philadelphia, PA: Westminster, 1962), 44–5.

16. See the helpful reply to Noth by Dennis J. McCarthy, "Exod. 3:14: History, Philosophy, and Theology," *Catholic Biblical Quarterly* 40 (1978): 311–22.

17. The following material is drawn from Allen, "Exodus 3 after the Hellenization Thesis," 179–96, reprinted as Chapter 2 in this volume.

18. Augustine, *Sermons*, vol. 1: *On the Old Testament* (The Works of Saint Augustine; ed. Edmund Hill; New York: New City, 1990), 7.7.

it on his own."[19] Our limits, however, are not naturally apparent but are revealed to us by God himself.

The Name of Mercy

In the next verse, a second name is given: "THE LORD, the God of your fathers, the God of Abraham, the God of Isaac, and the God of Jacob, has sent me to you" (v. 15). God is identified within particular narratives, the stories of the Israelites and their God. Robert Jenson has heralded this emphasis: "Asked who God is, Israel's answer is, 'Whoever rescued us from Egypt.' Asked about her access to this God, Israel's answer is, 'We are permitted to call on him by name.'"[20] Of course, this is to skip ahead several steps, for God has not yet redeemed Israel. A broader point is pertinent, though, and deserves emphasis: God here says that he may be identified by giving attention to the stories of Israel. He specifically refers to the patriarchal narratives, but one can rightly infer Jenson's point as a logical and narratival corollary (the impending action of redeeming Israel also identifies God—eventually, the resurrection of Jesus fulfills a similar function).

The crucial issue is how the two names are to be related. Does the name of mystery minimize the import of the name of mercy? Conversely, does the name of mercy render the mystery null and void? Here exegesis and dogmatics converge.

First, we must see that they are distinct names. Some would demur. As Donald Gowan argues:

I see Ex. 3:14-16 to be the same kind of etymologizing wordplay. The name of the God of Israel was Yahweh. It had no definition, as the names of other gods did… a way of expressing the freedom of the subject, in order to emphasize the human inability to know God's "being." What Israel could know about God follows immediately in verses 16b-22.[21]

Yet this is reductionistic, failing to see the repetition of verse 15 in verse 16b. Both speak of the historical availability of this YHWH, a point remarkably different from the initial naming of verse 14. As Augustine puts it, the two names can be distinguished by a contrast between "that name in himself, this one for us."[22] The first points to the fact that our knowledge will be limited, while the second offers a promise of adequate (if not perfect) naming.

Second, we must see that the second name comforts where the first name has challenged and perplexed. Just as law drives one to look for Gospel, so the name

19. Augustine, *Sermons*, 7.7.
20. Robert W. Jenson, *Systematic Theology*, vol. 1: *The Triune God* (New York: Oxford University Press, 1997), 44.
21. Gowan, *Theology in Exodus*, 85.
22. Augustine, *Sermons*, 7.7; cf. F. Bourassa, "Theologie trinitaire chez saint Augustin," *Gregorianum* 58 (1977): 675–725.

of mystery propels one to seek a name of mercy: in both cases, God provides. We do not comprehend God, but we do apprehend him in this redemptive history recorded in these biblical texts. So the two names exemplify a rhetorical and spiritual dynamic not to be missed: awe at God's vastness and transcendence, matched by assurance of God's nearness.

The exegetical task (and that of biblical dogmatics) is to affirm all that the canonical writings pressure us to affirm, even when our logical intuitions suggest that they may be contradictory. Here we must find ways to honor the integrity of both divine names. We thus honor revelation and locate mystery at the appropriate place in theological pursuit.

The Implications

When the bush burnt, light was shed on many facets of biblical truth. While focusing on the doctrine of God, this concluding section ought to point at least to other areas of doctrinal concern that are elucidated or complexified by Exodus 3.

Divine Transcendence

The first divine name points to the otherness of God. Strictly speaking, God is simply himself. He is not a conflation or collection of parts. He is singular. He is simple. Theologians from Augustine to Thomas have argued that Exod. 3:14 teaches the simplicity of God, that is, the oneness and unity of God; for example, Thomas says that "Moses after then was more fully taught about the simplicity of the divine essence when he was told, *I am who I am*."[23] Simplicity is contrasted with complexity here. It bears saying that God's simplicity is what makes human knowledge of God very complex. Humans are complex beings, made up of constituent parts from arms and legs to minds and spirits. We experience all of life amidst complex beings and things, whether automobiles or corporations, that can be parceled out and pieced together again. We, therefore, have no comparison that fits God's being perfectly, because all our categories of thought are complex and finite. This is the point made by the first naming: God cannot be identified with anything else, however much he might identify himself amidst the events of world history.

Is this metaphysical teaching? Étienne Gilson claimed: "Of course we do not maintain that the text of Exodus is a revealed metaphysical definition of God; but if there is no metaphysic *in* Exodus there is nevertheless a metaphysic *of*

---

23. Thomas, *Summa Theologiae*, 2a2ae.174.6, reply. A Christian version of divine simplicity was not only a Western fixation; it was also achieved in the theological work of the Cappadocian fathers, according to Andrew Radde-Gallwitz, *Basil of Caesarea, Gregory of Nyssa, and the Transformation of Divine Simplicity* (Oxford Early Christian Studies; Oxford: Oxford University Press, 2009).

Exodus."[24] We do well to follow Matthew Levering in observing that metaphysics is not thought about abstract things; rather, metaphysics is abstract thought about very concrete things.[25] In this case, Exod. 3:14 identifies a particular character (YHWH) as a unique being in a class all by himself (*sui generis*). As Augustine says in *De Trinitate*, Exod. 3:14 makes God "difficult to contemplate."[26]

We can usefully link the doctrine of divine simplicity with the biblical nature of divine transcendence. Kathryn Tanner has served us well by clarifying the analytical difference between "quantitative" and "qualitative" forms of divine transcendence.[27] Whereas "quantitative" approaches assume a univocal relation between God's attributes and ours (with the difference being that God simply exemplifies them *more*), "qualitative" transcendence actually involves God's existence outside the very categories of creaturely life. God is not simply more loving in the same way that we are, or more good in the same manner that our friends are. Rather, God is good and loving in the way that God is; *he* is who *he* is. He exists on a wholly different plane of being—not a higher plane or a more fully realized plane, but a wholly distinct plan of being.

Divine Presence

The second divine name suggests the immanent presence of God in this world, more particularly, in the covenantal history of Israel.

According to Franz Rosenzweig, "all those who find here notions of 'being,' of 'the-one-who-is,' of 'the eternal,' are all Platonizing ... God calls himself not 'the-one-who-is' but 'the one-who-is-there,' i.e. there for you, there for you at this place, present to you, with you or rather coming toward you, toward you to help you."[28] Rosenzweig falsely construes transcendence and immanence as a zero-sum game, whereas the two namings here in Exodus 3 suggest that God's transcendence is what allows for his immanence. Indeed, the God who is thoroughly different from us is, nonetheless, "nearer to us than we are to ourselves."[29] As noted above, the canon pressures us to affirm both transcendence and presence; biblical exegesis

24. Étienne Gilson, *The Spirit of Medieval Philosophy* (New York: Charles Scribner's Sons, 1940), 433.

25. Matthew Levering, *Scripture and Metaphysics: Aquinas and the Renewal of Trinitarian Theology* (Challenges in Contemporary Theology; Oxford: Blackwell, 2003).

26. Augustine, *De Trinitate*, I.3.

27. Kathryn Tanner, *God and Creation in Christian Theology: Tyranny or Empowerment?* (repr.; Minneapolis, MN: Fortress, 2004), chs. 2–3; cf. idem, *Jesus, Humanity, and the Trinity: A Brief Systematic Theology* (Minneapolis, MN: Fortress, 2001), 1–14.

28. Franz Rosenzweig, "A Letter to Martin Goldner," in Martin Buber and Franz Rosenzweig, *Scripture and Translation* (trans. Lawrence Rosenwald with Everett Fox; Bloomington: Indiana University Press, 1994), 191.

29. Karl Barth, *Church Dogmatics* II/1: *The Doctrine of God* (ed. T. F. Torrance and G. W. Bromiley; Edinburgh: T&T Clark, 1957), 314.

and dogmatics will honor the breadth and coherence of the full canonical portrait even if it cannot fully explain how this is metaphysically compatible.

Again, Kathryn Tanner provides help: "What makes God different from creatures is also what enables God to be with what is not God rather than shut up in self-enclosed isolation ... Immanence and transcendence, closeness and difference, are simply not at odds in God's relations with us."[30] Eventually, we will learn that a person is both divine and human: Jesus can have two natures, because the two natures are ontologically different or distinct. His divinity and transcendent glory is highlighted time and again by his identification with the divine name given in Exod. 3:14 (see Phil. 2:5-11; Heb. 1:1-4; the various "I AM" sayings of John's Gospel).[31] A non-competitive relationship between the divine/transcendent and the human/immanent is essential as an ontological framework if the Incarnation is to make any sense whatsoever.[32] Maintaining the truthfulness of both divine transcendence and presence allows us to maintain the full mystery of what the Bible pressures us to confess of God's economy of salvation; it does not explain away the mystery, but it locates it properly. Unfortunately, many theologians in the modern period have domesticated the transcendence of God, rendering it less than qualitative and, thus, causing systematic problems in various doctrinal *loci* by jettisoning one of the names revealed here.[33]

30. Tanner, *Jesus, Humanity, and the Trinity*, 12, 13.

31. David S. Yeago, "The New Testament and the Nicene Dogma: A Contribution to the Recovery of Theological Exegesis," *Pro Ecclesia* 3 (1994): 152–64; C. Kavin Rowe, "Romans 10:13: What Is the Name of the Lord?," *Horizons in Biblical Theology* 22, no. 2 (2000): 135–73; C. Kavin Rowe, "Biblical Pressure and Trinitarian Hermeneutics," *Pro Ecclesia* 11 (2002): 295–312; Richard Bauckham, *God Crucified: Monotheism and Christology in the New Testament* (Grand Rapids: Eerdmans, 1998); Christopher R. Seitz, "Handing Over the Name: Christian Reflection on the Divine Name YHWH," in *Figured Out: Typology and Providence in Christian Scripture* (Louisville: Westminster John Knox, 2001): 131–44.

32. I have developed this argument in *The Christ's Faith: A Dogmatic Account* (T&T Clark Studies in Systematic Theology; London: T&T Clark, 2009), ch. 4. While I have misgivings with elements of parts 3 and 4 in this fourth chapter (with Chapter 7 in the present volume offering a modification on part 3 regarding the fallen/unfallen nature debate), I continue to think this fundamental argument about divine transcendence and Reformed Christology continues to be a point of fundamental significance (and it has since been further articulated with great explanatory power by more volumes from Rowan Williams, Aaron Riches, and Ian McFarland).

33. William C. Placher, *The Domestication of Transcendence: How Modern Thinking about God Went Wrong* (Louisville, KY: Westminster John Knox, 1996). Not all of Placher's historical work was equally shrewd (e.g., ch. 9 is less than satisfactory), yet his overarching narrative is cogent, persuasive, and important.

Mediation

Because the holy God is known amidst the life of Israel, the creaturely realm is shown to have integrity and value. While God is different from creation and cannot be reduced to what is visible in the life of the covenant, covenant and creation do really witness to God's being. Exodus 3 manifests this mediation in two ways.

Language: Naming God

Karl Barth wisely affirmed that "as ministers we ought to speak of God. We are human, however, and so cannot speak of God. We ought therefore to recognize both our obligation and our inability and by that very recognition give God the glory."[34] Here we see that God continues to allow humans to name him, to address him, to pick him out of the heavenly crowd. Indeed, God responds to such prayer, as Exod. 2:23-25 makes very plain. "God heard their groaning," to be sure, but, more importantly, this led to deeper action: "God remembered his covenant with Abraham, with Isaac, and with Jacob." Then "God saw the people of Israel" and, therefore, "God knew." Because the language of prayer and divine address is valid and has real integrity, humans can summon God's engagement.

We need not engage in exegetical flights of fancy regarding where God might have been prior to this hearing and seeing Israel's groaning. For example, Donald Gowan thinks that Exodus 1-2 exemplify "the absence of God" (as does the book of Job).[35] Quite apart from the earlier mention of God's actions in blessing the faithful and daring Hebrew midwives (Exod. 1:20-21), the emphasis of these two chapters is clearly not on God's absence so much as the reality of Israel's plight in all its raw texture. Only after the reader sees the plight and the mire of slavery does groaning ensue and, then, God hears and sees and knows. The point does not seem to be that God was absent or disinterested, but, rather, that human words have great importance in the divine economy, whether they be prayerful groanings or prophetic witness.

So, as Christopher Seitz reminds us:

> *What is at stake is whether we are entitled to call God anything at all.* The proper question is whether we have any language that God will recognize as his own, such that he will know himself to be called upon, and no other, and within his own counsel then be in a position to respond, or to turn a deaf ear.[36]

God does hand over a name, as Seitz says, and so we can speak of and to God. Scholastic theologians employed a distinction between comprehensive and

---

34. Karl Barth, "The Word of God and the Task of the Ministry," in *The Word of God and the Word of Man* (trans. Douglas Horton; London: Hodder and Stoughton, 1928), 186.

35. Gowan, *Theology in Exodus*, 1-24.

36. Christopher R. Seitz, "The Divine Name in Christian Scripture," in *Word without End*, 252 (emphasis in original).

apprehensive knowledge of God, as well as a distinction between *archetypal* and *ectypal* theology, to honor the nature of this speech about God. We know God as finite humans can know an infinite and transcendent LORD. While adequate and even good, such knowledge and talk is neither divine nor perfect. Even when glorified, we shall still see the glory of the LORD with creaturely, limited eyes. Yet we shall see, and we will praise. God honors such language—so should we.

Creaturely Objects: The Burning Bush

If God's identification with a name is jarring, then God's appearance amidst a burning bush is downright scandalous. God is not only evident in the stories of Israel, he is also dwelling in a particular plant at one point in time.

That words and objects can be employed for God's own purposes shows that creation is not inherently flawed or unfit for God's presence. Of course, the book of Exodus will later make much of the particular circumstances in which God can dwell somewhere, namely, the Tabernacle. Yet our consideration of such details must not trump the astonishing affirmation that nature can be used for supernatural purposes. We may not have perfect linguistic capacity for comprehensively defining God or concrete presences of God in every place and time, but God does promise to be with us, to give us everything that we need.[37]

Throughout the centuries that followed, Jews and Christians found themselves identified by that burning bush. Many Jews later interpreted their people as burned yet not consumed, and eventually Protestants would see the church as constantly suffering yet promised victory over the gates of hell.[38] In many ways, of course, this is to load the burning bush with meaning that it does not carry in its original context. Exodus 3 does not suggest that the burning of this plant is a bad or painful thing, rather it highlights the vivid and surprising nature of a burning bush that is still standing resolute. The symbol does not hint immediately at fortitude amidst suffering (though that is surely a biblical emphasis) but about God's presence in the midst of creaturely life and human history. The bush must be interpreted by the naming: God can be named as the one involved with the patriarchs, and now as the God of enslaved Israel.

God comes near and works amidst the physical. There are dangers in rewriting history and projecting oneself backward: as if this story is really about the presence of God with the poor. But there is reason to make good and reasonable inferences, bringing "the past, the story of Israel, to bear upon the present," as Jon

37. Stanley Hauerwas and Samuel Wells, "The Gift of the Church and the Gifts God Gives It," in *The Blackwell Companion to Christian Ethics* (Blackwell Companions to Religion; ed. Stanley Hauerwas and Samuel Wells; Oxford: Blackwell, 2004), 13–27.

38. Liberation theologians have gone even further, identifying the bush with the marginalized, oppressed, and poor. Against such links, Jon D. Levenson has shown how the book of Exodus specifically deals with the liberation of a people promised blessing in covenantal form by their own God ("Exodus and Liberation," 127–59).

Levenson says.[39] Eventually, this has implications for Christology, bibliology, and sacramentology. In every case, there is an identification of something creaturely with the presence of God. These creaturely objects are not themselves divine (even in Christ: while there is a hypostatic or personal union of the creaturely with the divine, nonetheless, the human nature does not itself become divine).[40] A salvation wrought "before the foundation of the world" (Eph. 1:4) unfolds by means of nails and blood and is passed along by water and wine as well as the feeble testimony of the saints through the ages. While gracious, the gospel involves the frame and fulfillment of nature.

Holiness

Finally, we cannot comment on Exodus 3 and covenantal mediation without noting the theme of holiness.[41] Moses is called to a particular bush to hear God's speech. There is a division of common and sacred, then, even in the setting. This distinction is clearly highlighted by God's warning: "Do not come near; take your sandals off your feet, for the place on which you are standing is holy ground" (v. 5).[42]

Holiness jolts Moses out of any sense of familiarity, and it does away with whatever privilege seems to flow from simple pedigree. When this fiery God reveals himself to Moses "I am the God of your father, the God of Abraham, the God of Isaac, and the God of Jacob" (v. 6), Moses does not reply with a relaxed or familiar tone. Instead, we are told that he "hid his face, for he was afraid to look at God" (v. 6). Reverence and awe are required from those who would encounter the living God of Israel. The Puritan John Owen, articulated what many have found here: "As Moses was then commanded to put off his shoes, the place whereon he stood being holy ground, so it will be the wisdom of him that writes, and of them that read, to divest themselves of all carnal affections and imaginations, that they may draw nigh unto this great object of faith with due reverence and fear."[43]

Thus, finally, Exodus 3 teaches about the special nature of God's presence—holiness and, as Leviticus will clarify soon, cleanness—and so we must conclude

---

39. Levenson, "Exodus and Liberation," 156–7.

40. John Owen exemplifies such an approach, as is described by Alan Spence, *Incarnation and Inspiration: John Owen and the Coherence of Christology* (London: T&T Clark, 2007) and Kelly M. Kapic, *Communion with God: The Divine and the Human in the Theology of John Owen* (Grand Rapids, MI: Baker Academic, 2007).

41. See further Michael Allen, *Sanctification* (New Studies in Dogmatics; Grand Rapids, MI: Zondervan Academic, 2017), esp. chs. 1–2.

42. R. W. L. Moberly argues that holiness was not a category of patriarchal religion, and it was first introduced here in Exodus 3 (*The Theology of the Book of Genesis*, 135–7).

43. John Owen, "Christologia: Or a Declaration of the Glorious Mystery of the Person of Christ," in *Works of John Owen*, vol. 1: *The Glory of Christ* (Edinburgh: The Banner of Truth Trust, 1965), 181.

with words about worship. Indeed, Exodus 3 moves from knowledge of God to concern for Israel's welfare to preparations for worship, as the whole book of Exodus makes these very moves.[44] God reveals himself as transcendent and yet immanently present with Israel; thus, they can trust in his deliverance brought about through the ministry of Moses. Because they will be redeemed from bondage and brought back into the land from their exile, they will be able to serve the LORD rather than Pharaoh. Freedom and revelation lead to worship of the one true God (Exod. 3:12, 18; 4:31). The presence of the divine in the midst of history brings salvation, to be sure, but it also puts the redeemed in a position of awe and gives them a reverence for the holy.

44. See the threefold structure argued by Levenson, "Exodus and Liberation," 142–4.

Chapter 4

DIVINE FULLNESS

Theologians have lots of words. Specifically, when speaking of God, the scope and mystery of the Godhead demand that we have many words to hand to attest his transcendent goodness and might. The reader will remember the words at the end of the Gospel according to John: "Now there are also many other things that Jesus did. Were every one of them to be written, I suppose that the world itself could not contain the books that would be written" (Jn 21:25). Attesting the breadth of the Savior's light requires many words, indeed too many for any one book to bear. How much more true must this be when we speak of the glory of the whole Godhead? While we speak of God being simple, one, and unified, the corollary of that claim is that we can only know him by rather complex and rich catenas of words meant to brim over and point to his excess.

Hence confessions and catechisms regularly make use of many attributes or character traits to insist that we keep our eyes upon the full breadth of God's goodness. For instance, the Westminster Shorter Catechism asks and answers: "What is God? God is a Spirit, infinite, eternal, and unchangeable, in his being, wisdom, power, holiness, justice, goodness, and truth" (WSC 4). While longer lists appear in Larger Catechism 7 and in the Confession of Faith chapter 2, even this short answer resorts to almost a dozen terms to attest the bare minimum which must be said of the divine character. These and other terms have been confessed and debated throughout the centuries. Interestingly, however, one divine attribute has not achieved the prominence it deserves: divine fullness. It does not appear overtly, for example, in any of the Westminster Standards, and that silence is by no means unique to that strain of Reformed theology or even to Protestantism more broadly. When one looks for fullness in the brilliant riches of Christian doctrine, ironically one typically finds only void and want.

We might seek to account for this modern reticence regarding the riches of the divine glory. Since John and Paul speak of God's fullness, why did it cease to capture our imagination? Why has the language of fullness fallen out of favor in recent Christian theology? Does this follow from a reaction to supposedly Hellenistic thought (and the purported Hellenization of the early church)? Does this silence somehow relate to modern rationalism which seeks to think by means of quantifiable elements rather than mysterious principles? Are particular exegetical trends related to the Greco-Roman backgrounds of Pauline and

Johannine teaching to account for this trend? Such anatomies of the modern silence would be no doubt significant, but they are beyond the bounds of this study. In this brief chapter, we will offer a sketch of divine fullness, seeking to note its biblical roots, taking in its relation to other elements of the doctrine of God, tracing its effects into the works of God in election, creation, incarnation, and beyond, and finally asking what practical uses the doctrine bears, that is, what ethical entailments follow from this particular divine reality. In so doing, we are attempting to reorient theological reflection with regard to a biblical theme that has been forgotten. Given the modern forgetfulness, perhaps a broad sketch can help reframe our imagination in a useful manner.

Introduction to a Dogmatic Sketch of Divine Fullness

Fullness is not a Christian word. We must go a step further than this even, admitting that divine fullness is not a Christian idea. In saying this, we do not deny the presence of such claims within the Christian tradition or even the Holy Scriptures. Rather, we note that the language is not exclusively or even originally Christian. It is common jargon and borrowed terminology. Fullness (the *pleroma*) regularly appears in pagan Greek literature prior to and contemporaneous with the New Testament writings. Taken from elsewhere, it becomes Christian.[1] Here we plunder the Egyptians (Exod. 12:36) by taking up language from the wider world and put it to the use of pointing to the incomparable one and his gospel.

Any time such common language, charged with metaphysical and moral entailments in a non-Christian manner, appears in holy writ, we do well to be vigilant in observing how it is used. Words do not carry meaning in and of themselves, but they mean things within contexts. While fullness would no doubt sound familiar to hearers or readers of the New Testament writings (which, of course, is part of its power), what is said there would be markedly unfamiliar in key respects. Thus we are reminded that we need to be alert to the Christian difference that situating language in the economy of the gospel has upon words like fullness (or other terms that are shared with pagan thought on God: infinity, omnipotence, eternity, goodness, and the like).

Dogmatic theology provides intellectual discipline by returning the mind again and again to the testimonies of the prophets and apostles. Dogmatics reminds us of the need to have our thought sanctified; with false presuppositions and assumptions confronted and mortified, and with new categories and concepts enlisted and vivified. Dogmatics prompts us to follow the Bible's teaching all along its way, never narrowing our focus and in so doing losing its breadth and wholeness. Given our propensity as individuals and groups to focus in on

---

1. We could argue that it is ontologically Christian and that other versions are degenerations of that principal designation; this ordering is both true in reality and yet backwards in historical and epistemological experience.

hobby-horses, this canonical contextualization is no small matter. Dogmatics also compels us to have our priorities and emphases shaped by those marked by Holy Scripture itself: in so doing, its repetitions, its logical connections, and its literary emphases reconfigure our hierarchy of values. When we so frequently misidentify first and second things, such schooling proves essential. Finally, dogmatics hones our approach to any single theme by showing the lineaments that connect it to other biblical doctrines. Dogmatics always returns us, sooner or later, to the God "from whom, through whom, and to him are all things" (Rom. 11:36).

As we seek to think biblically about divine fullness, then, we do well to have our thoughts ordered by the whole Bible. We will consider the topic in four movements: the fullness in God (wherein life and bounty are his own in and of himself), the fullness from God (whereby he shares that life and bounty with his children), the fullness by God (whence comes all that is needed to share that life and bounty with his children), and the fullness before God (which traces the ways in which human faithfulness bears the marks of divine fullness). Good theology must lead eventually to ethics, prayer, and praise, but it may do so only in such a way that the graciousness of those human actions has been described by means of contemplating God and his works on our behalf, through Christ and the Spirit.

Fullness in God: Life and Bounty in and of Himself

Divine fullness is first and foremost a reality within the divine life. God is rich and full with life, light, and all bounty. He possesses these realities in and of himself as the triune God, such that his fullness is that of the eternal triune relations and of the distinctly Trinitarian unity. His riches are owned by he who is without beginning or end and thus who is characterized by aseity. Yet his bounteous bliss goes beyond mere self-existence or self-sufficiency to also require that we attest his excess, wealth, and fullness. All that he has, he is, and he has all and more.

The doctrine of the Trinity not only identifies God by his singular name, as Father, Son, and Holy Spirit (Mt. 28:19), but also depicts the relational character of God's life. The persons share perfect bounty and life in and of themselves; for instance, the way in which the Son shares that self-sufficiency and fullness in and of himself with the Father is attested by Jesus: "For as the Father has life in himself, so he has granted the Son also to have life in himself" (Jn 5:26). While Bonaventure speaks of the Father as "fullness as source," the Son and Spirit possess fullness as generated and spirated, each in their own personal mode of subsistence.[2] God is full, not only of power or knowledge but also of love within the triune communion. Father, Son, and Holy Spirit have shared perfect charity with one another for all eternity, such that their actions toward us do not begin their life of love but only express the public overflow of what has marked their own unity from everlasting unto everlasting. Only with such an understanding can we confess not simply that

---

2. Bonaventure, *Commentary on Sentences*, 1.27.1.

God acted lovingly or that God took upon himself a loving posture but that "God is love" (1 Jn 4:8; see also 1 Jn 4:16). John presses home the eternal nature of God's love in that the divine demonstration of love in sending his Son is immediately described as an occasion for "making manifest among us" that love, rather than initiating or beginning that love (1 Jn 4:9).

The divine fullness has also been expressed in part by the doctrine of divine aseity. This confession of the self-existence of God speaks to the fact, negatively, that God does not receive being from another and, positively, that God possesses life in and of himself. Aseity is not equivalent to the well-intentioned but logically mangled notion of being *causa sui* or cause of one's own being. Aseity speaks, rather, to existing apart from any cause and, thus, it removes God's existence from the same sort of category as that of every other being. While God has being, his being, then, is not of a type or sort to be likened unto or related nearly to human or creaturely being. Traditionally, language of the *analogia entis* has been intended to emphasize both the shared fellowship and the marked and qualitative distinction between God's way or mode of existing and that of all creatures.[3] We do not share existence univocally, though we do both exist (and hence equivocation regarding being cannot be appropriate). The realm of analogy means to acknowledge being with a difference. While the notion took on a very different sort of meaning in late modern theology and, thus, received brutal responses from some in the Protestant world (such as Karl Barth), we can appreciate its classical concern to express the very biblical principle of the Creator–creature distinction (signaled by texts such as Exod. 3:14 and others) alongside the equally scriptural reality of fellowship in being.

Aseity gestures toward fullness, though it does not comprehend the doctrine. Aseity specifically signals the fullness or self-sufficiency of God's existence.[4] Fullness moves beyond that claim to make a still further one. God has "life in himself" (Jn

3. For helpful analysis of classical Reformed endorsement of the *analogia entis*, albeit in the vein of Thomas Aquinas rather than his later interpreter Cajetan, see Richard A. Muller, "Not Scotist: Understandings of Being, Univocity, and Analogy in Early-Modern Reformed Thought," *Reformation & Renaissance Review* 14 (2012): 127–50. Muller finds affirmation in Maccovius, Junius, Zanchi, Voetius, and others, at several points disagreeing with the argument presented by J. Martin Bac, *Perfect Will Theology: Divine Agency in Reformed Scholasticism as against Suarez, Episcopius, Descartes, and Spinoza* (Leiden: Brill, 2012). Unlike some later renderings of the *analogia entis* (especially after modifications to the doctrine at the hands of Cajetan and Suarez), the key focus in classical Reformed renderings was on proportionality. For a nuanced reflection on late modern declensions and their Protestant rebuttal by Barth, see Keith L. Johnson, *Karl Barth and the Analogia Entis* (T&T Clark Studies in Systematic Theology; London: T&T Clark, 2010), esp. ch. 2.

4. On a positive account of aseity, see John Webster, "Life In and Of Himself," in *God without Measure: Working Papers in Christian Theology*, vol. 1: *God and the Works of God* (London: T&T Clark, 2015), 13–28; and especially Augustine, *Tractates on the Gospel of John 11-27* (Fathers of the Church 79; Washington, DC: Catholic University of America Press, 1988), tract. 22.

5:26), but he is also blessed "from everlasting unto everlasting" (Neh. 9:5). God not only possesses mercy but is "rich in mercy" (Eph. 2:4) and has "riches of his glory" (Rom. 9:24). Whereas aseity is necessary to fullness, touting the self-possession of God's existence, aseity is not itself sufficient to signal the overflow that is the divine fullness. God is not only without beginning or end as *a se*, that is, the "first and the last," but also the "living one" who is replete and filled to overflowing with vitality (Rev. 1:17-18). Indeed, he is not only "Alpha and Omega," but also the one "who is and who was and who is to come, the Almighty" (Rev. 1:8; see also Rev. 4:8).[5] This fullness marks God out to be the one known by the high priest as "the Blessed One" (Mk. 14:61),[6] the "blessed God" (1 Tim. 1:11), and "God, the blessed and only ruler, the king of kings and lord of lords" (1 Tim. 6:15). When we attest the blessedness and richness of God in and of himself, we indicate his reality as the one who possesses all fullness and whose own character is rich. He not only has what he has by himself—rather than from another—but he has it excessively.

Fullness from God: Sharing That Life and Bounty with Others through Election, Creation, and Incarnation

God's fullness does not leave God locked up in himself. The logic of the gospel's God runs in just the opposite direction. Precisely out of his fullness, God overflows in grace and free favor unto others, and he gives lavishly without thereby giving himself away. Indeed, one of the most significant features in tracing out the divine fullness is the new perception we may now possess of grace, for the bestowal of a blessing to another can only truly be called grace (undeserved favor of one sort or another) when the one bestowing the gift has all that they need and needs nothing from the object of that gift. We can see how his rich possession of all blessings in and of himself shapes and marks the manner of his election, creation, and incarnation.

First, divine fullness marks the election of God's children not for anything foreseen in them but by God's mysterious will alone. "He chose us in him [Christ] before the foundation of the world" (Eph. 1:3-4). And this divine predestination in Christ Jesus flows from the "God and Father of our Lord Jesus Christ" who is himself "blessed" (Eph. 1:3-4).[7] The unconditional nature of divine election flows

---

5. Rev. 1:17 and 4:8 surely seek to render an amplification of Exod. 3:14, expanding on that text's temporal underdetermination and amplifying it in all three tenses.

6. Some translations (e.g., ESV) simply render "the Blessed" here.

7. On Eph. 1:3-4 and election, see Wesley Hill, "The Text of Ephesians and the Theology of Bucer," in *Reformation Readings of Paul: Explorations in History and Exegesis* (ed. Michael Allen and Jonathan Linebaugh; Downers Grove, IL: IVP Academic, 2015), 143–64; on election in Romans 9, see also David Gibson, *Reading the Decree: Exegesis, Election, and Christology in Calvin and Barth* (T&T Clark Studies in Systematic Theology; London: T&T Clark, 2009); Ben Dunson, *Individual and Community in Paul's Letter to the Romans* (WUNT 2:332; Tübingen: Mohr Siebeck, 2012).

not from arbitrariness as if election is randomness, but we speak of unconditional election as coming from or arising out of nothing in and of the human object of election. This reality was relayed powerfully by Moses (Deut. 7:6-8) and later by Paul (Rom. 9:6-29). Election does come from somewhere, though, and it does express wisdom. It comes not from a wisdom or logic based on reciprocity and of the blessing of those who merit, deserve, or will make best use of a gift. Rather it comes to the dead, and it expresses the wisdom and logic of divine generosity. We can refer to this as a logic and not mere arbitrariness, because it flows from God's self-possession of the fullness of life and bounty. Should God need supplementation or fulfillment, it would make all the sense in the world for him to elect those with potential. In light of his fullness, however, his electing love flows seamlessly to seek out the small, insignificant, and even sin-drenched.

Second, divine fullness shapes the very character of creation itself, wherein nothing is needed or utilized other than the divine voice. The doctrine of *creatio ex nihilo* speaks not only of the distinction between uncreated being and created being but goes a step further to attest that the creative activity of the uncreated one does not find its origination, supplementation, or coordination in any input from the created order. It is not for nothing that the prologue of John states that "all things were made through him [the Logos, who is with God and is God], and without him was not anything made that was made," and then it immediately shifts to say that "in him was life" (Jn 1:3,4).[8] The vitality—and possession of not only his own life but that of all—leads to the creation. The text makes this plain then by saying further that "the life was the light of men" (Jn 1:4). In other words, God's own life—his full life within the triune being of God—illumines and spreads. The metaphor of light is apt because the sun's rays spread without in any way diminishing the luminosity of the sun itself. God's spreading and sharing—specifically here, his act of creating all things with the input or help of no other—does not in any way diminish God.

Third, divine fullness comes within the realm of the creaturely in the person of the Son. The chosen vessel of God's care for his elect people is the Messiah, "who is God over all, blessed forever" (Rom. 9:5). "In him all the fullness of God was pleased to dwell" (Col. 1:19); indeed, Paul presses further to emphasize the human frame of his divine condescension, "for in him the whole fullness of deity dwells bodily" (Col. 2:9). Donald Carson has argued that this incarnational fullness of deity within human being through personal union marks out a greater grace than that known through the law in his interpretation of the Johannine teaching that "from his fullness we have all received grace upon grace" (Jn 1:16). Carson suggests that "grace upon grace" be read in terms of an antithesis that highlights the still greater mercy shown in the incarnation.[9] While the law was a prior grace,

---

8. Cyril makes a similar point in interpreting Jn 3:36 relating this text to Jn 1:4; see Cyril of Alexandria, *Commentary on John*, vol. 1 (ed. Joel Elowsky; trans. David Maxwell; Ancient Christian Texts; Downers Grove, IL: IVP Academic, 2013), 115.

9. D. A. Carson, *The Gospel According to John* (Grand Rapids, MI: Eerdmans, 1991), 132.

it has been replaced by Christ as the means of experiencing the presence of God, which can now be known in a much greater display of grace precisely because Christ possesses the divine fullness. His fullness has been accented already in the famous claim that "the Word became flesh and dwelt among us, and we have seen his glory, glory as of the only Son from the Father, full of grace and truth" (Jn 1:14). The incarnate Son's glory marks out his character as overflowingly rich with the very characteristics of yhwh (for "grace" and "truth" are terms which render the divine attributes of Exod. 34:6-7). Cyril of Alexandria speaks of how, possessed of the fullness, the Son's grace is one which then "gushes forth to each soul" such that the "creature receives" this gift "as from an ever-flowing spring."[10] The gospel of the Son speaks not only of the righting of wrongs but the glorifying of the ordinary through the mediation of the incarnate Son, himself full to the brim with the Father's glory and quick to make common those riches for his brothers and sisters.

Fullness by God: Doing All Needful for Sharing That Life and Bounty with Others through Applying Salvation and Extending His Mission

God's fullness leads to action for the sake of creaturely renewal in salvation through Christ Jesus. In doing so God offers all to the creature without receiving any benefit or recompense from the creature. Paul attests to this divine weightiness in his remarks at the Areopagus: "The God who made the world and everything in it, being Lord of heaven and earth, does not live in temples made by man, nor is he served by human hands, as though he needed anything, since he himself gives to all mankind life and breath and everything" (Acts 17:24-25). God is full to the brim; no closeness or communion with us, whether in creation or temple or any other fellowship, serves to fill him up. "Yet he is actually not far from each one of us, for 'in him we live and move and have our being'" (Acts 17:28, likely citing Epimenides of Crete). To the divine fullness in himself there is also divine fullness for others, and in that divine fullness for others there is a sufficient provision enacted by God.

First, God goes still further in applying that work of Christ, fulfilling the needful task of working out salvation by including or enfolding others into his life and death. The goal of knowing God in Christ is such that "you may be filled with all the fullness of God" (Eph. 3:19). Regularly, we read of the work done for us by Christ as "bestowing his riches on all who call on him" (Rom. 10:12) or as "the riches of his grace, which he lavished upon us" (Eph. 1:7-8). We can see the fullness of God expressed in the human bearing found in the person and life of Jesus, for we are to "all attain to the unity of the faith and of the knowledge of the Son of God, to mature manhood, to the measure of the stature of the fullness of Christ" (Eph. 4:13). The salvific work of Christ not only meets the bare minimum of our needs, but offers an excessive largesse. For this reason Hebrews can speak

10. Cyril of Alexandria, *Commentary on John*, vol. 1, 67 (on Jn 1:16).

of "so great a salvation," not only in its cause and cost (in terms of incarnation and sacrificial atonement) but also in terms of its conferral (Heb. 2:3). Ultimately, the sufficiency or fullness of God's work flows from the character of his mercy in his very being, for "our God is full of compassion" (Ps. 116:5) and "rich in mercy" (Eph. 2:4).

Second, God's fullness presses beyond these two prior graces to still wider provision in enabling Christian mission and actualizing his kingdom here upon earth. Paul tells the Corinthians that "in every way you were enriched in him in all speech and all knowledge—even as the testimony about Christ was confirmed among you—so that you are not lacking in any spiritual gift" (1 Cor. 1:5-7). The provision of God's enrichment enables attestation or testimony; Christian witness flows from God's continuing provision. Divine gifts are not only the origin of mission and the content of its proclamation; the overflowing fullness of God is the very context for and energy unto Christian witness. Indeed, for this reason the church can be likened as "his body, the fullness of him who fills all in all" (Eph. 1:23). The head works through the body—the church—such that it expresses and extends his fullness to the world in mission.[11] The church does not become Christ, nor does the church fill him; just the opposite, he "fills all in all." But the church does become identified with him and even with his "fullness."

Think of the remarkable grace shown to men and women that God not only gives us reconciliation in Christ but even enlists us as ambassadors or instruments of reconciliation (2 Cor. 5:17-20) and goes a step further to speak of us as those "working together with him" (2 Cor. 6:1). We might consider this a remarkable risk; when a project matters, we tend to make sure we do not place its results in the hands of the weak. Yet Paul has noted that these Corinthians who are fellow workers with God are not wise or fitting (1 Cor. 1:20-21). God can enlist weak disciples because God lacks nothing; his mission flows out of his very vitality. God's fullness enables the frail and fallen to be employed in kingdom work, as his abundance proves to be more than enough to ensure the accomplishment of his intended goals. The blessing pronounced by Paul in Rom. 15:13 invokes the filling of God: "May the God of hope fill you with all joy and peace in believing." It leads to personal transformation that can only be characterized as abundance: "so that by the power of the Holy Spirit you may abound in hope." But God's abundant filling spills over immediately into service and ministry: "I myself am satisfied about you, my brothers, that you yourselves are full of goodness, filled with all knowledge and able to instruct one another" (15:14). God fills by his Spirit, abundantly enriching our hope, filling us with goodness, that we may be filled with knowledge so as to

---

11. Maintaining the distinction between head and members is no doubt pivotal and attested even in the immediate context here, wherein Paul has just said "And he put all things under his feet and gave him as head over all things to the church" (Eph. 1:22). "All things under his feet" surely includes the church itself. Indeed, we can speak of the lordship of Christ over the church as a preparatory microcosm of his wider reign over all creation, which will eventually bow the knee as his ecclesia has done so already.

teach and instruct others. The recipient of God's filling, then, is brought into his centrifugal movement which ever always reaches out to bring more into its blessed possession of all good riches.

Fullness before God: The Resulting Character of Creaturely Holiness as Faithful Prayer and Praise

The fullness of God shapes the faithfulness of human creatures in Christ. Because God's character is displayed in the gospel, human knowledge and service to God are re-shaped accordingly. To the nature of God corresponds the life and behavior of his creaturely subjects. How does our following the way of Jesus bear the marks of divine fullness? What elements of our covenantal devotion demonstrate the effects of this divine attribute?

First, divine fullness reminds us that we always depend upon God and never out-run our need for his provision. We have received grace and count our lives to be his own (Rom. 14:8-9; Phil. 1:21). Yet when we ask: "what shall I render to the LORD for all his benefits to me?" we answer "I will lift up the cup of salvation and call on the name of the LORD" (Ps. 116:12,13). Indeed the Psalmist identifies this action as paying his "vows" to the LORD (Ps. 116:14,18). We see, however, that these vows are not made good on by doing something other than calling for more generosity from God and, thereby, going more deeply into one's dependence upon him.[12] The image of lifting up the cup of salvation is one like Oliver Twist asking "More?" Because God is a Deity of fullness, not lacking but possessing all within himself, we never shift into the mode of returning discrete goods to God. Even our thanksgiving takes the form of calling upon him for still more deliverance (Ps. 116:17).[13] Divine blessedness and its expression through blessing others cultivate the Christian ethic of prayerful dependence and a life always marked by faithful trust in the triune God.

Second, divine fullness prompts us to reduce all things ultimately to God and, correspondingly, to return all things to him in praise. The art of reduction is an intellectual exercise of tracing things back to their deepest cause or principle. We reduce a bodily malady not by forgetting or overlooking it, but by appreciating its deeper roots in a virus or other illness. Similarly, we do not negate, minimize, or disrespect creaturely realities in reducing them to God, but we do accurately

---

12. For further reflection on how sanctification is always by faith alone, though not of faith alone, see John Owen, *Pneumatologia* (Works of John Owen 3; Edinburgh: Banner of Truth Trust, 1965), esp. 413–6; G. C. Berkouwer, *Faith and Sanctification* (Studies in Dogmatics; trans. John Vriend; Grand Rapids, MI: Eerdmans, 1952), ch. 2; Michael Allen, *Sanctification* (New Studies in Dogmatics; Grand Rapids, MI: Zondervan Academic, 2017), ch. 10.

13. Calling upon God's name involves a cry for his rescue, as can be seen earlier in Ps. 116:4.

assess them in light of his fullness. In this drama of human blight and glory, there is genuine integrity and blissful good within the creaturely realm. These graces are spread far and wide. But we cannot envision these graces separated from the wider orbit of gospel truths, for we see them flowing forth from him; we appreciate them as suspended through him; we see them as purposed unto return to him. "For from him and through him and to him are all things"; Paul hereby locates all reality within the movement of God's fullness. Thus, he voices an ethical implication: "To him be glory forever" (Rom. 11:36). The blessed abundance of God's being leads to the wide extent of God's provision which leads in turn to all glory, laud, and honor being his own. Divine fullness—and its overflow into the gracious economy of his works—shapes the ethic of Christian praise.

Conclusion: Confessing the Fullness of God Yesterday and Today

Let us return to where we began: Is fullness truly absent from recent theology? While the dominant strands of contemporary theology in the wider academy have tilted toward either some form of process theology or to what may be termed evangelical historicism, which is an over-identification to or reduction of God's being to that action in the economy of the gospel, we can observe some retrievals of the fullness of God. John Webster has sought to refocus attention upon the perfection of God and to think all other realities of the divine or the divine economy always relative to that preponderant beauty.[14] My colleague Scott Swain has sought to reorient contemporary approaches to the trinity (specifically countering those of the Lutheran Robert Jenson and the Presbyterian Bruce McCormack, advocates of leading versions of evangelical historicism) in a similar manner by beginning with the riches that are God's own:

> The triune God is inherently rich, "the everlasting well of all good things which is never drawn dry." To the gospel's "blessed God" (1 Tim. 1:11) belong the immeasurable fullness of greatness, power, glory, victory, and majesty, an immeasurable fullness that God enjoys in and of himself (1 Chron. 29:11; Ps. 145:3; Jn. 5:26; Rom. 11:33-35). The divine works *ad extra* are consequently the free and generous overflow of God's fontal plenitude. (Ps. 36:8-9; Jn. 1:4; 5:21-25; Rom. 11:33-36; Jas. 1:17)[15]

Swain has turned a discussion about divine aseity and self-sufficiency, more restrictive jargon, to the deeper font of divine fullness, biblical and classical

14. While present in numerous works now, see most recently the essays published in John Webster, *God without Measure: Working Papers in Christian Theology*, vol. 1: *God and the Works of God* (London: T&T Clark, 2015).
15. Scott R. Swain, *The God of the Gospel: Robert Jenson's Trinitarian Theology* (Strategic Initiatives in Evangelical Theology; Downers Grove, IL: IVP Academic, 2013), 152–3.

language which speaks not only of sufficiency but of excess and resplendence. And he has turned away from history and the dramas of redemption's story and creational engagement to the deep sublime of God's eternal repose. Still further, as with Webster's arguments, he has then tried to show how this divine richness does not undermine the economy or the covenant, but helps show its singular nature: unlike other relations, here is one of grace, true and free.

If there are some voices reminding us of the riches of divine fullness today, we might ask if fullness is really missing from the Westminster Standards? While the specific terms "fullness" and "full" are not to be found on the surface of the text, it is perhaps appropriate to see the judgment present implicitly in the structure of the argument. Westminster Shorter Catechism 4 identifies God as "a Spirit, infinite, eternal, and unchangeable in his being, wisdom, power, holiness, justice, goodness, and truth." Notice that three terms—"infinite, eternal, and unchangeable"—qualify the way in which we hear the final seven terms. God's being, for example, is one that is infinite, eternal, and unchangeable. Here we see the doctrine of divine simplicity put to grammatical usage, in that the structure of the sentence exemplifies that tenet's affirmation that God's attributes are unified in reality.[16]

How do we read Westminster's litany of divine attributes in light of divine simplicity? Each of the attributes of God is his own infinitely, eternally, and unchangeably; this provides a matrix for interpreting each attribute as interpenetrating the others. They are simple in themselves; for us, knowing them requires dialectical thought to appreciate their oneness. The profusion of terms and their substantive inter-relations, however, point to the weighty fullness of the divine being. God has excessive or rich possession of all his characteristics, such that neither time, space, nor anything else might limit or diminish them. The combination of terms found therein—"infinite, eternal, and unchangeable"— intermingles together and attests to the notion of fullness. Each of God's qualities or attributes bears the fullness or richness which exceeds any single place (infinity) or time (eternity) or any episode or circumstance which might ebb or flow (immutability or unchangeableness). Taken together, then, these terms speak to the self-sufficient blessedness of God. God brims over in excess with each and every one of his many-splendored attributes.

16. For defense and analysis of divine simplicity, see Steven J. Duby, *Divine Simplicity: A Dogmatic Account* (T&T Clark Studies in Systematic Theology; London: T&T Clark, 2015). A number of criticisms have been launched regarding this doctrine, the most significant of which include Wolfhart Pannenberg, *The End of Metaphysics and the Idea of God* (trans. Philip Clayton; Grand Rapids: Eerdmans, 1990), 11–12; and T. F. Torrance, *The Christian Doctrine of God: One Being, Three Persons* (Edinburgh: T&T Clark, 1996), 246–50. Analytic theologians and philosophers of religion have also protested, most notably Alvin Plantinga, *Does God Have a Nature?* (Milwaukee, WI: Marquette University Press, 1980), 1–9; and Eleonore Stump and Norman Kretzmann, "Absolute Simplicity," *Faith and Philosophy* 2 (1985): 353–82.

It is worth making explicit that implicit logic, for divine fullness provides a remarkable lens for seeing the movement of Christian theology as a whole. Fullness speaks directly of God and then, secondarily, of other beings from God, in God, and unto God. Fullness bespeaks the reality of Christ by nature and of the body of Christ by grace. Fullness points back to the Alpha of God's eternal self-sufficiency while also gesturing forward to the Omega of God's limitless provision for his glorified saints. Fullness reminds us that the triune God of creation is rich and enriching, that the lordly king of our salvation is blessed from everlasting to everlasting and blesses his saints forevermore. Fullness reorients us to one who, in the gospel, gives without giving himself away. Not surprisingly, then, language of fullness appears (under the idiom of blessedness, riches, or fullness) regularly alongside calls to and demonstrations of prayer and praise. Such a God as this one summons forth our songs, our prayers, our very selves and all we have.

Chapter 5

TRINITY: CONTEMPLATIVE AND PRACTICAL WISDOM

Reading the Bible well involves dealing with its matter, namely, the triune God, for the living and true God is present in and through its varied means or its literary multiformity. Thinking about hermeneutics in a manner that is biblically rooted demands attention be given to the doctrine of the Trinity. The Trinity serves as a focal point but also a nexus, a lodestar for our contemplation as well as a searchlight for our pathways. In tending to the hermeneutical centrality of the Trinity, the supposed modern revival of interest in Trinitarian theology warrants analysis.[1] Beginning with the work of Karl Barth and Karl Rahner, both Protestants and Roman Catholics of all stripes have given themselves to engagement of this doctrine in its material form as well as its methodological significance. Trinity has functioned as a central hermeneutical means but also as a lens for hermeneutical ends.

This supposed revival may not be truly vivifying; much of its purported historical assessment has been shown subsequently to be rather uninformed and not surprisingly a good many of its material judgments are thereby malformed, including at key junctures.[2] Even so, it has helped re-emphasize the centrality of

---

1. Exemplary instances of the so-called revival are Christoph Schwöbel (ed.), *Trinitarian Theology Today: Essays on Divine Being and Act* (Edinburgh: T&T Clark, 2000); and Stanley J. Grenz, *Rediscovering the Triune God: The Trinity in Contemporary Theology* (Minneapolis, MN: Fortress, 2004). The former volume also includes an essay-length synopsis from John Zizioulas, whose work has been perhaps the most frequently cited text in the so-called revival: *Being as Communion: Studies in Personhood and the Church* (Crestwood, NJ: St. Vladimir's Seminary Press, 1997).

2. Summary of the historical reassessment exceeds the bounds of this essay yet warrants mention. For a synopsis of so-called "new canon" historiographic research, see the perceptive essay by Michel Rene Barnes, "The Fourth Century as Trinitarian Canon," in *Christian Origins: Theology, Rhetoric, and Community* (ed. Lewis Ayres and Gareth Jones; London: Routledge, 1998), 47–67; as well as monograph-length analyzes including Lewis Ayres, *Nicaea and Its Legacy: An Approach to Fourth Century Trinitarian Theology* (Oxford: Oxford University Press, 2004); John Behr, *Formation of Christian Theology*, vol. 1: *The Way to Nicaea* and vol. 2: *The Nicene Faith* (Crestwood, NJ: St. Vladimir's Seminary Press, 2001–4) and a host of more specific studies on various figures (including Arius, Athanasius,

the works of God as the place whereby God is made present and known; hence an emphasis upon the economy or the economic Trinity has been a first principle in much recent Trinitarianism. Similarly, it has paired this economic focus with a second principle, namely, that the doctrine of the Trinity cannot be isolated but must also be employed or put to use in shaping other doctrines and concerns; hence the proliferation of Trinitarian theologies of this, that, and the other. In this chapter, I will explore ways in which these two principles help shape a Trinitarian reading of the Bible productively, at least if they are handled in a wise manner and so long as overreach is avoided. In one sense the Trinitarian theology of Kevin J. Vanhoozer has brought much of twentieth-century reflection on the Trinity to something of a transition: offering a chastened account of the economy of the gospel and then applying that theology to the task of practical wisdom in what he deems a theodramatic form, so we will see his contribution in each regard. In this chapter these two principles are examined in the course of recent Trinitarian formulation, in each case also offering brief suggestions for how they might be most capably put to hermeneutical work.

Principle 1: The Turn to the Economy: The Supposed Revival

Theologies in the twentieth century turned emphatically and, at least at times, exclusively to the economy of God's works. In an attempt to avoid speculation, they began with the missions of the incarnate Son of God (the Word) and the sending of the *Paraclete* (the Spirit), from which alone can any judgments about God's inner life be ventured. To grasp this foundation in the divine economy, the Trinitarian theology of Karl Barth, Karl Rahner, Jürgen Moltmann, and finally Kevin Vanhoozer will be assessed.

Karl Barth: The God Who Elects to Self-Reveal

Karl Barth's doctrine of God was offered as a salve to a wounded Protestant body. That body manifested itself in symptoms such as a theologically weakened backbone incapable of standing up to National Socialism in the 1930s or to the prior war efforts in the 1910s, but the roots of that malady were far deeper. Weakness in liberal theology stemmed from missteps in earlier Orthodox dogmatics, especially regarding the doctrine of God. "We stand here before the fundamental error which dominated the doctrine of God of the older

---

Basil, Gregory Nyssa, Gregory Nazianzus, Augustine, and Thomas Aquinas) and a range of topics (divine simplicity, eternal generation, inseparable operations, the *filioque*, *perichoresis*, patristic exegesis, divine impassibility, aseity, and the divine processions). For perspective on the claims of the so-called revival, see Stephen R. Holmes, *The Quest for the Trinity: The Doctrine of God in Scripture, History, and Modernity* (Downers Grove, IL: IVP Academic, 2012).

theology and which influenced Protestant Orthodoxy at almost every point. For the greater part this doctrine of God tended elsewhere than to God's act in revelation, and for the greater part it also started elsewhere than from there."[3] Barth was a student of the post-Reformation Reformed dogmatics, viewing them as personally invaluable for his own preparation as a university professor in the early 1920s, and yet he deems them to have made a misstep at just this point, namely, beginning to study God elsewhere than his self-revelation (whether later historical work shows Barth's judgment here to be valid or not has been and should be debated).

For himself, Barth begins the doctrine of God otherwise. "It is by the grace of God and only by the grace of God that it comes about that God is knowable to us."[4] But what does that divine grace for knowledge of God involve? "God reveals Himself. He reveals Himself through Himself. He reveals Himself."[5] The triune God reveals himself and in revealing himself, he graciously does all that is needed for humans to know him, and in so providing all, he reveals himself to be triune: Revelation yes, but also, Revealer and Revealedness.

Divine self-revelation does not remain nebulous or abstract, however, as Barth ties it more specifically to the coming of the incarnate Word of God and the sending of his promised Holy Spirit. "If God gives Himself to man to be known in the revelation of his Word through the Holy Spirit, it means that He enters into the relationship of object to man the subject."[6] That Word is the singular revelation of God, and "therefore our first and decisive transcription of the statement that God is, must be that God is who He is in the act of His revelation."[7] Barth scholars continue to debate just how deep that material judgment goes— whether divine being in the act of divine self-revelation means that there is no anterior divine life or not[8]—but the broader point has kick-started a modern emphasis upon the divine economy of Word and Spirit as the matrix within which God makes himself to be known. Similarly influential (albeit, in hindsight and with the benefit of more recent studies in the primary sources, historically questionable) was Barth's historical judgment that this constitutes a turn not merely from liberal platitudes that identified culture with divine spirit but also from Orthodox dogmatics that conflated Christ and Divine Wisdom with the capacities of human rationality.

3. Karl Barth, *Church Dogmatics*, II/2: 261.
4. Barth, *CD*, II/1: 69.
5. Barth, *CD*, I/1: 296.
6. Barth, *CD*, II/1: 9.
7. Barth, *CD*, II/1: 262.
8. See especially Bruce McCormack, "Grace and Being: The Role of God's Gracious Election in Karl Barth's Theological Ontology," in *Cambridge Companion to Karl Barth* (ed. John Webster; Cambridge: Cambridge University Press, 2000), 92–110; and Paul Molnar, *Divine Freedom and the Doctrine of the Immanent Trinity* (2nd ed.; London: T&T Clark, 2017).

Karl Rahner: Transcendental Existential and Self-Giving Communication of God

Barth's Protestant prophecyings, with both their lament of supposed ills and their summons to new life for the doctrine of God, were matched by the Trinitarian judgments of the Roman Catholic theologian, Karl Rahner. His work was scattered across various essays, but his influence has stemmed largely from a work that has circulated under the title *The Trinity*.[9] The treatise begins with two sections of descriptive work wherein, first, Rahner speaks of the isolation of the Trinity from Roman Catholic piety and, second, of the problematic relation of theological attempts to relate divine unity and trinity. "Despite their orthodox confession of the Trinity, Christian are, in their practical life, almost mere 'monotheists' … should the doctrine of the Trinity have to be dropped as false, the major part of religious literature could well remain unchanged."[10] Not merely piety, though, but also the doctrine of God could be left unchanged, for "it looks as if everything which matters for us in God has already been said in the treatise 'On the One God'" and nothing notable remains to be said in the following treatise "On the Triune God."[11] Like Barth, Rahner judges both practice and theory to be malformed.

What prescription does Rahner offer to this illness in Roman Catholic theology and life? "The doctrine of the 'missions' is from its very nature the starting point for the doctrine of the Trinity."[12] Here Rahner uses language developed in the tradition to speak not of the life of God in himself but of God's transitive actions wherein Word and Spirit, the second and third persons of the Godhead, extend God's own life toward others. Thus Barth's emphasis upon Word and Spirit is matched here by Rahner's focus upon the missions of God, each identifying these works of the divine economy as the starting point for Trinitarian theology. Rahner, like Barth, also identifies them not merely as an inception point but an ongoing fundament or baseline, as he says that "we must always return to the original experience of salvation history" in our theology.[13]

To express this method, Rahner offers a maxim: "The 'economic' Trinity is the 'immanent' Trinity and the 'Immanent' Trinity is the 'economic' Trinity."[14] The language of "economic Trinity" speaks of the Godhead moving outward in those Trinitarian missions of the divine economy. The mention of the "immanent Trinity" speaks, however, of God's own life in himself, which Rahner explicitly notes is nowhere explicitly addressed in the Bible (not even in texts such as Jn 1:1-14).[15] What Rahner here calls a "thesis" has since been referenced as "Rahner's

9. Karl Rahner, *The Trinity* (trans. Joseph Donceel; London: Herder & Herder, 1970).
10. Rahner, *Trinity*, 10–11.
11. Rahner, *Trinity*, 17.
12. Rahner, Trinity, 48.
13. Rahner, Trinity, 106.
14. Rahner, Trinity, 22.
15. Rahner, Trinity, 22.

Rule."[16] Rahner went on to speak of the "methodological importance of our basic thesis" in as much as it prompts theologians to start with and found all that is needed of divine knowledge in salvation history (what early fathers called the economy), even that which we need to know of the immanent life of God in himself.[17] Rahner will speak more widely of human transcendental knowledge of God who is revealed in our existential self-awareness of need for more, though that revelation of God as the transcendental existential" is most focused in the way in which God is revealed in salvation history or the divine economy. Rahner says that "the divine self-communication possesses two basic modalities: self-communication as truth and as love ... His self-communication, insofar as it occurs as 'truth,' happens in history; and that insofar as it is happens as 'love,' it opens this history in transcendence towards the absolute future."[18] In other words, God is known in the economy of both historical self-revelation (of the Son) and existential transcendence (through the Spirit); in both cases, though, God's own being or inner life is known in and through, and normed and limited by God's economy of works, both public and private. In this regard Rahner has extended Barth's emphasis upon the economy to include not merely the singular history of redemption but also the existential presence of the triune God in all times.

Jürgen Moltmann: The Suffering Trinity and Divine Reciprocity

The projects of Barth and Rahner both identified problems in faith and practice and sought to refashion a Trinitarianism without abstractions, largely by grounding their efforts upon the divine economy. Later theologians would take up the task and extend it still further. While a host of figures might be considered here (including Wolfhart Pannenberg, Eberhard Jüngel, Robert Jenson, Colin Gunton, or Stanley Grenz), Jürgen Moltmann has most vigorously and widely illustrated the trajectory.

Moltmann shares a sense that something has gone amiss. He juxtaposes an approach to the doctrine of God via God as "the supreme substance" with an alternative affirmation wherein "God is the absolute subject."[19] Yet Moltmann finds both approaches lacking: "In distinction to the trinity of substance and to the trinity of subject we shall be attempting to develop a social doctrine of the Trinity" and in so doing will draw on "panentheistic ideas."[20] To grasp the negations as well

---

16. See especially Fred Sanders, *The Image of the Immanent Trinity: Rahner's Rule and the Theological Interpretation of Scripture* (Issues in Systematic Theology 12; Peter Lang, 2004).

17. Rahner, *Trinity*, 40.

18. Rahner, *Trinity*, 98. See also Stephen J. Duffy, "Experience of Grace," in *Cambridge Companion to Karl Rahner* (ed. Declan Marmion and Mary Hines; Cambridge: Cambridge University Press, 2006), 43–4 and 46.

19. Moltmann, *The Trinity and the Kingdom of God: The Doctrine of God* (trans. Margaret Kohl; London: SCM, 1981), 10–12.

20. Moltmann, *Trinity and the Kingdom of God*, 19.

as the appeal of panentheism, his concern for the works or deeds of God must be appreciated.

What of the economy in Moltmann's social approach? "The New Testament talks about God by proclaiming in narrative the relationships of the Father, the Son and the Spirit, which are relationships of fellowship and are open to the world."[21] Fellowship within the Godhead appears in the triune works of creation and of new creation, the moments in the divine economy. Indeed, unity "lies in their fellowship, not in the identity of a single subject."[22] Moltmann has no place for divine substance and resolves all Trinitarian unity in these interpersonal relations. These divine works also reveal God's openness to the world, which picks up on the influence of panentheism. He defines "Christian panentheism" must later as "the idea that the world is inherent in the nature of God himself from eternity. For it is impossible to conceive of a God who is not a creative God."[23] This creative and open portrait of God brings with it vulnerability: "The relationship between God and the world has a reciprocal character, because this relationship must be seen as a living one."[24]

This reciprocity runs two ways, positively and negatively. Positively, "if God is love, then he does not merely emanate, flow out of himself; he also expects and needs love."[25] Negatively, this divine need for reciprocal concern opens him up to suffer. A Christological example illustrates this approach to divine limitation: "If we are to understand the suffering of Christ as the *suffering of the passionate God—* it would seem more consistent if we ceased to make the axiom of God's apathy our starting point and started instead from the axiom of God's passion."[26] Here a material turn to the divine economy has led to a more revisionary approach, precisely because the divine economy has been interpreted with God operating as a figure amongst other figures, neither as a substance nor as an Absolute figure or subject above all others; rather God's being has been interpreted panentheistically as always creative and thus as always limited and possible (in what Moltmann calls the "self-humiliation of God"[27]).

Moltmann's emphases on divine vulnerability and passibility as perceived in the divine economy could be seen in the work of others, from Jon Sobrino to

---

21. Motlmann, *Trinity and the Kingdom of God*, 64.

22. Moltmann, *Trinity and the Kingdom of God*, 95 (see also 157).

23. Moltmann, *Trinity and the Kingdom of God*, 106.

24. Moltmann, *Trinity and the Kingdom of God*, 98.

25. Moltmann, *Trinity and the Kingdom of God*, 99.

26. Moltmann, *Trinity and the Kingdom of God*, 22 (italics original). For more on this subject, both divine passibility and patripassianism, see Moltmann, *The Crucified God: The Cross of Christ as the Foundation and Criticism of Christian Theology* (trans. R. A. Wilson and John Bowden; London: SCM, 1974).

27. The language of self-humiliation, though, distinguishes an inward life (wherein such "inward self-humiliation" occurs) from the outward economy (wherein "outward incarnation" manifests the inward move) at least at places in Moltmann's argument: see *Trinity and the Kingdom of God*, 118–19.

Paul Fiddes. One might debate whether some interpreters or improvisers upon the approach of Barth, such as Robert Jenson and Bruce McCormack, do not also wind up logically in much the same place. At the turn of the millennium, this turn to the economy seemed to lead to a revisionary doctrine of God which would be juxtaposed to the God of Protestant liberalism and post-Reformation Orthodoxy (as in Barth), to modern piety and even scholastic theologies of the Roman Catholic churches (as in Rahner), and even to the catholic tradition of the fathers which was now seen to be Hellenized (as in Moltmann). With the work of Moltmann and others, the economic Trinity has led to a radical revision of the divine attributes and of the task of Christian theology as a whole.

Kevin Vanhoozer: Communicative Theism and the Project of Remythologizing

We have already alluded to ways in which the historiographic judgments of this supposed Trinitarian revival have been questioned. The so-called Hellenization thesis has been challenged.[28] Former understandings of post-Reformation Orthodoxy have been overturned.[29] Much of recent Trinitarian theology just won't do. Yet the focus upon the economy, begun by Barth and Rahner and shorn of the excesses of Moltmann and the others, has not simply been tossed in more recent years (and for good reason). No one has shown a critical approach to upholding the emphasis upon the economy apart from that kind of iconoclasm more than Kevin Vanhoozer in his project to remythologize the doctrine of God. His stated goal in *Remythologizing Theology* is "to explore the ontology of the one whose speech and acts propel the theodrama forward."[30] He does not ditch the priority of the economy: "The proper starting point for a doctrine of God is thus the biblical depiction of God as a speaking subject whose breathed ('Spirited') voice is expressed supremely in the Christological Word made flesh and secondarily in the canonical polyphony that in turn presents Jesus Christ."[31] Economy takes in neither only incarnation and passion nor even simply Pentecost but also the apostolic emissaries and their ecclesiastical instruments, the writings that serve as the canonical voice of Jesus Christ. Vanhoozer expands the divine economy, then, to include the speech performative acts of God making Scripture holy: past, present, and

---

28. See, e.g., Andrew Radde-Gallwitz, *Basil of Caesarea, Gregory of Nyssa, and the Transformation of Divine Simplicity* (Oxford Early Christian Studies; Oxford: Oxford University Press, 2009); and Sarah Coakley (ed.), *Re-thinking Gregory of Nyssa* (Directions in Modern Theology; Oxford: Blackwell, 2005).

29. See especially the four volumes of Richard A. Muller, *Post-Reformation Reformed Dogmatics: The Rise and Development of Reformed Orthodoxy, ca. 1520 to ca. 1725* (2nd ed.; Grand Rapids, MI: Baker Academic, 2003).

30. Kevin J. Vanhoozer, *Remythologizing Theology: Divine Action, Passion, and Authorship* (Cambridge Studies in Christian Doctrine; Cambridge: Cambridge University Press, 2010), xiv.

31. Vanhoozer, *Remythologizing Theology*, 24.

future. Whereas Rahner expanded in the direction of existential transcendentals, Vanhoozer pushes toward what he calls a "communicative theism" fixed upon canonical Scripture.

What sort of Trinitarianism flows from this question? Who and what must God be to speak thus? Here Vanhoozer speaks of "remythologizing" as a means of rebutting the attempt (post-Bultmann) to disentangle divine being and presence from the so-called mythos of sacred scripture.

> To remythologize theology we must focus not on the being of God considered in the abstract but on the identity of God considered in the historically and canonically concrete. God is not a story, however; hence to remythologize also entails seeking the implicit logos in the mythos, and that means reflecting on the "what" of the divine "who." Theology must do more than retell the old, old story, but it need not follow that we have to choose between narrative and metaphysics. On the contrary, the way forward is to develop a theological ontology whose basic framework and categories are generated by (or, if borrowed from elsewhere, revised in light of) the divine self-presentation in the gospel of Jesus Christ and its canonical attestation.[32]

In so doing Vanhoozer speaks of how "God's being is in communicating" himself and his speech. Vanhoozer addresses what he calls "kenotic-perichoretic relational ontotheology" (his term for what Moltmann and others such as Philip Clayton are proposing), seeking to counter the recent affirmations of divine passibility. Over against the supposedly vulnerable and empathetic theologies that have dominated recent theology, Vanhoozer suggests that "only the communicating God can help."[33] Such a God must be seen in his economy, though not merely in incarnation and passion and those depths of humiliation but also in resurrection and ascension and his exalted session on high.[34] Vanhoozer's argument here reminds one of the quips from the late Herbert McCabe, namely, that "the temptation to attribute suffering to God as God, to the divine nature, is connected with a failure to acknowledge that it is really God who suffers in Jesus of Nazareth."[35]

A range of questions remain with his project. Does Vanhoozer's description of Trinitarian communicative theism most fully express the kind of communicative project revealed in the economy and the scriptures? Where he says that "the three persons are distinct communicative agents that share a common communicative agency,"[36] one might question whether that's not exactly backward. Would it not better reflect their communicative action and the biblical breadth of

---

32. Vanhoozer, *Remythologizing Theology*, 182–3.

33. Vanhoozer, *Remythologizing Theology*, 504.

34. Vanhoozer, *Remythologizing Theology*, 501.

35. Herbert McCabe, "The Involvement of God," in *God Matters* (London: Mowbray, 1987), 51.

36. Vanhoozer, *Remythologizing Theology*, 247.

God-speech (inclusive of texts such as Rom. 8:12-17 especially) to say they are one communicative agent active in distinct communicative agencies? Such would parallel classical language of inseparable operations and of the one divine will perhaps more smoothly while also affirming the singular covenantal plan of God, adopting women and men into the family of God via union by grace with the eternal, now incarnate Son of God, in whom all such communication occurs by the Spirit.[37]

Such questions noted, Vanhoozer's project should nonetheless be appreciated as an exegetically infused recalibration of the modern turn to the economy, in so doing taking in more of that divine economy (including not only the full span of the Christological works of God, not least the heavenly session, but also the scriptural instruments employed directly by God in making his own goods common through human speech acts). Vanhoozer does not merely turn to the narrative elements of the biblical drama but also attends to passages that provide a metaphysical context within which that drama fits.[38] Reading the Bible for the trinity involves not merely picking up the divine character(s) in the story, but also reading all the breadth of that inscripturated Word. Doing so necessarily alerts the reader to the unique character of the triune God of Israel, who is near and yet other, whose way is in our midst and yet wholly unfamiliar. While Trinitarian theology is to be gleaned from the economy, that economy takes the form not only of redemptive historical acts (say, virgin birth through Pentecost) but also of their redemptive-historical canon (the scriptural witness of prophets and apostles), which illumines not only a major plotline but also its metaphysical context. If the economy fills the verses of the Triune, scriptural hymn, then the recurring chorus (apart from which the varied stanzas make little sense) is that pointed affirmation of the metaphysics of God and creation revealed just as pointedly in biblical verse.

Principle 2: The Call for Practical Wisdom: Trinitarian Theologies of This, That, and the Other

The supposed turn to the Trinity also has involved a marked emphasis upon the value or utility found in viewing other subjects in a Trinitarian manner. Supposedly Christian faith and practice could subtract all Trinitarian reference, Karl Rahner had said, without suffering any real change.[39] Similarly, Robert

---

37. In this regard I construe the communicative agency of the three in Rom. 8:12-17 differently than Sarah Coakley, *God, Sexuality and the Self: An Essay "On the Trinity"* (Cambridge: Cambridge University Press, 2013), 100–51 (esp. 111–21).

38. See also Matthew Levering, *Scripture and Metaphysics: Aquinas and the Renewal of Trinitarian Theology* (Challenges in Contemporary Theology; Oxford: Blackwell, 2003); and Wesley Hill, *Paul and the Trinity: Persons, Relations, and the Pauline Letters* (Grand Rapids, MI: Eerdmans, 2015).

39. Rahner, *The Trinity*, 10–11.

Jenson said that "God's first debility in the Enlightened West is that he has become useless."[40] Immanuel Kant surely agreed as he averred that "absolutely nothing can be acquired for practical life from the doctrine of the Trinity."[41] If there was a worry about a discrete and insular doctrine of the Trinity (as voiced by Rahner and others), then twentieth- and twenty-first-century theologians sought to employ the trinity as a lens for perceiving reality in its multifaceted nature.

If ever that were really true (and there are reasons to doubt neither its truthfulness at points nor its endorsement in the thought of folks ranging from Kant even to doctrinal theologians such as Rahner but at least to question the extent of its applicability[42]), today such could not be said of increasing swathes of doctrine, ethics, and exegesis. The second emphasis of recent Trinitarian theology has been its insistence that the Trinity opens up space for viewing other topics more genuinely, serving not only hermeneutically for reading the Bible but also for constructing a coherent Christian faith and practice.[43] To explore the application of trinity as a lens for viewing other biblical concerns, Karl Barth, Miroslav Volf, Sarah Coakley, and then Kevin Vanhoozer will be considered.

Karl Barth: The Triune Doctrine of the Word of God

Barth not only kick-started this modern focus on the economy; he also showed how Trinitarian thought functioned to illumine other stretches of Christian

---

40. Robert W. Jenson, "The Christian Doctrine of God," in *Keeping the Faith: Essays to Mark the Centenary of* Lux Mundi (ed. Geoffrey Wainwright; London: SPCK, 1989), 27.

41. Immanuel Kant, "Der Streit der Fakultäten," in *Werke in sechs Bänden* (ed. W. Weischedel; Dormstadt: Wissenschaftliche Buchgesellschaft, 1964), 50.

42. Fred Sanders, *The Deep Things of God: How the Trinity Changes Everything* (2nd ed.; Wheaton: Crossway, 2017).

43. Ironically this trend arose simultaneous to what has been a widespread castigation of Augustine's Trinitarian theology (see, e.g., John Zizoulas, *Communion and Otherness: Further Studies in Personhood and the Church* [London: T&T Clark, 2006], esp. 33–4; and Colin Gunton, "Augustine, the Trinity, and the Theological Crisis of the West," *Scottish Journal of Theology* 43, no. 1 [1990]: 33–58; for critical, historiographic pushback, see Lewis Ayres, "Augustine, The Trinity and Modernity: Colin Gunton's *The One, the Three and the Many*," *Augustinian Studies* 26 [1995]: 127–33.). This inverse relationship is ironic given that Augustine's *de Trinitate* provides the paradigmatic example of looking at the Trinity (as revealed in the economy [books 1-4] and named via creedal terminology [books 5-7]) as well as looking along the trinity at creaturely realities [books 8-15]). See Rowan Williams, "*Sapientia* and the Trinity," in Collectanea Augustiniana: Mélanges T. J. van Bavel, (ed. Bernard Bruning, Mathijs Lamberigts, and J. Van Houtem; *Bibliotheca Ephemeridum Theologicarum Lovaniensium XCII-A*. Louvain: Leuven University Press, 1990), 317–32; Michael Hanby, *Augustine and Modernity* (Radical Orthodoxy; London: Routledge, 2003); and Matthew Drever, "The Self before God? Rethinking Augustine's Trinitarian Thought," *Harvard Theological Review* 100, no. 2 (2007): 233–42.

dogmatics. The doctrine of the Trinity in volume one of his *Church Dogmatics* not only identifies the God to be confessed but also addresses methodological prolegomenon. Indeed, the first part volume turns to Trinity as a means of grasping the God who reveals Himself; while it is his lengthiest discussion of Trinity, the volume is technically titled *The Doctrine of the Word of God* (to be followed by volume two, *The Doctrine of God*, which concerns the attributes of God and God's election). Trinity and the doctrine of revelation are bound together in Barth's presentation.

Later volumes would see parallel instances of Trinitarian (or Christological) reflection employed not merely as topics in their own right but as lenses for appreciating the depth of faith and practice. So volume four of the *Church Dogmatics* turns to the doctrine of reconciliation and to Christology. Analysis of the two natures of Christ and his single person provide entryways to analyzing human sin (as pride, sloth, and falsehood and condemnation), human transformation (as justification, sanctification, and vocation), Christian community (as gathered, upbuilding, and sending), and ethics (faith, love, and hope). Here Trinitarian theology, focused predominantly though not exclusively on the Son of God, offers a framework for a textured account of all human transformation, both individual and corporate.

Miroslav Volf: Triune Politics

More commonly, Trinitarian theology in the vein of Moltmann—what may trade under the name of "social Trinitarianism"—has been employed for cultural or sociopolitical purposes. A range of theologians have offered such analysis: Catherine LaCugna, John Zizioulas, Jon Sobrino, Leron Shults, and Stanley Grenz, to name but a few prominent voices. Volf, a student of Moltmann, took up the ecclesiological imprint of the Trinity in his volume, *After Our Likeness: The Church as the Image of the Trinity.*[44] His aim was blunt: "I have tried to develop a nonhierarchical but truly communal ecclesiology based on a nonhierarchical doctrine of the Trinity."[45] He did not deem the link controversial at the time; in fact, he could note that "today, the thesis that ecclesial communion should correspond to trinitarian communion enjoys the status of an almost self-evident proposition."[46]

Now Volf alerts us to the "limits of analogy."[47] He also admits that "within interpersonal relations there is nothing that might correspond to the numerically identical divine nature."[48] And he notably points to the "strict impossibility of

---

44. Grand Rapids, MI: Eerdmans, 1998. See also idem, "'The Trinity Is Our Social Program': The Doctrine of the Trinity and the Shape of Social Engagement," *Modern Theology* 14, no. 3 (1998:, 403–23.

45. Volf, *After Our Likeness*, 4.

46. Volf, *After Our Likeness*, 191.

47. Volf, *After Our Likeness*, 198–200.

48. Volf, *After Our Likeness*, 204.

human correspondence to perichoresis."[49] But he does proceed to describe the "catholic self," arguing that "every person is a catholic person insofar as that person reflects in himself or herself in a unique way the entire, complex reality in which the person lives."[50] This catholic personhood comes only within relationships and cannot be experienced in isolation.[51] And, further, this personal reality is a gift of the Spirit, for "it is not the mutual perichoresis of human beings, but rather the indwelling of the Spirit common to everyone that makes the church into a communion corresponding to the Trinity, a communion in which personhood and sociality are equiprimal."[52]

For Volf, then, "the church reflects in a broken fashion the eschatological communion of the entire people of God with the triune God in God's new creation."[53] While he tries to not merely make but manifest the analogical limits of this fit between triune and human communion, much more might be asked.[54] Not least would be examination of ways in which the divine nature has to function in any such correspondence, given that the divine nature and will exist in a fashion that drastically outstrips any creaturely commonality. Human unity is not on the order of divine unity and singularity; it merited saying, "Hear, O Israel, the LORD your God, the LORD is one" (Deut. 6:4). Volf's approach to a Trinitarian approach to community typifies recent trends to use the doctrine, or at least slivers of the doctrine, as a map for a distinctive politics.

Sarah Coakley: Gender, Transforming Desire, and Trinity

Not all applications of Trinity to other issues provide such a smooth transition from the divine to the ideals of human flourishing regnant today. Trinity can function as a lens that challenges as well as validates Christian thought in other arenas. The first of a projected four-volume systematic theology by Anglican theologian and philosopher of religion Sarah Coakley—the whole project titled *On Desiring God*—fixes upon the Trinity, though not discretely and definitely not atomistically. She begins by claiming that "no cogent answer to the contemporary Christian

49. Volf, *After Our Likeness*, 210, 213.
50. Volf, *After Our Likeness*, 212, 213.
51. Volf, *After Our Likeness*, 280.
52. Volf, *After Our Likeness*, 213.
53. Volf, *After Our Likeness*, 235.
54. See the trenchant critique in Mark A. Husbands, "The Trinity Is Not Our Social Program: Volf, Gregory of Nyssa, and Barth," in *Trinitarian Theology for the Church: Scripture, Community, Worship* (ed. Daniel J. Treier and David Lauber; Downers Grove, IL: IVP Academic, 2009), 120–41. Volf and I have discussed these matters at greater length in a conversation soon to be published as "The Trinity in Dialogue: A Conversation on Social Trinitarianism and Classical Trinitarianism: Miroslav Volf and Michael Allen," in *The Orthodox Doctrine of the Trinity: What's at Stake in Recent Debates* (ed. Matthew Barrett; Downers Grove, IL: IVP Academic, forthcoming).

question of the Trinitarian God can be given without charting the necessary and intrinsic entanglement of human sexuality and spirituality in such a quest: the question of right contemplation, right speech about God, and right ordering of desire all hang together."[55]

Coakley pushes back on the "doctrinal criticism" of an earlier generation of Anglican divines (typified by Maurice Wiles) by noting that "the modern textbook account of the development of the doctrine of the Trinity has largely obscured these crucial points of connection, often by concentrating more on philosophical issues of coherence than on the fathers' biblical exegesis or ascetical exercise."[56] She turns then to mine resources rarely related to Trinitarian theology, not least the ascetical treatises of Gregory of Nyssa and other fathers of the church, and she seeks to explore what it means that God is the object of our desires, which overlap and entangle themselves with other desirings (inclusive of, though not subsumed by, sexual desires). In so doing she seeks to reassert systematic theology as a life-giving discipline by showing how it plays a role in the transformation of human desire, and how the doctrine of the Trinity makes sense of that transformative experience at a basic level (what she calls "explicitly prayer-based access to the workings of the divine").[57]

Her *théologie totale* wagers that systematic theology "does not convey the hubristic idea of a totalizing discourse that excludes debate, opposition, or riposte; but on the other hand, it does not falter at the necessary challenge of presenting the gospel afresh in all its ramifications—systematically unfolding the connections of the parts of the vision that is set before us."[58] In so doing she believes systematic theology, viewed as a rational and ordered path to the purgation of desire via prayer-based access to the triune God, helps forward the feminist cause: by challenging the "idolatrous desire to know all that fuels "onto-theology," by undercutting the "imperious desire to dominate that inspires 'hegemony,'" and by transforming the "'phallocentric' desire to conquer that represses the feminine."[59] In Coakley's hands, then, a systematic theology of the Trinity evokes the dispossession of meeting God, specifically the triune God who enlivens us (by the Spirit) in a way that intensifies and simultaneously purges our desire.[60] This kind of Trinitarianism challenges hubris and weaponized power—not least in its misogynistic forms—not by dulling the edges of the Creator–creature distinction but by dispossessing humans of any control. In this regard Coakley's feminist project continues a path

---

55. Coakley, *God, Sexuality, and the Self*, 1–2.
56. Coakley, *God, Sexuality, and the Self*, 3.
57. Coakley, *God, Sexuality, and the Self*, 6; on the transformation of desire, see 11–22 especially.
58. Coakley, *God, Sexuality, and the Self*, 11.
59. Coakley, *God, Sexuality, and the Self*, 51–2.
60. On the simultaneity and pairing of intensification and purgation of desire, see Coakley, *God, Sexuality, and the Self*, 13.

that stands a good bit askance from identity politics or the mainstream of that movement in any of its waves.[61]

Crucial to Coakley's project is a kenotic approach to Christology that emphasizes the self-emptying of God within which Christians participate.[62] Thus, the call to empty our voices (in silent prayer) as a means of more deeply emptying our weak and wayward desires finds roots in Trinitarian and Christological thought, though this humiliating form and the rather narrow breadth of that Christological root might be questioned. The exalted Christ and his heavenly session does not yet play a significant role in her Trinitarian reasoning (though that may well emerge in later volumes). Even so, those and other hesitations aside, it should be appreciated that a Trinitarian schema grounds her ascetical and feminist project, the latter facet of which really finds its own way (amongst other feminisms on offer) only because of that Trinitarian/Christological mooring.

Kevin Vanhoozer: Theo-Dramatic Wisdom

Kevin Vanhoozer has also shown how the Trinity is employed as a lens or viewpoint for other theological and formative concerns. Throughout his works he has taken the language of drama to frame the task of Christian discipleship, wherein fittingness shapes the formation of women and men who follow the stage prompts and the script (not to mention the guidance of the Director) as participants in the company of the gospel.[63] He continues to speak of the economy of God and addresses the two supposed divine missions (i.e., the sending of the

61. On her project *vis à vis* mainstream feminism, see Sarah Coakley, *Powers and Submissions: Spirituality, Philosophy, and Gender* (Challenges in Contemporary Theology; Oxford: Blackwell, 2002). My analysis would differ rather starkly from Lynn Tonstad, *God and Difference: The Trinity, Sexuality, and the Transformation of Finitude* (Gender, Theology, and Spirituality; New York: Routledge, 2017), though Tonstad's concern to avoid what she terms "corrective projectionism" remains needful, even if not exactly applicable as a critique of Coakley (esp. 13–14, 17).

62. See especially Coakley, "Kenosis and Subversion: On the Repression of 'Vulnerability' in Christian Feminist Writing," in *Powers and Submissions*, 3–38 (see 16-25 for her disentangling various iterations of kenosis throughout history).

63. See especially Kevin J. Vanhoozer, *The Drama of Doctrine: A Canonical-Linguistic Approach to Christian Theology* (Louisville, KY: Westminster John Knox, 2005); idem, *Faith Speaking Understanding: Performing the Drama of Doctrine* (Louisville, KY: Westminster John Knox, 2014); the performance theme arises from the project of Hans Urs von Balthasar (his *Theo-Drama*) and from the influence of his doctoral supervisor: see Nicholas Lash, "Performing the Scriptures," in *Theology on the Way to Emmaus* (London: SCM Press, 1986), 37–46. The language of the theodrama has also been taken up recently by David Ford, *The Future of Christian Theology* (Oxford: Blackwell, 2011), 23–4; and by Ben Quash, *Theology and the Drama of History* (Cambridge Studies in Christian Doctrine; Cambridge: Cambridge University Press, 2005).

Son and of the Holy Spirt): "The purpose of the two missions, then, is communion and community: a sharing in the truth and love—the very life—of God."[64]

Vanhoozer offers what he repeatedly calls a "directive" theory of doctrine which leads to wisdom.[65] To that end, his book offers "new metaphors for theology (dramaturgy), Scripture (the script), theological understanding (performance), the church (company), and the pastor (director)."[66] To what end? "The task of theology is to enable hearers and doers of the gospel to respond and to correspond to the prior Word and Act of God, and thus to be drawn into action."[67] If there is a beneficial emphasis to Vanhoozer's argument, it is that scripture is related overtly and theologically to the acts of God. We are drawn into participating in a play that has a script, one given by a figure who not only authors but immerses himself also in the drama itself. Thus, the kind of self-dispossessive posture so heralded by Coakley finds an epistemological prompt here as the Christian receives not only their stage prompt but their being in the Word of the Lord. Similarly, the version of communal leveling that is spoken to those who natively measure worth by their power, as in Volf's argument, here finds that there's a more highly directed and more concretely bounded definition given to that unitive community.

Vanhoozer has used trinity as a lens for other things in the past: for grasping speech-act theory in a threefold manner in *Is There a Meaning in This Text?*, even for thinking more specifically of triune action involved in the inspiration and also interpretation of Holy Scripture as "triune discourse."[68] His most developed application of triune thought—that which employs the triune economy as the matrix for describing a directive approach to doctrine for the sake of forming faithful improvisers or disciples who follow in the way of Jesus—matches his approach to the economy in *Remythologizing Theology*, namely, by tying the missions of Word and Spirit in redemptive history to the agency of Word and Spirit also in the prophetic ministry of God's Holy Word. While other applications of the triune lens are crucial and while Vanhoozer's actual enunciation of it in *Drama of Doctrine* is not the most effusive, his pairing of triune reasoning and exegetical protocols is most promising for thought about theological method and

64. Vanhoozer, *Drama of Doctrine*, 70.
65. Vanhoozer, *Drama of Doctrine*, xii, xiii, 22.
66. Vanhoozer, *Drama of Doctrine*, xii.
67. Vanhoozer, *Drama of Doctrine*, 44.
68. Kevin J. Vanhoozer, *Is There a Meaning in This Text? The Bible, the Reader, and the Morality of Literary Knowledge* (Grand Rapids, MI: Zondervan, 1998); idem, "Triune Discourse: Theological Reflections on the Claim That God Speaks (Parts 1 and 2)," in *Trinitarian Theology for the Church: Scripture, Community, Worship* (ed. Daniel J. Treier and David Lauber; Downers Grove, IL: IVP Academic, 2009), 25–78. See Daniel J. Treier, "Introduction: Evangelical Hermeneutics in Dialogue with Kevin J. Vanhoozer," in *Hearing and Doing the Word: The Drama of Evangelical Hermeneutics* (ed. Daniel J. Treier and Douglas A. Sweeney; London: T&T Clark, 2021), especially section 38a on the Trinitarian implications present in these essays.

biblical hermeneutics, showing how the triune splendor of God might cast light upon other facets of Christian theology and ethics.

Principled Steps for the Practice of Future Trinitarian Theology and Hermeneutics: A Brief Conclusion

In his essay "Meditation in a Tool-Shed," C. S. Lewis spoke of the difference between "looking at" something and "looking along" that same thing. It is one thing to look at the overwhelming vibrancy of a skylight pouring like a laser beam into a darkened shed, though it is altogether something different to stand in that beam, as it were, such that functions like a floodlight within which all other things are illumined.[69] Recent Trinitarian theology has sought to extend both facets of thinking the trinity: looking at who God is by means of his self-revelation in the divine economy (especially, as in Vanhoozer's work, as construed not merely in the redemptive historical acts of Word and Spirit but also in the redemptive historical adumbration of those acts in the prophetic and apostolic canon of that Word and Spirit), but also looking through this triune God to see how all things hold together in him and how trinity functions as a lens for all other doctrines (again not least in Vanhoozer's concern that such triune logic be directed by scriptural prompts to all future theological improvisation). In so doing, Vanhoozer's project can be seen to bring to maturity major trends in modern theology: a reassertion of the particular deity who is illumined as triune and also of the global significance of that character for grasping all else in its light. Precisely here the one (living and true, triune God) and the many (all arenas of life made new by this triune gospel of Christ) are shown to be unified.

In future doctrinal and exegetical work, perhaps more attention should be paid to the interstices, that is, to how "looking at" conjoins with "looking along". If the supposed turn to Trinitarian theology in the late twentieth century did involve a renewed verve in "looking at" the triune God as revealed in the divine economy as well as a new focus upon "looking along" the Trinity to grasp other realities in its light, then perhaps what is needed most is a refocusing upon contemplative wisdom as a fundamental theological vocation.[70] Perhaps doing so will help alert

---

69. C. S. Lewis, "Meditation in a Toolshed," in *God in the Dock* (Grand Rapids, MI: Eerdmans, 1970), 230–4.

70. For examples, see Matthew Levering, "*Sacra Doctrina*; Wisdom, Scripture, and Metaphysics," in *Scripture and Metaphysics: Aquinas and the Renewal of Trinitarian Theology* (Challenges in Contemporary Theology; Oxford: Blackwell, 2003), 23–46; idem, "Friendship and Trinitarian Theology: A Response to Karen Kilby," *International Journal of Systematic Theology* 9, no. 1 (2007): 39–54; Katherine Sonderegger, *Systematic Theology*, vol. 1: *The Doctrine of God* (Minneapolis, MN: Fortress, 2015), esp. 19, 24, 456; John Webster, *God without Measure*, vol. 1: *God and the Works of God* (London: T&T Clark, 2015), on which see Michael Allen, "Toward Theological Theology: Tracing the Methodological Principles of John Webster," *Themelios* 41, no. 2 (2016): 236 n. 106; and especially Sarah Coakley, *God, Sexuality, and the Trinity*, 18–30, 43–52.

scripture readers, hermeneutically speaking, that more is going on in those texts than the mere transmission of a redemptive history and that God is revealed as more than another character. Possibly a reassertion of theology's contemplative role will also help remind all of us that the triune God has bearing on all things but is never to be used for the sake of anything. While it is not only rightful but necessary to develop a theological and thus Trinitarian perspective on every facet of life, the way of applying Trinitarian jargon to projects of our own devising is to flirt with idolatry and to fall foul of the third commandment, namely, taking the name of the Lord in vain. Only beholding the beauty of the Lord in worship and learning via contemplation to make out the character, resplendent and majestic, of the living and true God can guard us, by God's grace, from weaponizing Trinitarian language as a religious ornament upon our academic and practical pursuits.

Recent Trinitarian theology—in its exegetical and doctrinal forms—manifests the practical turn of a wider culture. Pragmatism does not merely influence laypersons who sit before Scripture, asking "what does this mean to me?" It also pressures the intellectual underpinnings of modern Christian theology by accentuating the active life and the works of God for us and with us. In so doing it opens up the reality that Scripture offers us good news (*evangelium*) and glad tidings of a God who is not far off (Jer. 23:23). Yet we must also beware lest we miss ways in which it also forecloses or disincentivizes other theological ventures, such as the contemplative and speculative task of knowing and loving God in and of himself, God for his own sake, God as only God is in the eternal divine life.[71] As we read Holy Scripture and participate in practice of Christian doctrine, may our watchfulness for God's action in our midst and God's relevance to our action be matched by our attentiveness to God himself.

71. Of significance in this regard would be places where Thomas Aquinas addressed the contemplative task: e.g., *ST*, 1a.1.4, reply and especially 2a2ae.180.4, reply. In her projected second volume, Sarah Coakley will take up the task of contemplation more directly as well.

Chapter 6

ETERNAL GENERATION AFTER BARTH

Introduction: Thinking Eternal Generation after Barth

I will examine two ways in which Karl Barth's doctrine of Christ prompts further theological exploration in significant and challenging directions. His doctrine of eternal generation is, in and of itself and strictly construed, especially uninteresting, which I would argue is not a bad thing.[1] But the systemic manner in which he connects this doctrine to ancillary topics or themes is remarkable and well worth our attention. First, we will consider the ways in which Barth connects this doctrine to *theologia*, the exploration of God's inner life and works. Second, we will examine the path by which Barth relates this doctrine to *oikonomia*, the scope and sequence of the gospel of the triune God.

Before turning to those topical and thematic connections, however, two preliminary matters are worthy of attention. First, I should comment briefly on how this exploration relates to contemporary debates regarding Barth's doctrines of election and of the Trinity. Second, I will briefly note the location of Christological material within the structures of dogmatic theology, noting its distributed nature and its interrelated connection to other key topics. Having considered those issues, we will be in a good position to reflect upon Barth's contributions and promptings to contemporary reflection on the doctrine of eternal generation. My goal is not to offer exposition of Barth's text so much as to note areas where his trajectory might lead, thus making good on my title: thinking *after* Barth about eternal generation.

---

1. For recent assessment of classic accounts by which one might make a judgment regarding the nature of Barth's doctrine of eternal generation as compared to, say, that of various patristic figures or later medieval, see the following helpful studies: Keith Johnson, "Augustine, Eternal Generation, and Evangelical Trinitarianism," *Trinity Journal* 32NS (2011): 141–63; John Webster, "Eternal Generation," in *God without Measure* (London: T&T Clark, 2015), 29–42.

Preliminary Matter #1: Relationship to the Debate on Election and the Trinity

How does my exploration relate to the suggestive account of evangelical historicism as developed in recent years by Bruce McCormack?[2] His account has implications, of course, for the doctrine of eternal generation, and he has begun to gesture toward that significance with some specificity by riffing in a Barthian manner of appropriating the Thomistic claim that that "the [divine] processions contain the [divine] missions."[3] I do not have time to mount any case for or against McCormack's proposal, but I should offer a couple comments regarding its influence and its viability.

First, regarding its influence: I regularly observe that Barth interpretation often occurs by people in situations markedly different from Barth himself, taking

---

2. There are precursors to much of McCormacks's argument in the German literature. For example, key elements can be found in this passage from Jüngel: "As the 'sum of the Gospel' and the 'very essence of all good news' God's election of grace is the beginning of 'all the ways and works of God.' In his ways and works God sets himself in relation. In speaking of a beginning of these ways and works, we mean a relation of God to that which he is not. For God himself 'has indeed no beginning.' It is thus a question of the beginning of God's *opera ad extra* [external works]. But as the beginning of all the ways and works of God, God's election of grace is not only an *opus Dei ad extra* [external work of God] or, more precisely, an *opus Dei ad extra externum* [external work of God directed outwards]; it is at the same time an *opus Dei ad extra internum* [external work of God directed inwards]. For election as such is not only a decision made by God and therefore also an election which also certainly concerns him; it is equally a decision which affects God himself 'because originally God's election of man is a predestination not merely of man but of Himself.' If, then, the decision of the election of grace not only affects elect humanity but also at the same time affects God in a fundamental way, then it is dogmatically consistent to treat the doctrine of predestination as a part of the *doctrine of God*" (Eberhard Jüngel, *God's Being Is in Becoming: The Trinitarian Being of God in the Theology of Karl Barth* (trans. John Webster; Grand Rapids, MI: Eerdmans, 2001), 82–4.

3. Bruce L. McCormack, "Processions and Missions: A Point of Convergence between Thomas Aquinas and Karl Barth," in *Thomas Aquinas and Karl Barth: An Unofficial Catholic-Protestant Dialogue* (ed. Bruce McCormack and Thomas Joseph White; Grand Rapids, MI: Eerdmans, 2013), 99–126. Thomas Aquinas distinguished between the acts of nature and of will in his account of the triune being of God. Bruce McCormack has made much of the Thomistic claim that the divine processions and divine missions are one act with two terms. This is true. But Thomas also says—elsewhere in his doctrine of God—that there is a distinction between God's necessary, characteristic acts and his freely willed, creative acts (*ST* 1a.41.2). McCormack has read one statement apart from its wider Trinitarian context. See further Matthew Levering, "Christ, the Trinity, and Predestination: McCormack and Aquinas," in *Trinity and Election in Contemporary Theology* (ed. Michael T. Dempsey; Grand Rapids, MI: Eerdmans, 2011), 244–73.

material claims of his and putting them to functional use quite opposite his own. For example, a number of American and Canadian students of Barth take him to be a beacon of a leftward-leaning version of evangelical theology, and he is viewed as an intellectual symbol of viability for a continuing evangelicalism shorn of its more mindless fundamentalisms. In my Presbyterian context, he has sometimes been taken to represent an orthodox but non-confessional theology upon which this tradition might venture forward. Of course, it is worth noting that Barth was responding to a very different context than American fundamentalism or to a traditional Presbyterianism (based on, for example, confessing the Westminster standards); he was responding to Harnack and later to Bultmann and to what they represented, above all else, the liberal theology of the European churches. It is ironic when a figure who fought to bring a confession-less church back toward orthodoxy becomes a symbol of a movement or desire to dial down the confessional standards or strictures of a very different denominational setting.

Something similar is occurring with regard to Barth's Christology and Trinitarian theology. Take this statement from Paul Dafydd Jones in his response to the claims of Paul Molnar regarding Barth's theology of the *logos asarkos*:

Molnar's mistake, then, is to suppose that Barth epitomizes what he presumes to be dogmatically needful in the present day, namely, "*a clear and sharp distinction* between the immanent and economic Trinity", the corollary of which is an affirmation of the *logos asarkos*. This dogmatic claim inflates regulative claims about the independence and provenience of God to the point at which they distract from Barth's own convictions about the divine being. The plain (and assuredly critical) fact of divine freedom tells only one part of the divine story. Barth's focus is on what God *does* with God's freedom. His suggestion is that the economic event of Christ ramifies in the time and space of God's immanent life.[4]

Jones is right. Barth's focus—his rhetorical passion—is to emphasize that God wills to be with us and not apart from us and, thus, can only be known as he makes himself known amongst us. Barth is a Christ-centered theologian, then, if ever there were one, and the driving argument of the *Church Dogmatics* hits its high points in affirming what Barth will elsewhere call the "humanity of God." But Molnar is right. Barth does affirm the *logos asarkos*; he does speak of the economy as "correlating" to (and not constituting) the inner life of God; and he does locate the roots of God's willed decision to elect the Christ-story as his own in God's own inner loving freedom. Viewing the two together requires a contextual sensitivity: Barth was responding in a time and to an intellectual milieu of cultural Christianity with a Christ-centered focus on the electing God; we do not live in such a time, at least not in the mainline religious traditions of North America. Our culturally compelling presuppositions about God are psychologistic and historicist, not

4. Paul Dafydd Jones, *The Humanity of Christ: Christology in Karl Barth's Church Dogmatics* (London: T&T Clark, 2008), 93.

anything driven by the categories of classical theism. While Barth's contextual and rhetorical focus in his day was to emphasize the economic focus of theology upon the Christ event (which Jones rightly attests), I can only imagine today that his concern would regard God's freedom, transcendence, and holiness (which Molnar champions). So our thinking about Barth's doctrine of God and any utility it might have for contemporary thinking needs to be mindful of changing contexts.

Second, regarding its viability as a historical and a systematic proposal: I do wish to suggest a thesis directly regarding Barth interpretation: that Barth overtly teaches a fundamentally traditional doctrine of the Trinity, and that Barth extensively provides a doctrinal matrix within which that traditional doctrine might be radically retooled. If one looks at his overt Trinitarian claims in I/1 and even later in his occasional comments in his final years, he upholds a classic approach to the doctrine of eternal generation, specifically, and the eternal character of the triune God, broadly speaking. But attention to his historicized Christology—in particular, to the way he reconfigures the two states of Christ and moves away from operative use of the language of "natures"– suggests a line of reasoning that might well lead elsewhere. "Two roads diverged" within the corpus of Karl Barth—I think honesty compels we acknowledge this reality.

I suggest we call an end to this focus upon the historical question and move instead to the dogmatic query. Is election an act of the divine will or an instance of divine self-constitution? Is God's triune being an object or implicate of God's free election of Jesus Christ? More specifically, can we speak of the antecedence of eternal generation to the Son's faithful embrace of his Father's sending? There remains a place for Barth studies as such, but the historical question is far less interesting than the more important theological question: which rubric better provides categories to keep us alert to the way in which Holy Scripture schools us regarding the character of the God of the gospel: evangelical historicism or reformed catholicity?

Paul Nimmo has mounted a provisional defense of McCormack's Barth, with respect to its constructive value. Against the charge that McCormack's view of the doctrine of God leaves us with a hidden God behind the decree of election and, thus, the decree to be triune:

> One might note initially that it betrays a very substantialist mode of thinking, wherein substances are complete and definable in themselves above any historical action or relation. The corollary to this is that in order for there to be an action, there must be a subject. This might be intuitively satisfying (and perhaps even true) for contingent beings such as human agents; but to assume that it holds for God without further analysis is nothing less than anthropomorphic speculation without biblical foundation.[5]

5. Paul T. Nimmo, "Election and Evangelical Thinking: Challenges to Our Way of Conceiving the Doctrine of God," in *New Perspectives for Evangelical Theology* (London: Routledge, 2010), 36.

The terminology of substance is beside the point here, in as much as it is an accidental reference to the doctrinal point made by McCormack's detractors (likely few of whom, if any, would defend Aristotelian substance metaphysics). Ultimately Nimmo's defense suggests that with respect to creatures, a subject precedes action, while, with respect to God, a subject may not need to precede action.

Without employing any of the language of substance, we can restrict ourselves to fundamental doctrinal terminology and convey the point. The perfect God acts to make himself present to others. Presence necessarily implies (logically) prior perfection. One might scroll through the divine economy to trace acts that demonstrate this rhythm: creation ex nihilo, unilateral covenant initiation, and, of course, the incarnation of the preexistent Son. In fact, I think the logic of the gospel requires us to say the exact opposite of that which Nimmo suggests. It is only with respect to creatures that acts precede a stable subject, for ours is a pilgrim existence. But with respect to God, any action flows forth from God's settled identity. Again, this is not the result of a substance metaphysics so much as it is simply an attempt to honor the logic of basic doctrines like the aseity of God, on the one hand, and creation ex nihilo, on the other hand.

All this is to say that my sympathies are with the classical rendering of Barth's Christology and Trinitarian theology, though it will soon be seen that some of Barth's most significant insights involve new or freshly rearticulated applications or implications of those classical teachings.[6]

Preliminary Matter #2: Christology in the Structure of Dogmatic Theology

A second preliminary observation warrants our attention. Christology—in particular, the doctrine of eternal generation—occurs at numerous locations in the *Church Dogmatics*. Having been addressed in volume I/1 as a part of the doctrine of "God the Son," it reappears in I/2 with other Christological material before surfacing yet again (at great length, both explicitly and implicitly) in volume IV/1 amidst the doctrine of reconciliation, specifically the section on "the way of the Son into the far country."

John Webster addresses "the place of Christology in systematic theology" in a recent essay. He notes:

6. Evangelical historicism does present a particular approach to the doctrine of eternal generation, but in doing so it does not actually present a novelty. Centuries ago, Wilhelmus à Brakel reflected upon such an approach. In his analysis of eternal generation, he addressed a number of "evasive arguments," the third of which was: "The second Person is called the Son because He agreed to assume the human nature in the Counsel of Peace, and for the accomplishing of the work of redemption was manifested in the flesh as the visible image of the invisible God" (Wilhelmus à Brakel, *The Christian's Reasonable Service*, vol. 1: *God, Man, and Christ* [ed. Joel Beeke; trans. Bartel Elshout; Grand Rapids, MI: Reformation Heritage, 1992], 150).

In much modern (and notably, but not exclusively, Protestant) systematic theology these matters have acquired a special prominence, because discrete teaching about the person and work of Christ has often annexed the fundamental role which earlier theologies more naturally recognized in teaching about the Trinity, and so has come to speak as the hallmark of the genuineness, purity and distinctiveness of Christian doctrine.[7]

Webster notes this tendency but observes that the distinctiveness of the Christ cannot be glibly elided into the primacy of Christology, in as much as attesting the Christ requires a whole spate of categories already at work with which the Christ is identified (e.g., God, the human, the covenant). Thus Webster prompts us to begin further back and address God himself (*theologia*) and all things "relative to him as their origin and end" (*oikonomia*).[8]

Does this distinction and order not privilege the abstract? Does it not make the incarnation and the mission of the Son a secondary or accidental matter? Webster notes such concerns and offers three clarifying comments to this schematic of theology and economy as the subjects of this intellectual and spiritual discipline. First, though theology is primary and economy is secondary, this distinction is not a separation. In other words, "The pre-eminence of theology does not mean that economy is an accidental or inessential element of systematic theology."[9] "[A] treatment of faith which did not proceed beyond the divine essence and triunity to the effects of God would be Christianly unthinkable. But these effects, including the incarnation of the Word, are just that: effects, only intelligible when their cause is grasped."[10] Second, while theology precedes economy materially, economy tells us of or reveals theology. Further, "The outer works of God are his works, not some remote operation which is not proper to him, and this continuity of acting subject means that God's economic acts elucidate his inner being, even though they do not exhaust it." Third, this talk of the material order and the epistemological order need not be matched necessarily by the pedagogical order. In other words, one could begin by talking of the economy, provided that one does so in a way that makes plain over the course of the exposition that in the order of being the economy is secondary. Pedagogy may be shaped by various needs of the time, place, and setting; the metaphysical primacy of God's inner life, however, must be attested in one way or another.

---

7. John Webster, "Christology, Theology, Economy: The Place of Christology in Systematic Theology," in *God without Measure*, vol. 1: *God and the Works of God* (London: T&T Clark, 2015), 44.

8. Webster, "The Place of Christology in Systematic Theology," 46, citing Thomas Aquinas, *Summa Theologiae*, 1a.1.7, reply. For further analysis of Thomas on this point, see Gilles Emery, "*Theologia* and *Dispensatio*: The Centrality of the Divine Missions in St. Thomas's Trinitarian Theology," *The Thomist* 74 (2010): 515–61.

9. Webster, "The Place of Christology in Systematic Theology," 46.

10. Webster, "The Place of Christology in Systematic Theology," 48.

Barth illustrates these principles in the architectonics of the *Church Dogmatics*.[11] While he does cycle back to address the doctrine of God amidst his Christology, he has already reflected upon God's inner life in *CD* I/1-I/2 and again in II/1. Still further, he locates election as an act of will rather than nature in II/2. One need not be convinced of the precise nature of his Christocentrism to appreciate the systemic application of his Christology consistently across the *CD*. I remain broadly unpersuaded that he has provided a coherent and viable way beyond natural theology and what he views as its two forms, Protestant liberalism and Roman Catholicism. And yet I marvel at the way in which he puts Christology to use by exploring how the Trinitarian relations of origin must be extended in the direction of relations of ongoing intra-Trinitarian communion and by showing how the mission of the incarnate Son corresponds to the eternal life of the Son. And how, in so doing, he continues to honor this distinction and ordered relation between theology and economy. It is to these connections that we now turn.

Theologia: *The Obedience of the Eternal Son*

Barth had already begun with and dealt with God—yet theology continued to haunt the *Church Dogmatics*. Quite literally, the doctrine of God had been addressed in volume 2, and yet there is no getting around the fact that volume 4, addressing the doctrine of reconciliation, returns to theological matters. In speaking this way, I am not making the rather obvious judgment that Barth continues to talk of matters which concern religious issues or regard divine things, as the term "theology" is employed in North America; nor do I make the slightly more particularly Christian claim that Barth addresses matters of Christian principle, as the term "theology" would be put to use in Great Britain; rather, I use the term "theology" in its classic, scholastic sense (*theologia*) to refer specifically to affirmations of God's own being (over against his relations to others). And I do so to note the startling reality that in this extended account of the incarnation, that central hub of God's involvement with others (when another nature is assumed by the second person of the Trinity), *theologia* returns as a matter for our consideration.

Why this? Why here? Barth's theological principles compel him to think theology whenever and wherever God reveals himself, and, we might add, nowhere else. In this vein, Barth continues the Reformed tradition's anti-speculative, iconoclastic approach. He adds his own spin to it, of course, in the way in which he articulates its scripture principle and in the distinctive Christocentrism that flavors his hermeneutical appropriation of that text.[12] Such matters, however, are

---

11. Webster, "The Place of Christology in Systematic Theology," 56–7.

12. See esp. Karl Barth, *Church Dogmatics*, vol. 4: *The Doctrine of Reconciliation*, part one (ed. G. W. Bromiley and T. F. Torrance; trans. G. W. Bromiley; Edinburgh: T&T Clark, 1956), 177.

not my concern in this chapter. I want to consider not where he draws theological matters from, but where he takes them at this point. In other words, it is worth highlighting the way in which God's self-revelation in the incarnation and the reconciling work of the incarnate Son apparently is an event (or a narrative cycle of such events) that tells us of God: his own being in and of himself. So right in the vortex of his exposition of the gospel narrative—the nexus of divine economic activity—Barth turns back to *theologia*.

Barth's application of that methodological return to theology is also noteworthy. In *Church Dogmatics* IV.1 §59.1 he turns to the obedience of the Son to the Father in his incarnational life and death as well as perfect life in the Godhead.[13] This discussion occurs amidst chapter XIV of the *Church Dogmatics*, on "Jesus Christ, the Lord as Servant," in other words, on the humiliation of the Son. More specifically this paragraph focuses upon "the obedience of the Son of God," to which later part volumes will offer contrasting and paired reflections upon "the exaltation of the Son of Man" (§64) and "the glory of the mediator" (§69). It will be followed in this chapters and part volume by reflections upon pride (§60), justification (§61), the Spirit and the gathering of the community (§62), and the Spirit and faith (§63). But the most pertinent material for our purposes is specifically found in §59.1, amidst his exposition of the "way of the Son of God into the far country."

What *theologia* is found in this reference to and rumination upon the incarnate Son's trek into the wilderness? Some say that Barth historicizes Christology and, in so doing, the Godhead.[14] And to the extent that he fails to do so consistently, we might press on further. For example, Bruce McCormack claims that §57, and specifically its attention directed to the methodological or epistemological rule played by God's self-disclosure as willed in the covenant of grace, "is significant for the treatment of the doctrine of the incarnation which will follow in §59.1 in that the door is closed firmly on the thought of the incarnation of a Logos understood along the lines of an abstract metaphysical subject."[15] Thus the economy is predicated of God, and, more strikingly, God is subject only of this economy and in no other way (though not only *in* this economy). In McCormack's rendering this will lead to an unease with a number of pieces of classical Christian divinity: divine impassibility and divine simplicity, for starters. His iconoclasm here stems not from a philosophical aversion to such ideas, but from an exegetical and hermeneutical conviction that they fail to be coherently confessed of the one whom the gospel narrative names as the eternal Son.[16] This one suffered—this one

---

13. Barth, *Church Dogmatics*, IV/1, 192–210.

14. Bruce L. McCormack, "Karl Barth's Historicized Christology: Just How 'Chalcedonian' Is It?" in *Orthodox and Modern: Studies in the Theology of Karl Barth* (Grand Rapids, MI: Baker Academic, 2008), 201–34.

15. McCormack, "Karl Barth's Historicized Christology," 219.

16. Barth, *Church Dogmatics*, IV/1, 192.

cannot be construed along the lines of simplicity—this one reveals the Father—and thus, the Godhead cannot be impassible or simple.[17]

As mentioned above (regarding preliminary matter #1), I will not be addressing this claim about genetic development within and beyond Barth. It is worth noting, however, that McCormack's approach has been followed by or, perhaps we might say, paralleled by a number of other significant figures doing constructive work downstream from volume four of the *Church Dogmatics*. Jüngel, Pannenberg, Moltmann, and Jenson each go some ways toward this kind of historicizing (albeit they tend to differentiate whether toward protology or eschatology). To each of them one might respond in many ways, perhaps most pointedly by noting that here in IV/1, Barth insistently uses the language of "correspondence" to speak of the link between *theologia* and *oikonomia*, a term that notes a distinction within a unity.[18] The route of reading divine eternity in or within history may not fit Barth's structural rhetoric here.

Another way might be pursued, however, which sought to honor Barth's theological principle—that the incarnation reveals the Father and, thus, our Christology must again return us to *theologia*—without discarding a classical Trinitarian theology and its (at least classically adjoined) complex of divine attributes.[19]

17. Admittedly, McCormack continues to develop his constructive arguments (as well as the historical excurses that relate to them, at least with regard to figures beyond Barth and movements deeper in the tradition), and thus any judgments regarding his project remain provisional. Thus far the widest portrait which he has sketched in a publicly accessible way is his series of Kantzer Lectures delivered at the Henry Center of Trinity Evangelical Divinity School in 2011 (available online: http://henrycenter.tiu.edu/kantzer-lectures-in-revealed-theology/past-lectures-publications/bruce-mccormack/). For an assessment of his project to this point (noting some modifications that have already been undertaken regarding the notion of divine freedom), see Scott R. Swain, "Grace and Being: Bruce McCormack on the Gospel's God," in *The God of the Gospel: Robert Jenson's Trinitarian Theology* (Strategic Initiatives in Evangelical Theology; Downers Grove, IL: IVP Academic, 2013), 208–27.

18. See, e.g., Barth, *Church Dogmatics*, IV/1, 187; also idem, *Church Dogmatics*, vol. 4: The Doctrine of Reconciliation, part two (ed. G. W. Bromiley and T. F. Torrance; trans. G. W. Bromiley; Edinburgh: T&T Clark, 1958), 43–4. Paul Jones uses the language of the incarnate Christ's election being "coincident" and "coordinate" with the inner life of the Trinity rather than being "constituted" by it, which appears to be a shrewd judgment of what is being implied with this terminology (*The Humanity of Christ*, 81 fn. 51).

19. It was Gregory of Nyssa, after all, who said that "obedience is part of his nature" ("Against Eunomius," in *Nicene and Post-Nicene Fathers*, vol. 5: *Gregory of Nyssa*, second series [ed. Philip Schaff and Henry Wace; trans. H. C. Ogle, William Moore, and Henry Austin Wilson; Peabody: Hendrickson, 1994], II.xi [122]).

In another place Scott Swain and I have sought to make good on this sort of project.[20] In that argument, we contend:

> The obedience of the eternal Son in the economy of salvation is the proper mode whereby he enacts the undivided work of the Trinity "for us and our salvation." More fully, the obedience of the Son is the economic extension of his eternal generation to a Spirit-enabled, creaturely life of obedience unto death, and therefore the redemptive foundation for his bringing "many sons to glory (Heb. 2:10)."[21]

A number of objections can be raised to such an approach, arising from both classical and modern motivations. First, can the idea of the Son's obedience, within the realm of *theologia* and not merely the incarnate *oikonomia*, be held alongside the conviction that the Godhead shares a single will? Second, would the Son's obedience in any way render his omnipotence (as the Almighty) problematic? Third, does any attempt to affirm the eternal Son's obedience within a classical Trinitarian theology not fall afoul of a wider problem, namely, the essentialism of a substance ontology? These questions would not exist, at least not in that form, for anyone taking Barth's Christology into a historicizing trajectory. These queries necessarily arise, however, for someone who remains committed to the attributes and Trinitarian metaphysics of classical Christian divinity and who seeks to honor the epistemological rule of the incarnation, *à la* Barth.[22]

Oikonomia: *The Faith of the Incarnate Son*

Barth's doctrine of eternal generation, and his wider Christological approach, not only leads to a methodological return to *theologia* in considering the obedience of the eternal Son, it also prompts further attention be given to the particularity of the Son's economic course. Specifically, we will see that the eternal receptivity of the Son, who is marked by filiation, flows forth out of his divine fullness into an economy of not only incarnation but of a life of trust and obedience to his Father's will.

---

20. Scott R. Swain and Michael Allen, "The Obedience of the Eternal Son," *International Journal of Systematic Theology* 15, no. 2 (April 2013): 114–34, reprinted as Chapter 8 in the present volume. Some significant parallels can be seen in Bruce D. Marshall, "The Unity of the Triune God: Reviving an Ancient Question," *The Thomist* 74 (2010): 1–32.

21. See Chapter 8.

22. Significant concern has been raised in a thoughtful way by Thomas Joseph White in the essay: "Intra-Trinitarian Obedience and Nicene-Chalcedonian Christology," *Nova et Vetera* 6, no. 2 (2008): 377–402. Swain and I have attempted to address his concerns, however, in our essay.

As mentioned above, the obedience of the eternal Son extends the eternal generation of the Son into the economy. Thomas Aquinas taught that the missions contain the processions, or, put otherwise, the processions extend outward to the missions. Yet this axiom precedes even that high medieval distinction, for Cyril of Alexandria elaborated on the manner in which the eternal generation of the Son necessarily shaped the revelation bestowed by the Son in his gracious economy of making the Father known.[23]

Might we press further and suggest that eternal generation not only finds extension in the reality of the incarnation but also in the patterns of that incarnate life? Barth's Christology prompts us to relate the humble and dependent manner of the lordly servant to his eternally receptive character in the Godhead.

Ought we to go this route? Barth's exegesis suggests that the New Testament—particularly the Pauline writings—does point toward this kind of economic specificity. Barth was well ahead of his time, as it were, in rendering the Pauline phraseology *pistis christou* in the manner of a subjective genitive ("Christ's faith") rather than an objective genitive ("faith in the Christ").[24] Whereas New Testament studies would come around to this translational and interpretive move only in the 1980s, Barth anticipated this move by decades.[25] Owing to his efforts, theologians were talking about the faith of the Christ (at least in oblique ways) long before Richard Hays and others led the charge to rethink Pauline studies in the 1980s and 1990s;[26] the notion had, by that point, already been mentioned or even discussed in the works of Gerhard Ebeling, Thomas Torrance, James Torrance, John Murray, Wolfhart Pannenberg, Jon Sobrino, and the United Presbyterian Church of the United States of America's "Confession of 1967."[27]

Exegetical reflection upon those *pistis christou* phrases remains debated. I confess that I remain convinced by the more traditional rendering of them as objective genitives ("faith in Christ"), for specific syntactical and rhetorical reasons and not due to any dogmatic presuppositions that would render the subjective

23. See especially his Commentary on Jn 12:49–50. For analysis, see Matthew R. Crawford, *Cyril of Alexandria's Trinitarian Theology of Scripture* (Oxford Early Christian Studies; New York: Oxford University Press, 2014), 20–1.

24. This phraseology occurs in the following Pauline texts: Rom. 3:22, 26; Gal. 2:16 (2x), 20; 3:22; Phil. 3:9; Eph. 3:12.

25. See, e.g., Karl Barth, *The Epistle to the Romans* (trans. Edwyn C. Hoskyns; 6th ed.; London: Oxford University Press, 1968), 96; idem, "Gospel and Law," in *Community, State, and Church: Three Essays* (trans. G. Ronald Howe; Garden City, NY: Anchor Books, 1960), 74. But note that Barth seems to render Phil. 3:9, at least, with the relevant phrase as an objective genitive: idem, *The Epistle to the Philippians: 40th Anniversary Edition* (trans. James W. Leitch; Louisville, KY: Westminster John Knox, 2002), 99–103.

26. The key work here is Richard B. Hays, *The Faith of Jesus Christ: The Narrative Substructure of Galatians 3:1-4:11* (2nd ed.; Grand Rapids, MI: Eerdmans, 2001).

27. Fuller bibliography can be found in Michael Allen, *The Christ's Faith: A Dogmatic Account* (T&T Clark Studies in Systematic Theology 2; London: T&T Clark, 2009), 17–22.

genitive questionable or problematic. Yet while I remain convinced by more traditional exegesis, it seems equally significant to note that Barth's broader point may find surer footing on other biblical grounds.[28] For example, the Epistle to the Hebrews addresses the incarnate life of the Messiah with greater pointedness than any of those Pauline texts (see Heb. 2:10-3:6; 4:14-5:10). This may be a case of bad texts being employed to prompt a good doctrine, if the Christ's faith is a significant facet of Christology that was rediscovered by questionable Pauline exegesis but finds better scriptural warrant in Hebrews and, possibly, the Gospels. Elsewhere I have explored the coherence of claims that the incarnate Son did exercise faith—anthropologically, covenantally, metaphysically—as well as the soteriological significance and ethical implications of such an attestation.[29] In that initial study on *The Christ's Faith*, I only hinted at the way in which the economic form of the Son's earthly life as a life of eccentric dependence mirrored or extended in a new way that intra-Trinitarian life of the eternally begotten Son. In a comparative dogmatic analysis of the place that the Christ's faith might hold within the theological schemas of Thomas Aquinas, the federal theologians, and, finally, Karl Barth, I noted that each had their own way of sustaining "this axiomatic claim that the works *ad extra* reveal the life *ad intra*," more specifically, that the "faith of the Christ would be construed by each of these dogmatic systems as the economic echo of eternal filiation which marks the Son in relation to his Father."[30] I noted that Aquinas uses the language of processions and missions, the federal theologians employ the doctrine of the covenant of redemption (*pactum salutis*), while Barth turns to the obedience of the Son of God and its relation to eternal generation at this axiomatic point.

I noted in that initial study that these three dogmatic systems each offered greater testimony of the immanent life of God than is currently on offer in many of the most notable approaches of the supposed Trinitarian renaissance of the last century. Each approach—Thomas, the federal tradition, and, yes, Barth—compels us to speak not only of the evangelical history of the Triune God, but of the fullness of that God's life from which that history receives its movement. And reflection upon the way in which the shape of that economy—specifically, the Son's obedience of faith before his Father and ours—can inform our account of that immanent triune life. Thus, I pressed forward in a more recent article to explore this connection between *oikonomia* and *theologia* still further.[31] In that account an attempt was made to note the widespread import of the Son's receptivity or fidelity. Thus, "The earthly fidelity

28. For accounts that are more deferential to the exegetical claims of a few recent New Testament scholars (e.g., Richard Hays), see David Stubbs, "The Shape of Soteriology and the *pistis Christou* Debate," *Scottish Journal of Theology* 61, no. 2 (2008): 137–57; Douglas Harink, *Paul among the Postliberals: Pauline Theology beyond Christendom and Modernity* (Grand Rapids, MI: Brazos, 2003).

29. Allen, *The Christ's Faith*.

30. Allen, *The Christ's Faith*, 180–1.

31. Michael Allen, "'From the Time He Took the Form of a Servant': The Christ's Pilgrimage of Faith," *International Journal of Systematic Theology* 16, no. 1 (2014): 4–24.

of Jesus is a distributed doctrine in as much as it manifests itself in every part of his earthly sojourn: the willingness of the eternal Son to assume human nature, the virgin birth, the patient apprenticeship of a Son being brought to perfection, the ministry, and, finally, the passion and bruising at the behest of his neighbors."[32] I also argued there, with Barth, that Christology must lead to a return to our doctrine of God. Thus, soteriology must be rooted in Christology, and I made the effort to "show that the Christological account flows forth from the eternal relations of the Trinity." In so doing, a thesis was unpacked: "In the eternal life of the perfect God, the divine Son pleases the Father in the Spirit and, therefore, the divine Son trusts the Father by the Spirit's power during his earthly pilgrimage."[33]

Much of that argument proceeded by way of engaging the biblical exegesis not of Karl Barth, but of early church fathers (especially Athanasius and Gregory of Nyssa), Thomas Aquinas, and some sixteenth- and seventeenth-century Reformed theologians (Bullinger, Ursinus, Polanus, Perkins, and Turretin play key roles in the argument). And more surely needs to be said than that which was expressed regarding the ways in which Spirit Christology's attempts to construe the incarnate action of the Son must be further rooted in a Logos Christology, whereby the single subject acts not only according to his Spiritually graced human nature but also according to his divine personhood and nature as the Word incarnate. Here Cyril of Alexandria could further enhance the argument, particularly by drawing on his anti-Nestorian polemic regarding the lived significance of the Son's divine nature during his earthly sojourn.[34] But all that patristic, medieval, and reformational conversation aside, it remains the case that Barth has prompted such attention. For this reason Kevin Vanhoozer has spoken of a need to engage the doctrine of God in terms of a "post-Barthian Thomism."[35]

Conclusion: Toward a Reformed Catholic Confession of Eternal Generation

This exploration has been brief and suggestive, noting ways in which Karl Barth's theological ruminations prompt doctrinal development in matters regarding the life of God in himself as well as the economy of the gospel. While his doctrine of eternal generation is remarkably unremarkable, in and of itself, his attempt to show its systematic vitality must be described as both vivid and provocative. I have tried to offer the briefest of descriptions of ways in which my own reflections on *theologia* and *oikonomia* have alike been stirred by his methodological and material concerns. I neither consider myself a Barthian nor wind up agreeing with many of his most central doctrinal moves. Nonetheless, as a systematic

---

32. Allen, "From the Time He Took the Form of a Servant," 5.
33. Allen, "From the Time He Took the Form of a Servant," 6.
34. See Crawford, *Cyril of Alexandria's Trinitarian Theology of Scripture*, 35–42.
35. See Kevin J. Vanhoozer, *Remythologizing Theology: Divine Action, Passion, and Authorship* (Cambridge Studies in Christian Doctrine; Cambridge: Cambridge University Press, 2010), esp. part 2.

and historical theologian, I must note with Vanhoozer that any Thomism or Augustinianism or Scotism or any other classical articulation of God's character today will benefit from being reiterated in a "post-Barthian" fashion. For Barth's central reminder and prompt is one deep at the core of biblical, patristic, and, yes, Reformed theology, namely, that all speculation must be tethered to and tested by God's self-revelation, most centrally in the person and work of the incarnate Son. We do well, as we think about the classical doctrine of eternal generation, to think forward to its connections with the specific shape of the gospel economy as well as backward toward its wider theological significance in the immanent life of God. In both facets of Christological reflection, while Barth may not provide the answers, he does prompt the right questions.

Chapter 7

CHRIST'S HUMANITY

The following dogmatic thought experiment regards the relationship of Jesus Christ to human sin. It traces the exegetical reasoning of the Epistle to the Hebrews, chapters two through four, regarding the person of Christ. It eventuates in an approach to modern conversations regarding the human nature of Christ—whether fallen or unfallen—but it does so by situating it amidst a wider biblical and Christological context and with engagement of a perhaps surprising doctrinal resource: the Westminster Standards, that is, the confessional documents produced by the Westminster Assembly (the Westminster Confession of Faith as well as the Larger and Shorter Catechisms). The argument moves in four steps followed by a fifth section that offers some summative remarks.

I

"For it was fitting that he, for whom and by whom all things exist, in bringing many sons to glory, should make the founder of their salvation perfect through suffering" (Heb. 2:10).

Sin is a terribly strange and odd thing. In as much as the gospel involves a story of perfection, we ought to step back and consider the doctrinal matrix within which any discussion of sin would occur. Sin is unnatural. The Christian tradition has stridently opposed any dualism in which sin or evil is eternal or equivalent to the goodness, truth, and beauty of the triune God. While theologians have disagreed upon the best ways to avoid this dualism, they have consistently insisted upon the necessity of doing so. We cannot allow familiarity or overexposure to lead us away from the appropriate response of shock at the very mention of sin: it is treachery, deceit, unfaithfulness, a tear in the very fabric of our fellowship one with the other (most of all, a fissure in our concord with God). That a word about God would speak also of sin is an odd and unexpected thing, in as much as God is righteous, truthful, faithful, and, above all, holy.

Another way to begin is to say that glory is fundamental in the gospel. God is glorious. This is the one confessed unapproachable and indescribable precisely due to his luminosity and his excess of resplendence. This is the one attested magnificent: King of kings and Lord of lords. This is the one whose fullness and life has been his own from eternity past: Father, Son, and Spirit enjoying the rich harmony of the ever-sufficient triune love. And this bejeweled King determines to share that majesty with others, glorifying his creature with the light that is his alone. This ever-glorious God is now declared to be "bringing many sons to glory." Surely the language of sonship—specifically in the male register—is intentional, drawing as it would on the ancient rites of inheritance, wherein the firstborn male receives the glory, laud, and honor that were the patriarch's alone. But here "many sons" participate in this glory of the Father; it is not only shared with another, but is shared with many children, given to daughters as well as sons.

God's children are brought to glory "through suffering." This is not an obvious connection and indeed, it is a startling characterization. In its preceding context, of course, the glories of the gospel have been described in heavenly and in angelic terms and, then "by signs and wonders and various miracles and by gifts of the Holy Spirit distributed according to his will" (2:4). But "it was not to angels that God subjected the world to come" (2:5); glory turns creaturely and human, as the anonymous author addresses its shape. Taking up the words of Psalm 8, he said: "You made him [man] for a little while lower than the angels; you have crowned him with glory and honor, putting everything in subjection under his feet" (2:7-8; citing Ps. 8:5-6). When the proclamation turns to Christ specifically, again it addresses his being "crowned with glory and honor" (2:9), but this majesty is "because of the suffering of death." The pathway to glory is a portrait of pain and discipline.

The text presents the beginning as the imprint of the end. "He, for whom and by whom all things exist," brought this salvation to pass through his Son (2:10). Alpha and Omega are united in their sovereign sway over "all things" in heaven above and earth below; the Creator—the language "by whom" surely emphasizes that he was not only the planner ("for whom") of all things but their very maker himself—holds the place of privilege and honor when it comes to refashioning. Psalm 102 attests to this subjection of creation to its Maker: "You, Lord, laid the foundation of the earth in the beginning, and the heavens are the work of your hands" (1:10; citing Ps. 102:25).

Perfection and sin. Glory possessed and glory shared. Glory known only through suffering. Creation and conclusion. Beginning and end. Each of these pairs attests the narrative fit of the gospel story. In each case possible dichotomies and oppositions are repaired by tracing the exegetical shape of the gospel's form. Hebrews uses the language of fittingness to speak of this sense. "For it was fitting that he, for whom and by whom all things exist, in bringing many sons to glory, should make the founder of their salvation perfect through suffering" (2:10). The claim that this movement is "fitting" (*eprepen*) does not attest to common sense or worldly wisdom; it registers the appropriate relationship of one feature with the wider shape of the gospel as revealed in the canon of prophetic, apostolic Scripture.

Thomas Aquinas is the master of arguments from fittingness (*ex convenientia*). "Fittingness" is not a doctrine itself, but it is a tool for thinking doctrines. "Fittingness" links the gospel of Jesus with the wider canonical portrait of God's self-revelation and his revelation of created being.[1] Whether discussing the virgin birth, Christ's death upon the cross, or the transfiguration, Thomas teases out the scriptural logic of fittingness, showing how the manifestation of the gospel matches its theological order in the history of redemption. Fittingness is not reference to mere foretelling or prophecy; it is a claim about narrative fit. Aristotle's notion of "dramatic coherence" pertains here (see *Peri Poietikes*, 1452a,3), where events happen "unexpectedly but on account of each other," so that "before each decisive event we cannot predict it, but afterwards see it was just what had to happen."[2]

The canonical logic of the gospel is neither the wisdom of the Greeks nor the miraculous expectation of the Jews (1 Cor. 1:22). There is a fit to the gospel, however, so long as one views it within the wider matrix of Christian doctrine and, more fundamentally, the breadth of that to which doctrine points, the "whole counsel of God" revealed in the writings of the prophets and the apostles. As we reflect further upon the relationship of Jesus Christ to the absurd reality of human sin, we do well to move incrementally from the widest possible orbit to increasingly more confined relations and to trace the unfolding argument of this apostolic epistle as well. In so doing we may avoid too easily identifying sin or its solution with matters close to our cultural or personal hand; in so doing our theological grammar can be disciplined by the arch of scripture's own theological presentation. We inquire whether specific Christological claims make sense or fit with the wider canonical teaching on the nature of God and of humanity, of sin and its redemption, and so forth. With that methodological concern in mind, then, we will turn to consider the incarnational union, the humanity of Christ, and the relationship of him to human sin.

II

"Since therefore the children share in flesh and blood, he himself likewise partook of the same things, that through death he might destroy the one who has the power of death, that is, the devil, and deliver all those who through fear of death were subject to lifelong slavery" (Heb. 2:14).

Hebrews 2 presses further to articulate a grammar for discussing the person of Christ. It does so with sin in mind, that is, as an antidote and answer to the mangling effects of "death." Heb. 2:14 unfolds this sphere of death by referring to "the one who has the power death, that is, the devil" as well as those with "fear of death" and thus "subject to lifelong slavery." Physical death alone does not encompass the sway of this struggle; no, it reaches out to take in "the power of death" and even "lifelong slavery" and subjection. The idioms of politics ("power"), the courtroom

---

1. See Frederick C. Bauerschmidt, *Thomas Aquinas: Faith, Reason, and Following Christ* (New York: Oxford University Press, 2013), 161ff., 171, 197–201.

2. Robert W. Jenson, *Systematic Theology*, vol. 1: *The Triune God* (New York: Oxford University Press, 1997), 64.

("devil" or "the accuser"), psychological malformation ("fear"), and sociological struggle ("slavery" and subjection) are all engaged to describe this multifaceted funk that is sin as well as its consequent death-dealing excess.

In this valley of sin and death the light shines upon the person of Christ. This one "partook of the same things," that is, the very "flesh and blood" of "the children." The relationship of Hebrews to Platonism continues to be debated in various ways; surely the author here intends to point to the pitiful reality of material flesh as now a part of the very person of Christ.[3] The text employs the language of sameness ("the same things") to convey that the flesh and blood or humanity of the Son is the same humanity identified with the rest of the children of the living God. The same flesh capable of being sawn in two (11:37), disciplined (12:5-13), and resurrected (13:20) is partaken of by the second person of the Trinity. Any use of Platonic idiom to express the timely logic of the gospel in Hebrews is chastened by the humane character of the Son's existence: embodied, temporal, and social being.

This assumption of humanity is not held at remove or at any distance. "He himself likewise partook" of this creaturely experience. Here is no maneuver toward an emanationist or angelic/mediatorial Christology; indeed, Heb. 1:4-14 has excluded any such approach. This one is "very God" or "fully God"—the repetition of the subject's identification ("he himself") attests to the specificity of the claim: this humanity is the Word or the Son's personal humanity. The classical dogmatic tradition has maintained this single subject Christology through the centuries; for example, the Westminster Confession of Faith attests to the reality of Christ in these words:

> The Son of God, the second person in the Trinity, being very and eternal God, of one substance and equal with the Father, did, when the fullness of time was come, take upon him man's nature, with all the essential properties, and common infirmities thereof, yet without sin; being conceived by the power of the Holy Ghost, in the womb of the virgin Mary, of her substance. So that two whole, perfect, and distinct natures, the Godhead and the manhood, were inseparably joined together in one person, without conversion, composition, or confusion. Which person is very God, and very man, one Christ, the only Mediator between God and man.[4]

Westminster reiterates Chalcedonian language—"without conversion, composition, or confusion"—in a Cyrillian fashion that fixes upon the single

---

3. For orientation to the issues regarding Hebrews and its relationship to varying Platonisms, see Luke Timothy Johnson, *Hebrews: A Commentary* (New Testament Library; Louisville, KY: Westminster John Knox, 2006), 17–21.

4. "Westminster Confession of Faith," in *Creeds of the Churches: A Reader in Christian Doctrine from the Bible to the Present* (ed. John H. Leith; 3rd ed.; Louisville, KY: John Knox, 1982), 203–4 (VIII.2).

subject: "The Son of God, the second person of the Trinity ... Which person ... one Christ, the only Mediator." Here God and humanity are not brought close or near; they are personally united in this one, the second person of the Trinity. They are not mingled into a third kind (*tertium quid*) but are existent in a personal union of a single subject. As Bonaventure said, "Even though the divine and human natures are distant from each other as the infinite is from the finite, yet they can be united in a hypostatic union in a way that preserves the properties of each nature. But divine nature itself never becomes finite, nor the human nature infinite."[5] The Son of God really partook of our experience as one who was genuinely both divine and human.

III

"Therefore, he had to be made like his brothers in every respect, so that he might become a merciful and faithful high priest in the service of God, to make propitiation for the sins of the people" (Heb. 2:17).

Hebrews speaks further of this fellow brother not only in terms of assumption but also in the language of growth and development (see later 5:7-8). Here the term "made" is indicative of this broader concern: it speaks not simply to his beginning, but to his whole narrative arch and personal maturation. In these dynamic terms he is "made like his brothers"—the language is also passive ("he had to be made ... so that he might become"). While this does not preclude his personal agency, a deeper theological point is highlighted here: his history has a depth deeper than his immediate volitional rule, a history that is embedded within that of his family.

In this history he has been "made like his brothers in every respect." The Apollinarian controversy is no doubt the most apposite moment wherein this claim was explored for its implications. There the incarnational logic of the apostolic kerygma was taken to imply that the Son assumed not only flesh and blood, but everything respecting human life and nature. In that historical moment, of course, human rationality or mind was the controverted topic. Based on varying theories of the human and their composition throughout the centuries, however, the focus of this logic might shift. Later an ecumenical council would need to address the notion of the human will (therein opposing monothelitism), and then medieval theologians would wrestle with the passions

---

5. Bonaventure, *Disputed Questions on the Knowledge of Christ* (Works of Saint Bonaventure IV; ed. George Marcil; trans. Zachary Hayes; St. Bonaventure, NY: Franciscan Institute, 1992), 170 (Q. VI). Bonaventure's claim is one of many examples of the catholic heritage underlying the famed *extra Calvinisticum*; for reflection on this line of Christological reasoning from the patristic era all the way into the work of Calvin and other reformers, see E. David Willis, *Calvin's Catholic Christology: The Function of the So-Called Extra Calvinisticum in Calvin's Theology* (Studies in Medieval and Reformation Thought 2; Leiden: Brill, 1967), especially 26–60.

more broadly (which include intellectual life but are not bounded by it).[6] In modern times, though, it was not compositional issues so much as psychological experience that became the focus of attention. Did the Son experience history as we do? This sort of question exercised the reformers, notably Calvin and the reformed tradition. Later questions of personal growth and development went to the fore, in as much as anthropological investigations—whether in sociological or psychological approach—enabled scholars to assess the contours of human nature in its continually dynamic flux.

"That he might become a merciful and faithful high priest." The point of this personal assumption of a human nature in all its dynamic entanglements is for the sake of service, specifically, that he might be active "in the service of God." The Westminster Larger Catechism draws out these emphases in its reflection on the Son's human mediation:

> Q. 39: Why was it requisite that the Mediator should be man?
> A. It was requisite that the Mediator should be man, that he might advance our nature, perform obedience to the law, suffer and make intercession for us in our nature, have a fellow feeling of our infirmities; that we might receive the adoption of sons, and have comfort and access with boldness unto the throne of grace.[7]

His humanity was for the sake of "advance[ing] our nature," that is, seeing the human through the full sweep of development and into the very presence of God. A priest serves to broker presence between two parties, making their intimacy possible by way of an ongoing ministry of intermediary activity (so Heb. 5:1). Hebrews insists on the ongoing nature of the Son's mediation and priesthood; indeed, Heb. 7:16 points to the reality of his intercession during his resurrected state (when he possesses that "indestructible life").[8]

His ministry not only continues beyond that of any other human mediator, but it presses closer in to the divine life. As Cyril of Alexandria put it, "The mediation of Moses, however, is ministerial, while the mediation of Christ is free and more mystical since he touches the parties that are being mediated and reaches both, I

---

6. On the character of these conversations regarding the passions, see Kevin Madigan, *The Passions of Christ in High-Medieval Thought: An Essay on Christological Development* (Oxford Studies in Historical Theology; New York: Oxford University Press, 2007).

7. "Westminster Larger Catechism 39," in *The Constitution of the Presbyterian Church (U.S.A.), Part I: Book of Confessions* (Louisville, KY: Geneva, 1996), 254.

8. On the resurrected character of Christ's priesthood here, see David M. Moffitt, *Atonement and the Logic of Resurrection in the Epistle to the Hebrews* (Supplements to Novum Testamentum 141; Leiden: Brill, 2011), although Moffitt unduly limits his priesthood office and service to the period of his heavenly session. See Chapter 2 in my companion volume, *The Fear of the Lord: Essays on Theological Method*, for further engagement of Moffitt's important volume.

mean the mediated human nature and God the Father."[9] His priesthood is merciful in that it reaches down to finite and fallen humans; yet it is also faithful in as much as it does not involve any infringement upon or diminution of the divine presence and its concomitant standards for purity and holiness. Genuine personal presence is made real for all personal demands are met in this high priest.

Most pointedly, he became this human priest and this perfect human "to make propitiation for the sins of the people." He suffers the death of the cursed and only then receives back indestructible life. His narrative arch follows the course of his brethren: he does not merely enjoy life abundant, but he sacrifices his own innocent life prior to receiving it back—glorified—again. Thus, his life truly is "for the sins of the people" in as much as it is offered up for their sakes and now devoted to their cause by its intermediary function in the heavenly throne room. In all these respects he must be what we are—"that which is not assumed is not healed," as the Cappadocians would put it—for there to be hope of peace and life as one of us. Hebrews is insistent, of course, that "it is impossible for the blood of bulls and goats to take away sins" (10:4). In that context Christ takes the words of Ps. 40:6-8 upon his own lips, contrasting his personal offering of himself with "sacrifices and offerings," more specifically, with "burnt offerings and sin offerings" in which "you [God] have taken no pleasure" (10:5, 6). "A body" is necessary for taking away sins—a mere sacrifice in the manner of old is not enough. But this body must be "prepared" for the high priest, suggesting that it must be made befitting this kind of propitiatory role. "And by that will we have been sanctified through the offering of the body of Jesus Christ once for all" (10:10).

IV

"We do not have a high priest who is unable to sympathize with our weaknesses, but one who in every respect has been tempted as we are, yet without sin" (Heb. 4:15).

Only now are we in a position to approach the question of Christ's own personal relationship to sin. In the last two centuries a debate has arisen regarding the precise nature of the humanity assumed by this Son: was it fallen or unfallen?[10]

---

9. Cyril of Alexandria, *Commentary on John*, vol. 1 (Ancient Christian Texts; ed. Joel C. Elowsky; trans. David R. Maxwell; Downers Grove, IL: IVP Academic, 2013), 175 (5:46).

10. For notable accounts, see arguments for a fallen human nature in Ian McFarland, "The Status of Christ's Will: Fallen or Unfallen?" in *In Adam's Fall: A Meditation on the Christian Doctrine of Original Sin* (Challenges in Contemporary Theology; Oxford: Blackwell, 2010), 117–40; Thomas Weinandy, *In the Likeness of Sinful Flesh: An Essay on the Humanity of Christ* (London: T&T Clark, 1993); and for an argument for an unfallen human nature, see Oliver D. Crisp, "Did Christ Have a *Fallen* Human Nature?" in *Divinity and Humanity: The Incarnation Reconsidered* (Current Issues in Theology; Cambridge: Cambridge University Press, 2007), 90–117.

Again we do well to pay attention to Hebrews and the dogmatic tradition and only then to consider recent polemics in light of that deep and broad context of Christological thought. I will suggest in so doing that careful attention to all that Hebrews and the dogmatic tradition are saying perhaps prepares us to appreciate the link between Christ and the humanity which he redeems without conflating his moral character and that of the sinners for whom he has come to deliver salvation. To that end, we should reflect upon his human finitude and weakness, his experience of temptation, his consistent sinlessness, and the soteriological implications of these three Christological claims.

First, sympathizing with weaknesses marks out the priestly exercise of this Son. He is able to offer sympathy. His weakness is not unique or different—it is ours. Jesus's weakness is typified in that he was compelled to lead a life of prayer: "In the days of his flesh, Jesus offered up prayers and supplications, with loud cries and tears, to him who was able to save him from death, and he was heard because of his reverence" (5:7). His entreaties to his God and Father are not only prayerful but supplicatory, invoking God's aid and help in time of crisis. They were blood-soaked: "with loud cries and tears" in the very face of death.

Second, in every respect he was tempted as we are. His weakness involved not only bodily constitution but also moral exposure. His journey through temptation constituted his path to maturity: "Although he was a son, he learned obedience through what he suffered" (5:8). His suffering was global: torture and death, false witness and blasphemy, rejection and isolation. In this sphere and amidst these challenges, "he learned obedience" as a son; indeed, Hebrews will later describe how this gauntlet exemplifies the matrix of maturation (12:5-13), extending from the life of Christ (12:1-3) to its wider application in the lives of his followers.[11] Jesus was "author and perfector of faith" (12:2), bringing human faithfulness to its apex by journeying trustingly through death itself.

Third, he was "yet without sin"—theologians on all sides of this debate have insisted that this and other scriptural judgments regarding the moral purity of Jesus must be affirmed, namely, that he never sinned himself against God. Indeed, his sinless maturity enables his salvific ministry: "And being made perfect, he became the source of eternal salvation to all who obey him, being designated by God a high priest after the order of Melchizedek" (5:10). This Son was not only reverent (5:7) but was "made perfect" through the long course of his faithful suffering. Indeed, "he has no need, like those high priests, to offer sacrifices daily, first for his own sins and then for those of the people" (7:27). This one never has possessed an unholy character; this one has never acted in an impure way.

Fourth, what of the soteriological importance of these claims? The Westminster Confession can serve again as a prompt: "The Lord Jesus, in his human nature

---

11. On "autobiographical Christology" wherein the mysteries of Christ are viewed as constitutive of the path of his people, see Andrew Hofer, *Christ in the Life and Teaching of Gregory of Nazianzus* (Oxford Early Christian Studies; New York: Oxford University Press, 2013), especially 91–193.

thus united to the divine, was sanctified, and anointed with the Holy Spirit, above measure, having in him all the treasures of wisdom and knowledge; in whom it pleased the Father that all fullness should dwell." And all this was "to the end that, being holy, harmless, undefiled, and full of grace and truth, he might be thoroughly furnished to execute the office of a mediator, and surety."[12] This mediator is capable to serve as a priest and does actually mediate the very presence of God by entering now as a human, sanctified and even glorified to be a priest in the holy of holies. He is both mediator and surety, one who descends into our hell and also who goes into the very holy of holies as our pledge. This so-called double grace (*duplex gratia*) is not merely the confession of Westminster or of John Calvin, but of the early church fathers. Cyril notes how this mediator is "both the altar of incense since he is the pleasing aroma of sanctification and the altar of burnt offering since he is the sacrifice for the life of the world."[13]

Considering this question only within the matrix of Christological teaching articulated in Hebrews and confessed at Nicaea and Chalcedon frees us from some overly hasty, yet theologically detrimental maneuvers that have plagued the modern conversation. We do well to note what has driven this conversation. On the one hand, any denial that Christ assumed a fallen human nature seems to fall prey to a series of questions: From where did Christ receive an unfallen human nature? What people will such a Christ save and take into the very presence of God: fallen or unfallen? Can such a Christ be confessed as a sympathetic high priest familiar with our sorrows and temptations? Indeed, failure to make such a confession that he assumed our nature—received from a sinner named Mary— seems to fall prey to the Cappadocian maxim: "that which is not assumed is not healed."[14] This would seem to be Christologically and soteriologically fatal. On the other hand, any approach to confess that Christ assumed a fallen human nature can easily tilt into a Spirit Christology that seems to fail to honor the specific divinity of the Son himself. Schleiermacher is surely the paradigm for such an approach, wherein the divinity of the Son is constituted by his pneumatically shaped God-consciousness.[15] Again, fatality seems the inevitable result, both in emptying one's Christology of the claims "God of God, Light of Light, Very God of Very God" and in ridding one's soteriology of any real identification of God with humanity in personal terms. Such have been the recent assessments of the two sides of the debate.

12. "Westminster Confession of Faith," 204 (VIII.3).

13. Cyril of Alexandria, *Commentary on John*, 256 (6:68).

14. Gregory of Nazianzen, *To Cledonius the Priest against Apollinarius* (ep. CI) (ed. Philip Schaff and Henry Wace; trans. C. G. Browne and J. E. Swallow; Nicene and Post-Nicene Fathers 2:7; n.p.: Christian Literature Publications, 1894; repr. Peabody, MA: Hendrickson, 1999), 440.

15. *contra* Kevin Hector, "Actualism and Incarnation: The High Christology of Friederich Schleiermacher," *International Journal of Systematic Theology* 8, no. 3 (2006): 307–22.

We do well to think beyond these false approaches. The virgin birth by the Spirit's power is crucial: "The Holy Spirit will come upon you," Mary is told, "and the power of the Most High will overshadow you; therefore the child to be born will be called holy—the Son of God" (Lk. 1:35). From conception this son is "holy"—a term that marks him out not only metaphysically as unique and singular but also morally as pure and righteous. Spirit Christology need not and ought not tilt into a denial of the divinity of the Son: the life-giving filling of the Spirit may supplement and not supplant the divinity of the Son provided that one identifies the Spirit's strengthening as terminating upon the human nature and, more specifically, the human will of the second person of the Trinity.[16] The scholastic distinction between the *anhypostatic* and *enhypostatic* facets of Christ's humanity may prove helpful here: his humanity does not exist as an independent person (i.e., it is *anhypostatic* in itself) and only exists in the person of the Son (that is, it is *enhypostatic* upon the assumption). Westminster provides categories for this nuance: "Christ, in the work of mediation, acteth according to both natures; by each nature doing that which is proper to itself."[17] This helps us appreciate Lk. 1:35 saying two things of this virgin-born son: he is "called holy," and he is "son of God." As the divine Son, he has been righteous forever; as the human son of Mary, he has been made holy "by the power of the Most High."

Further there is every reason to confess that this sanctification of his human nature took place at the very moment of his conception. Citing Lk. 1:35, John Owen comments: "For the *pollution of our nature*, it was prevented in him from the instant of conception … He was 'made of a woman' (Gal. 4:4); but that portion whereof he was made was sanctified by the Holy Ghost, that what was born thereof should be a holy thing."[18] This specification that the Spirit worked a miracle at the point of the virginal conception such that Mary's flesh was not received by the Son as sinful or fallen flesh means that language of Christ being kept from fallen flesh should be used here.[19] It is for people like us, thus Christ must have assumed flesh like ours. But it is good news, thus Christ must have sanctified our flesh and done so all the way from his first moment of human life onward to glory. Here we must note that

---

16. For further argument toward a Spirit Christology that extends rather than usurps Nicaea and Chalcedon, see R. Michael Allen, *The Christ's Faith: A Dogmatic Account* (T&T Clark Studies in Systematic Theology; London: T&T Clark, 2009), 135–42. I would want to supplement that argument further now with further engagement of Cyril of Alexandria's anti-Nestorian treatises from the 420s. The great example in this regard, however, is the seventeenth-century theologian John Owen, especially his Trinitarian texts *Christologia* and *Pneumatologia*.

17. "Westminster Confession of Faith," 205 (VIII.7).

18. John Owen, *Communion with the Triune God* (ed. Kelly M. Kapic and Justin Taylor; Wheaton, IL: Crossway, 2007), 166 (italics original).

19. Indeed, such was the position of John Calvin, *Institutes of the Christian Religion* (Library of Christian Classics; ed. John T. McNeill; trans. Ford Lewis Battles; Louisville, KY: Westminster John Knox, 2006), 481 (II.xiii.4).

some, such as Edward Irving, have taken the language of the fallen human nature of Christ to suggest not only that he was born of a fallen human mother, but that his own substance was fallen.[20] Irving's intent was surely to honor the union between Christ and humanity, but his approach is disastrous. Christ in this depiction is not only amidst us, but he is one of us in ways that are both authentically human (traits rooted in creation) and in accidents of history (distortions rooted in the fall). Irving offers an account of the sustaining of Christ's humanity (such that the Spirit keeps it from acting sinfully moment by moment), but not of the sanctification or transformation of it (such that it is, in substance, sinless, unfallen, and holy).

It is this sanctification of human flesh—in this time after the fall and in this place east of Eden, a fallen nature—that is enacted by the Spirit and is crucial for the economy of the God's new covenant (Heb. 7:27-28; 9:7, 14). Otherwise, the Son's human will would be sinful and lead him into sin and thus render him incapable of being a high priest, much less a sacrifice for sin. Obviously, this would be catastrophic. Not only that but even the possession of a fallen nature would be culpable, for the very existence of a depraved will or nature is itself heinous to God our Heavenly Father. Either sin in character or in action would render him privy to the limits of the old priesthood, which was divinely given, useful for a time, but ultimately ineffectual in the face of our profound need for final atonement. But this counterfactual need not detain us, for the apostles point us in a different direction. This second Adam never submitted his will to the allure of temptation and was never himself fallen, unholy, or sinful. He was "sanctified," "anointed," and he was one "in whom it pleased the Father that all fullness should dwell." Westminster opens to us the direction of a Spirit Christology that honors the integrity of Christ's human nature, its dynamic sanctification by the Spirit (and not owing to some other source than God's will), and the fact that this is not an alternative to but an augmentation of the claim that this one is himself "very God of very God."

He is born from the fallen flesh of Mary, and yet his human will and nature was sanctified by the very Spirit of God, such that he does not have or possess a fallen human nature.[21] While he is dust and does return to that mire, he is also "yet

---

20. See C. G. Strachan, *The Pentecostal Theology of Edward Irving* (London: Darton, Longman, and Todd, 1973), 27; for wider attestation in Irving's corpus, see vol. 5 of *The Collected Writings of Edward Irving* (London: Alexander Strahan, 1865). The critical analysis of Donald Macleod is particularly helpful in engaging not only the problematic approach of Irving, but also some of its effects in the work of Karl Barth, T. F. Torrance, and James B. Torrance (see *The Person of Christ* [Contours of Christian Theology; Downers Grove, IL: InterVarsity Press, 1998], 222–9).

21. It should be observed that the Roman doctrine of the immaculate conception of Mary leads, logically, to an infinite regress. One must ask: If a pure Christ cannot be born of a sinful mother, then why can that mother be born pure from her own sinful parents? In other words, while the immaculate conception may be argued for on the basis of exegetical parallels (Mary as the new temple or tabernacle), it certainly raises metaphysical and covenantal questions about what is possible: for the birth of Mary and of her son.

without sin" or, in the language of Westminster, "holy, harmless, undefiled, and full of grace and truth." Recent approaches to the question of Christ's human nature are often viewed as dropping one or another facet of this teaching:

> On the one hand, those who seek to affirm that the Son assumed a *fallen* human nature (or sinful flesh) are often interpreted as sacrificing the sinlessness of Jesus and thus leaving believers still in need of a Savior. On the other hand, those who affirm that the Son assumes an *unfallen* human nature (cf., Adam *prior to the fall*) are often charged with presenting a generic Jesus who is not truly man, thus losing the soteriological significance of his life, death, resurrection and ascension.[22]

But the New Testament—in particular Hebrews—attests to his consubstantiality with us as well as his sanctification and even glorification by the Spirit. Dogmatics does well to attend to both affirmations deep within the apostolic witness.

To honor these emphases at the same time, we argue that while the eternal Son assumed his nature from a fallen mother, he was never a sinner and never possessed a fallen human nature for his humanity was sanctified immediately by the Holy Spirit. In technical or scholastic terminology, we might say that the act of assumption, then, is from (*a quo*) but not of or to (*ad quem*) a fallen human nature (since the only fallen nature is that of his human mother, Mary); we might further say that the act of assumption is not from (*a quo*) but of and unto (*ad quem*) an unfallen human nature (since his human nature is always unfallen, pure, sinless).[23] That his human nature comes from that of a fallen human mother honors his commonality with those he will redeem. That his human nature itself is and always remains pure, holy, and unfallen preserves his moral and covenantal singularity. Both are essential if he is the focus of the gospel.

The language of the Westminster Confession proves helpful here: "The Son of God ... did, when the fullness of time was come, take upon him man's nature, with all the essential properties, and common infirmities thereof, yet without sin; being conceived by the power of the Holy Ghost, in the womb of the virgin Mary, of her substance" (VIII.2). Note that the assumption (expressed with the claim "take up him") includes all facets or "essential properties" as well as those accidental realities due to sin which can be called "common infirmities thereof," with but one

22. Kelly M. Kapic, "The Son's Assumption of a Human Nature: A Call for Clarity," *International Journal of Systematic Theology* 3, no. 2 (2001): 154.

23. These distinctions between assumption *a quo* and *ad quem* were absent in my earlier account of this issue, thus hindering the argument found there in *The Christ's Faith: A Dogmatic Account* (T&T Clark Studies in Systematic Theology 2; London: T&T Clark, 2009), 126–35.

specific exception: "yet without sin." Westminster specifically uses the language "of her substance" to describe the origins of the Son's human nature (*a quo*), but it also notes that the event of assumptive conception, by the Spirit's power, terminated in (*ad quem*) the beginning of a life and a human nature that was "without sin." The Son's assumption was *from* a fallen human nature (that of Mary) but it was not *of* a fallen human nature (as his own substance was sanctified and, thus, pure, holy, and always unfallen). And this is soteriologically essential: the great High Priest comes from us but is not of our fallen condition; therefore, he may enter the holy of holies evermore to offer himself a pure sacrifice for sin and to intercede always on our behalf.

V

By way of conclusion we should note the way in which this argument has proceeded in contrast to many recent engagements. First, we have approached a thorny contemporary debate by way of setting the stage. Dogmatics is meant to enable exegesis to function well and, we might add, to lay the groundwork even for productive theological polemics (as was provoked in the nineteenth century by the work of Edward Irving). In many cases, this simply means that good theology forces the biblical interpreter or the polemicist to start back two or three steps and to take cognizance of the wider intellectual and canonical terrain when moving forward. This chapter has considered four things—scriptural fittingness, the incarnational union, the humanity of Christ, and his relationship to human sin—believing that though distinct, these items are related and are best considered in that sequence and order.

In this short thought experiment, second, we have stayed close to the text of the Epistle to the Hebrews. This is not ornamental or merely illustrative. Christian reasoning regarding the person of Christ principally flows from biblical exegesis. Unfortunately, recent debates regarding the character of Christ's humanity (whether fallen or unfallen) have tended to happen at great remove from the idiom and categories of Scripture. While we need not remain restricted to the lingo of the prophets and apostles alone—translation being essential to Christian intellectual and missional faithfulness—we do tend to see loss of both spiritual verve and of focused meaning when theological conversation occurs at too great a distance from that scriptural world.

Third, we have regularly touched down and related our Christological argument to one of the most important touch points of Western Christian theology, namely, the Westminster Confession of Faith. It is merely one confessional example of biblical reasoning, but it has proven to be a decisive one in the last half millennium (both inside and outside the ecclesiastical communions directly tied to its formal authority). Against the claims of some detractors of this confessional theology—ranging from the nineteenth-century voices of Edward Irving and John Macleod Campbell to the twentieth-century campaigns of T. F. Torrance and James B.

Torrance[24]—we have seen that the teachings of Westminster provide categories in which we are compelled to keep alive to the many-splendored glory that Hebrews, and the wider apostolic witness, reveals of the incarnate Son and his priestly service on behalf of the fallen children of Adam. This confessional language keeps us alert to Hebrews' teaching that while Jesus dwells in our midst, he does so in a manner unlike us: he is one holy by nature, not by grace. And from that nature he then shares grace with us, going so far as to share his own glory with his joint heirs. With respect to the topic of Christ and the plague of sin, this must be our final word: a word of shared glory by means of sin's overcoming in the priestly ministry of the spotless Lamb of God.

24. These accounts also suffer from confusion of incarnation and atonement, as if the act of assumption or the mere existence of an incarnate God itself provides atonement for sinful humanity. Their logical and rhetorical tendency toward some version of universalism (though we must note that this is a tendency that is often explicitly denied by some of the aforementioned authors) flows from this incarnational approach to the atonement.

Chapter 8

THE OBEDIENCE OF THE ETERNAL SON

SCOTT SWAIN AND MICHAEL ALLEN

I

One of the most interesting dogmatic theses to emerge from the twentieth century is the claim that the Son's obedience to the Father in accomplishing the work of salvation is not merely a consequence of the humble existence he assumed in the incarnation but rather constitutes his *opus proprium* within the *opera Trinitatis ad extra*, the Son's distinctive manner qua Son of executing God's undivided saving will. This thesis originates with Karl Barth, who gives it penetrating exposition in *Church Dogmatics* IV.1 § 59.1, and enjoys wide acceptance, both among those who are self-consciously indebted to Barth's theological program and among those who are not. In each instance, warrants for this *theologoumenon* are drawn from the broad New Testament witness to the one who declares: "I have come down from heaven, not to do my own will but the will of him who sent me" (Jn 6:38).[1]

Affirming the obedience of the only-begotten Son has in many cases entailed significant revisions to classical Trinitarian metaphysics. Whether in Barth's historicizing of the doctrine of God, the significance of which remains fiercely debated among his interpreters,[2] or in von Balthasar's lavish metaphysics of Trinitarian kenosis,[3] identifying obedience as the Son's personal property has led theologians to reconfigure the nature of the Father–Son relation and to reformulate traditional understandings of the divine being. In evangelical circles,

1. A survey of the NT witness to this theme may be found in Richard N. Longenecker, *Studies in Hermeneutics, Christology and Discipleship* (Sheffield: Sheffield Phoenix Press, 2004), ch. 6.

2. For an early assessment of Barth's historicized doctrine of God, see Eberhard Jüngel, *God's Being Is in Becoming: The Trinitarian Being of God in the Theology of Karl Barth*, (trans. John Webster; Grand Rapids, MI: Eerdmans, 2001). More recently, see the debate between Bruce McCormack, Paul Molnar, George Hunsinger, and others, essays of which are collected in Michael T. Dempsey, ed., *Trinity and Election in Contemporary Theology* (Grand Rapids, MI: Eerdmans, 2011).

3. Hans Urs von Balthasar, *Theo-drama*, vol. 5 (San Francisco, CA: Ignatius, 1998), 236–9.

revision has often meant replacing eternal generation with obedience as the Son's distinguishing personal property (usually identified as the Son's "role" in the Trinity), and adopting (a sometimes unreflective) social Trinitarianism, which affirms three centers of self-consciousness and willing within the triune God.[4] Such revisions seem inevitable in view of the history of Trinitarian doctrine, where the Son's obedience is most commonly attributed to the *forma servi* that he assumed in the economy, as opposed to the *forma Dei* that he eternally shares with the Father or the personal *modus essendi* whereby he is and acts "from the Father."[5] Thus Gregory of Nazianzus states: "In his character of the Word he was neither obedient nor disobedient ... But, in the character of the form of a servant, he condescends to his fellow servants, nay, to his servants, and takes upon him a strange form."[6] Similarly Augustine: "In the form of a servant, he did not come to do his own will, but the will of him who sent him."[7] If obedience can only qualify as a human attribute within the metaphysical complex of pro-Nicene Trinitarianism, as a form that is "strange" in relation to the *forma Dei*, then the apostolic witness to the Second Person's obedient saving embassy seemingly demands that dogmatics develop a more thoroughly evangelized metaphysic than that on offer in the tradition. On the basis of the apostolic witness to Jesus's divine filial obedience, we must conclude that obedience is proper to God's being, with all the metaphysical revisions that this entails.[8] Doctrinal development in this vein takes the form of sending the classical catholic and Reformed Trinitarian tradition packing.

4. Representative examples of these moves may be found in Wayne Grudem, *Systematic Theology: An Introduction to Biblical Doctrine* (Grand Rapids, MI: Zondervan, 2000), ch. 14 and appendix 6; J. Scott Horrell, "Toward a Biblical Model of the Social Trinity: Avoiding Equivocation of Nature and Order," *Journal of the Evangelical Theological Society* 47 (2004): 399–421; and Bruce Ware, *Father, Son, and Holy Spirit: Relationships, Roles, and Relevance* (Wheaton, IL: Crossway, 2005).

5. This threefold classification of biblical descriptions of Christ is found throughout patristic writings. For representative examples, see Athanasius, *Orations Against the Arians*, 3.29–36 in *The Christological Controversy* (ed. Richard A. Norris, Jr.; Philadelphia, PA: Fortress, 1980), 87–96; Gregory of Nazianzus, *Oration*, 29.18; 30.20 in *Christology of the Later Fathers* (ed. Edward R. Hardy; Louisville, KY: Westminster John Knox, 1954), 172–3, 190–2; Augustine, *The Trinity*, trans. Edmund Hill (Brooklyn, NY: New City Press, 1991), 2.2–4.

6. Gregory of Nazianzus, *Oration*, 28.6 in *Christology of the Later Fathers*, 180.

7. Augustine, *The Trinity*, 1.22. Compare the above cited quotation, however, with Augustine's comments on Jn 5:19 in *The Trinity*, 2.5 and also with his treatment of Jn 5:19-30 in his *In Johannis evangelium tractatus*, helpfully discussed in Keith E. Johnson, "Augustine's 'Trinitarian' Reading of John 5: A Model for the Theological Interpretation of Scripture?" *Journal of the Evangelical Theological Society* 52 (2009): 799–810.

8. Thus Karl Barth *Church Dogmatics*, 4 vols. in 13 pts (ed. G. W. Bromiley and T. F. Torrance; Edinburgh: T&T Clark, 1956–75) (hereafter *CD*), IV/1, 192–210.

The purpose of the present article is to question the seeming inevitability of this form of modern doctrinal development. Note well: We do not wish to challenge the claim that obedience constitutes the proper form of the Son's divine work in the economy of salvation.[9] We wish to challenge what is perceived to be the necessary *implication* of this claim, i.e., that affirming the obedience of the eternal Son requires a revision of traditional Trinitarian metaphysics in the classical catholic and Reformed tradition.[10] Our strategy for issuing this challenge is not primarily critical but constructive. We do not intend to engage directly the various modifications of Trinitarian theology that have emerged in the wake of our modern *theologoumenon* but to demonstrate how this *theologoumenon* fits— indeed, supremely so—within the orbit of traditional Trinitarian metaphysics, and to address some of the most significant objections that might be posed against this

---

9. This is not to say, however, that we endorse the lush kenotic approaches to the Trinity *in se* as proposed by Balthasar and others; for helpful concerns on this front, see Bruce D. Marshall, "The Unity of the Triune God: Reviving an Ancient Question," *The Thomist* 74 (2010): 26–31. Marshall wisely suggests that a recovery of the distinction between divine processions and divine missions enables us to avoid the "unhappy results" of Balthasar's Trinitarian maneuvers (p. 30). We would add that the distinction between the common and proper attributes of the divine persons must also be recovered, as well as the necessary redoubling that must mark any faithful characterization of the particular divine persons (see below).

10. Cf. Steven D. Boyer, "Articulating Order: Trinitarian Discourse in an Egalitarian Age," *Pro Ecclesia* 18 (2009): 255–72; and Thomas Joseph White, "Intra-Trinitarian Obedience and Nicene-Chalcedonian Christology," *Nova et Vetera* 6 (2008): 377–402. Boyer engages some of the issues raised in the present article and argues that certain (mainly) patristic precedents provide warrant for thinking about the obedience of the divine Son. Conversely, White engages Barth's thesis and argues, from a Thomistic perspective, against the current thesis, though he does propose a reformulated version of pretemporal "obedience" of the Son (construed as a statement about the mission, though not the procession of the Son). White has expanded his case in two more recent essays: "Classical Christology after Schleiermacher and Barth: A Thomist Perspective," *Pro Ecclesia* 20 (2011): 229–63; "On Christian Philosophy and Divine Obedience: A Reply to Keith L. Johnson," *Pro Ecclesia* 20 (2011): 283–9. The *Pro Ecclesia* exchange with Keith L. Johnson and Fritz Bauerschmidt does not really move the conversation regarding this topic forward, precisely because it ranges so widely over the terrain of modern theology after Schleiermacher and Barth. For a somewhat similar attempt to understand the theological implications of the Son's economic obedience within a Thomistic metaphysics, see Michael Waldstein, "The Analogy of Mission and Obedience: A Central Point in the Relation between *Theologia* and *Oikonomia* in St. Thomas Aquinas's *Commentary on John*," in *Reading John with St. Thomas Aquinas: Theological Exegesis and Speculative Theology* (ed. Michael Dauphinais and Matthew Levering; Washington, DC: Catholic University of America Press, 2005), 92–112; cf. Keith L. Johnson, "When Nature Presupposes Grace: A Response to Thomas Joseph White, O.P.," *Pro Ecclesia* 20 (2011): 264–82: "The obedience of Jesus of Nazareth on the cross cannot be held at a distance from God, as if it does not tell us something essential about God's being as God; rather, this obedience reveals God's innermost being" (268).

claim in the current theological climate. In so doing, we will argue that the church's tradition of Trinitarian reflection, and specifically its Thomist representation, has resources which actually enable this development to proceed (e.g., the distinction between common and proper attributes of the triune persons, the distinction between the divine processions and divine missions). We envision this argument as an attempt at catholic and Reformed *ressourcement*—neither mere repristination nor rejection of this classical tradition, but traditioned reasoning within this tradition in fresh and faithful form.

Our thesis, then, is as follows: The obedience of the eternal Son in the economy of salvation is the proper mode whereby he enacts the undivided work of the Trinity "for us and our salvation." More fully, the obedience of the Son is the economic extension of his eternal generation to a Spirit-enabled, creaturely life of obedience unto death, and therefore the redemptive foundation for his bringing of "many sons to glory" (Heb. 2:10). We will endeavor to establish this thesis in two steps. First, we will consider the relationship between the Son's eternal generation and his economic obedience following the direction of the medieval dictum: *modus agendi sequitur modus essendi* (sections II-III). Second, we will attempt to address three major objections that might be raised against our proposal: two classical and one modern (section IV).

II

As the economic extension of his eternal generation, the Son's obedience to the Father in the economy of salvation constitutes the proper filial mode whereby he executes the Trinity's undivided work of salvation. The present claim is a particular application of the more general Trinitarian rule: mode of acting follows mode of being (*modus agenda sequitur modus essendi*). Attempts to follow this rule—by grounding Trinitarian missions in processions or by considering God's inner-Trinitarian depths prior to the economic acts which flow there from—are commonly regarded as excessively speculative, even "disastrous" for Trinitarian theology.[11] Such endeavors, it is argued, transgress the boundary of evangelical revelation within which alone God's being may be known. Even among those who would affirm the aforementioned Trinitarian rule regarding the ontological priority of the divine being over the divine works, it is often assumed that the order of knowing (*ordo cognoscendi*) follows an order different to that of the order of being (*ordo essendi*): first, we come to know God's works; then, we infer the nature of God's being on the basis of those works.[12] We wish to dispute both perspectives and this on the basis of the apostolic order of teaching (*ordo docendi*).

11. See Robert W. Jenson, *The Triune Identity: God According to the Gospel* (Philadelphia, PA: Fortress, 1982), 125–31.

12. Bruce McCormack discusses this strategy and its attending logic in *Orthodox and Modern: Studies in the Theology of Karl Barth* (Grand Rapids, MI: Baker, 2008), 58; and more fully in *Karl Barth's Critically Realistic Dialectical Theology: Its Genesis and Development 1909–1936* (Oxford: Clarendon, 1997), 350–8.

That the Son's mode of acting follows from his mode of being is not merely a statement about the order of being. As strange as it may seem to Kantian sensibilities, it is also a statement about the order of knowing insofar as the order of knowing follows the scriptural order of teaching, which in many instances presents the *identity* of the Son as propaedeutic to understanding the *action* of the Son. As Thomas Aquinas observes, the Apostle John's contemplation of the Word was "full" because he was able to consider "not only the essence of the cause, but also its power":

> Since John the Evangelist was raised up to the contemplation of the nature of the divine Word and of his essence when he said, "In the beginning was the Word; and the Word was with God," he immediately tells us of the power of the Word as it extends to all things, saying, "Through him all things came into being." Thus his contemplation was full.[13]

In other words, the "order"[14] of the Fourth Evangelist's contemplative teaching is to reveal to us the *nature* of the divine Word in order that we may appreciate both the character and the consequence of his *action*. Because the Word is the Father's perfect self-communication (Jn 1:1), dwelling in eternal repose at the Father's side (Jn 1:18), his mission can result in the perfect revelation of the unseen God (Jn 1:18), and not simply the witness to a greater light (cf. Jn 1:6-8).

The Gospel of Mark also provides a key example of the scriptural *ordo docendi* in this regard. Though the nature of Jesus's messianic sonship remains a riddle to human characters within the narrative until the end of the Second Gospel, the truth of his divine filiation is made known to Mark's readers from "the beginning" (Mk 1:1, 11). At the beginning, middle, and end of his Gospel, Mark identifies Jesus the Messiah as "the Son of God" (1:1, 11; 9:7; 15:39),[15] as one whose filial way is "the way *of the Lord*" (1:3).[16] The structural location of these identifications within Mark's narrative lends support to Kingsbury's argument that the primary secret which Mark seeks to disclose to his readers is not so much the so-called "*messianic secret*" as it is the secret concerning Jesus's "divine sonship."[17] This is the secret that God knows, that Jesus knows, and that the unclean spirits know as well (1:11; 3:11; 5:7; 9:7). It is moreover the secret that is not revealed to human characters in the Gospel until Jesus breathes his last on the cross. In his lordly self-offering as a

---

13. Thomas Aquinas, "Prologue to the Gospel of John," in *Commentary on the Gospel of John, Chapters 1–5* (trans. Fabian Larcher and James A. Weisheipl; Washington, DC: Catholic University of America Press, 2010), 3.

14. Aquinas, "Prologue to the Gospel of John," 3.

15. Joachim Gnilka, *Das Evangelium nach Markus*, vol. 2 (Zürich/Neukirchen-Vluyn: Benziger/Neukirchener, 1979), 171.

16. On Jesus's identity as Israel's one Lord in Mark's Gospel, see Richard Bauckham, *Jesus and the God of Israel*: God Crucified *and Other Studies on the New Testament's Christology of Divine Identity* (Grand Rapids, MI: Eerdmans, 2008), chap. 8.

17. Jack Dean Kingsbury, *The Christology of Mark's Gospel* (Philadelphia, PA: Fortress, 1983), 14.

ransom for many (cf. 10:45), wherein he fulfills the role scripturally patterned for the beloved son in the Binding of Isaac (the *Aqedah*),[18] the Gentile centurion comes to see what Mark has made known to his readers from the beginning: "Truly this was the Son of God!" (15:39). Mark's story of the wicked tenants thus summarizes in parabolic form the characteristic pattern of evangelical revelation: the Father *has* a beloved Son; the Father *sends* a beloved Son; and the ensuing rejection and vindication of the beloved Son constitute the *realization* of the divine counsel, a counsel graciously unveiled to us through the evangelical witness in order that we might understand that "*this* was *the Lord's* doing," and that this the Lord's doing might be "marvelous in our eyes" (Mk 12:1-12).

To be sure, the knowledge of the Trinity rendered in the sacred writings is ectypal theology not archetypal theology, with all the limitations that this entails. However, the distinction between these two modes of knowledge is not to be understood as a distinction between epistemology and metaphysics, or as a distinction between phenomenal form and transcendental condition. No: God reveals *both* his triune being and action to us through his prophetic-apostolic Word. And this revelation—delivered by the divine rhetor in a form wisely suited to the needs of creaturely wayfarers[19]—enables an ectypal contemplation of the relation between Trinitarian being and action as that relation obtains in its archetypal foundation. It is the Father's sovereign good pleasure to reveal unto babes both his unique knowledge of the Son and his unique knowledge of the Son's status as one fully invested with all things requisite to our salvation (Mt. 11:25-27).

These assertions run contrary to contemporary assumptions about the nature of Trinitarian revelation. Contrary to what is commonly supposed, Holy Scripture does not portray the economic Trinity as the more accessible starting point from which we may infer the more inaccessible depths of the immanent Trinity.[20]

---

18. See Ernest Best, *The Temptation and the Passion: The Markan Soteriology* (2nd ed.; Cambridge: Cambridge University Press, 2005), 167–72. For other associations of the *Aqedah* with divine sonship, see *Testament of Levi* 18.6-7; Jn 3:16; and Rom. 8:32.

19. That is, a form which "imparts to us wayfarers as much knowledge of the First Principle as we need to be saved" (Bonaventure, *Breviloquium*, Works of Saint Bonaventure, vol. 9 [Saint Bonaventure, NY: Franciscan Institute, 2005], 1.1.2).

20. In emphasizing the present point, we do not wish to deny that when it comes to the knowledge of God available through general revelation there is a sense in which the "things visible" are better known to us than the "things invisible" (Rom. 1:20) and therefore that "from the effect we proceed to the knowledge of the cause" (Thomas Aquinas, *Summa theologiae*, trans. Fathers of the English Dominican Province, 5 vols. [New York: Benziger Bros., 1948], 1a.2.2). However, when it comes to the knowledge of the divine persons, and therefore to a knowledge that is not available to us through general revelation, Scripture's characteristic order of teaching is to instruct us concerning the identity of the divine persons in order that we may fully appreciate the action of the divine persons, which would otherwise remain shrouded in mystery. As Aquinas says, a revealed knowledge of the divine persons is necessary if we are to arrive at right ideas about the divine acts of creation and salvation (*Summa theologiae*, 1a.32.1).

According to scriptural testimony, neither God in himself (*theologia*) nor God's economy (*oeconomia*) is transparent to naked reason in its fallen state. Both are "hidden" from the wise; and both are "revealed" only to babes (Mt. 11:25; cf. 11:1ff).[21] The meaning of Jesus's saving work is not so transparent that it can be "read-off" the surface of that work in any straightforward manner. His enigmatic work repeatedly provokes *questions*—"Who then is this … ?" (Mk 4:41). And answers are not easily found by either friend or foe in the evangelical narratives, or among auditors of the apostolic preaching (cf. 1 Cor. 1:23). An understanding of Christ's person, and the appreciation of his work which accompanies it, is a gift rendered by the Gospels' "omniscient" narrators, who invite Spirit-illumined readers to understand the nature of Jesus's messianic action by unveiling to them the secret of his messianic identity.

Some will no doubt worry that the present line of thought threatens to saddle the biblical portrait of the drama of the divine persons (*dramatis Dei personae*) with an alien "essentialism" or "substance ontology." We will address this worry in due course. The point to emphasize at present, however, is that the apostles, not Aristotle, direct theological reason to the conclusion that mode of operation follows mode of being.[22] T. F. Torrance well summarizes the canonical pointers in this regard:

> What Jesus is toward us he is antecedently and eternally in himself, in God … Were that not so, the revelation we are given in Christ would not have eternal validity or ultimate reality. That is why the fourth Gospel begins with the wonderful prologue of the eternity of the Word in God, for it is from the eternal God that the Word proceeded, and all that follows in the Gospel—all that Jesus said and was in his dependence as the incarnate Son upon the Father—goes back to and is grounded in that eternal relation of Word to God within God. Similarly, the Epistle to the Hebrews begins its exposition of the high priestly work of Christ by teaching that the Son came forth from the Godhead, the Son by whose word all things were created. It is that Son who came and manifested himself, and now in the incarnation stands forth as the divine servant Son to fulfill his work of atonement in entire solidarity with man, eternal Son of God though he was. But all that Jesus did has reality and validity just because it rests upon that eternal relation of the Son with the Father, and therefore reaches out through

21. In this (and only this) sense, we move from economy to theology, namely, that God's revelation of his own identity occurs within his works (and, thus, that revelation is a part of the divine economy). So the context of our knowledge is surely an economic form of knowledge—we did not exist or commune with God apart from this economy. But the shape of revelation within the economy—following the Scriptural order of teaching— moves from his identity in himself (*theologia*) to his works (*economia*).

22. For further exegetical argumentation along these lines (see, e.g., Jn 16:28; 17:8; 15:26; 13:14), see Gilles Emery, "*Theologia* and *Dispensatio*: The Centrality of the Divine Missions in St. Thomas's Trinitarian Theology," *The Thomist* 74 (2010): 543–4 (515–61).

and beyond the span of years in his earthly ministry into God. Again, what Christ is in all his life and action, in his love and compassion, he is antecedently and eternally in himself as the eternal Son o f the Father.[23]

It is this canonical directive that must be our guide for dogmatic reasoning, regardless of what metaphysical ancillaries might have proven or may yet prove serviceable to theological reason in bearing witness to the one who came to do his Father's will.[24]

III

In light of the general rule that guides our discussion, it is time to focus our attention directly and specifically upon the relationship between the Son's eternal generation and his economic obedience.[25] As we will see, the Son's distinctive *modus essendi* as the Father's only-begotten determines his distinctive *modus agendi* as the Father's obedient emissary. In order to appreciate this link between the Son's eternal generation and his economic obedience, it will be helpful to turn a brief glance to John's initial characterization of the Word in his Prologue as the one "through whom" all things were created. This brief glance, along with the important Trinitarian concept that it provides, will serve us well as we then turn to consider one of the primary biblical texts that establishes our thesis, Jn 5:19-30.

Aquinas begins his commentary upon Jn 1:3 with a statement that recalls his earlier observation about the "fullness" of John's contemplation of the Word: "After the Evangelist has told of the existence and nature of the Divine Word, so far as it can be told by man, he then shows the might of his power."[26] In other words, having considered the Word's subsistence in relation to God ("the Word was with God") as God ("the Word was God" [1:1]), John considers the Word's agency in creation: "All things were made through him" (1:3). Aquinas immediately rules out a number of possible misinterpretations of this verse, including, for example, those which would take the Word as God's "instrumental cause" for creating (as when a man makes a bench "through" a hammer) or which would take the Word as God's "efficient cause" for creating (as when a man makes a bench

23. T. F. Torrance, *The Incarnation: The Person and Life of Christ* (ed. Robert T. Walker; Downers Grove, IL: IVP Academic, 2008), 176–7.

24. For further criticism of the strategy of deriving necessary transcendental arguments about God's being *in se* from God's actions *pro nobis*, see Nicholas M. Healy, "Karl Barth, German-Language Theology, and the Catholic Tradition," in *Trinity and Election in Contemporary Theology*, 240–3.

25. Space forbids a lengthy discussion and defense of the doctrine of eternal generation. For a fuller consideration of the doctrine, see John Webster, "Eternal Generation," in *God without Measure*, vol. 1: *God and the Works of God* (London: T&T Clark, 2015).

26. Aquinas, *Commentary on the Gospel of John*, 30.

"through" the direction of a carpenter). He also surveys a number of orthodox alternatives by which the meaning of this verse might be illumined. Among these, he mentions Augustine's suggestion that texts like Jn 1:3 reflect a common pattern of Trinitarian "appropriation" whereby the undivided work of the Trinity *ad extra* is considered to flow "from" the Father "through" the Son "in" the Spirit.[27] He concludes, however, that John's statement in verse three should not be taken as mere appropriation but rather as referring to a mode of divine agency that is "proper to the Word." Creation comes into being "through" the Word because the Word performs the common Trinitarian work of creation in a manner consistent with his distinctive mode of being: "The statement, 'The Father does all things through the Son,' is not [mere] appropriation but proper to the Word, because the fact that he is a cause of creatures is had from someone else, namely the Father, from whom he has his being."[28]

Aquinas's interpretation of the Word's activity in Jn 1:3 invokes the theologically fundamental distinction between what is "common" versus what is "proper" to the persons of the Trinity. According to this distinction, whereas the Father, the Son, and the Spirit hold in common one divine substance, wisdom, will, and activity, they are distinguished from one another by the unique or proper way in which they hold the one divine substance, wisdom, will, and activity in common. Each person's unique or proper way of being God is indicated by the personal names themselves: i.e., Father, Son, and Spirit. As Aquinas observes, the personal names "signify *processions*,"[29] or what we may characterize as "communicative relations." It is proper to the Father to father/beget the Son and, with the Son, to spirate/breathe the Spirit. It is proper to the Son to be fathered/begotten of the Father and, with the Father, to spirate/breathe the Spirit. And so forth. These processions, it must be emphasized, do not involve the coming into being of a product by a producer (contra Arianism). Nor do they involve the transition of a cause into a new relationship with its effect (contra modalism). The processions of the divine persons are *internal* to the simple and indivisible being of God.[30] They signify the unique ways in which the one divine being of God is eternally *communicated* to or by each person within the eternal fecundity that is the triune God.[31] With reference to the Son, eternal generation thus refers to "a communication of essence from the

---

27. Aquinas, *Commentary on the Gospel of John*, 30–4. Cf. also Gregory of Nyssa: "There is one motion and disposition of the good will which proceeds from the Father, through the Son, to the Spirit" (*An Answer to Ablabius: That We Should Not Think of Saying There Are Three Gods*, in *Christology of the Later Fathers*, 262).

28. Aquinas, *Commentary on the Gospel of John*, 34. Cf. Aquinas, *Summa theologiae*, 1a.39.8: "The word *by* is not always appropriated to the Son, but belongs to the Son properly and strictly, according to the text, *All things were made by him* (Joh. i. 3); not that the Son is an instrument, but as *the principle from a principle*."

29. Aquinas, *Summa theologiae*, 1a.27.1.

30. Aquinas, *Summa theologiae*, 1a.27.1.

31. Aquinas, *Summa theologiae*, 1a.27.5.

Father (by which the Son possesses indivisibly the same essence with him and is made perfectly like him)."[32] The Son's personal property—that which is "proper" to him and to him alone within the Godhead—is finally nothing other than the *subsisting filial relation* in which he eternally stands to the Father *as a receptive communicant* in the undivided divine essence.[33]

This discussion sheds light on the nature of a "proper" act. For Aquinas, a proper act is one in which a divine person "acts in the distinct mode of his relation with the other persons" in carrying out the undivided work of the Trinity.[34] This concept, found not only in the Dominican master but also in Reformed Orthodoxy, is a direct application of the principle, *modus agendi sequitur modus essendi*. When it comes to the external works of the Trinity, there can be no distinction *between* the works of the persons. Because they share one being, they also share one principle of action. Nevertheless, there can be—indeed must be—distinctions *within* the common work of the persons in their external operations.[35] Because they share one being in tripersonal modification, they also share one principle of action in tripersonal modification. Thus Zacharias Ursinus: "The works of the Trinity are indivisible, but not in such a sense as to destroy the order and manner of working peculiar to each person of the Godhead."[36] With respect to the Son, therefore, the concept of a "proper" act requires us to confess that "as the Son is from the Father, so he works from the Father."[37] As the Son's proper mode of being God consists in

32. Francis Turretin, *Institutes of Elenctic Theology* (ed. James T. Dennison, Jr.; Phillipsburg, NJ: Presbyterian & Reformed, 1992), vol. 1, 293. Cf. Aquinas, *Summa theologiae*, 1a.41.3.

33. Because it is intrinsic to God's eternal and wholly realized identity, the Son's "receptive" stance in relation to the Father involves no passivity or passibility. The Son has "by nature what he receives" (*Summa theologiae*, 1a.33.4). Gilles Emery states: "The fact of being begotten does not imply any 'passivity' in the Son. To be begotten is an action. And when one says that the Son 'receives the divine nature from the Father,' this 'reception' refers to a pure relation of the Son to the Father; this is the relation of origin" ("The Immutability of the God of Love and the Problem of Language Concerning the 'Suffering of God,'" in *Divine Impassibility and the Mystery of Human Suffering* [ed. James F. Keating and Thomas Joseph White; Grand Rapids, MI: Eerdmans, 2009], 69 n. 139). For further reflection, see Aquinas, *Summa Theologiae*, 1a.27.1-3.

34. Gilles Emery, *Trinity, Church, and the Human Person: Thomistic Essays* (Naples, FL: Sapientia Press, 2007), 129. In contrast to a "proper" act, an "appropriated" act or attribute is one that is common to all three persons but that, because of its affinity with a particular person, leads "to a better understanding and knowledge of what is proper" (Bonaventure, *Breviloquium*, 1.6.1).

35. Cf. Eugene F. Rogers, *After the Spirit: A Constructive Pneumatology from Resources Outside the Modern West* (Grand Rapids, MI: Eerdmans, 2005), 11–16, 45–6.

36. Zacharias Ursinus, *Commentary on the Heidelberg Catechism*, trans. G. W. Williard (repr. Phillipsburg, NJ: Presbyterian and Reformed, n.d. [1852]), 120.

37. Turretin, *Institutes*, vol. 1, 282. The principle upon which the above quoted statement rests: "the order of operating follows the order of subsisting" (281).

the pure relation wherein he receives his being from the Father, so the Son's proper mode of acting as God consists in the pure relation wherein he receives his actions from the Father. "Receptive filiation" is the Son's proper mode of being and acting as the one true and living God.

How does this concept illumine the matter under discussion? We may gather an answer to this question by looking at Jn 5:19-30, a text devoted to vindicating Jesus's right to perform his Father's works. The occasion for this defense is a Sabbath healing described earlier in chapter 5, which has provoked the ire of "the Jews," and which Jesus defends as a work performed in imitation of his Father: "My Father is working until now, and I am working" (5:17). To the minds of his accusers, Jesus's defense amounts to claiming that God is "his own/proper Father [πατέρα ἴδιον]," and therefore that he is "equal with God" (5:18). The *topos* of this passage, then, concerns the way in which Jesus's *manner of working* follows from the fact that God is his *proper Father*.

In expanding upon this theme, Jesus juxtaposes two claims that, taken together, present a perennial challenge to Johannine interpreters. The first claim is that Jesus does *nothing* on his own initiative, but *only* what he sees the Father doing. The second claim is that Jesus, in following his Father's lead, does *everything* that his Father does. "The Son can do nothing of himself, unless it is something he sees the Father doing; for whatever the Father does, these things the Son also does in like manner" (5:19). The problem facing interpreters is not that the Fourth Gospel would make a claim implying the Son's inferiority to the Father. Nor is it that the Fourth Gospel would make a claim implying the Son's equality with the Father. Taken in isolation, these claims could be understood as evidence of different redactional layers or of authorial inconsistency. The problem facing interpreters is that the Fourth Gospel makes these seemingly contradictory claims *within the same context*.[38] Indeed, Jn 5:19 insists that the former claim is the basis for the latter claim: *because* the Son always only follows the Father's initiative, he always performs all of the Father's works. The remainder of the passage focuses upon one particular divine work that Jesus performs with his Father at his Father's behest, a work that far outstrips any Sabbath healing (5:20) and whose power to perform lies uniquely with the one true God of Israel: the power to kill and to make alive (5:21-29).[39] Jn 5:19-30 concludes by recapitulating the principle that explains Jesus's *modus operandi*: "I can do nothing on my own. As I hear, I judge,

---

38. C. K. Barrett summarizes the interpretive challenge thusly: "Those notable Johannine passages that seem at first sight to proclaim most unambiguously the unity and equality of the Son with the Father are often set in contexts which if they do not deny at least qualify this theme, and place alongside it the theme of dependence, and indeed of subordination" (*Essays on John* [Philadelphia, PA: Westminster, 1982], 23).

39. See Deut. 32:39; Isaiah 26; with Marianne Meye Thompson, *The God of the Gospel of John* (Grand Rapids, MI: Eerdmans, 2001), 118–19; and Andrew Lincoln, *Truth on Trial: The Lawsuit Motif in the Fourth Gospel* (Peabody, MA: Hendrickson, 2000), 210.

and my judgment is just, because I seek not my own will but the will of him who sent me" (5:30).

Some interpreters take our text's description of the Son's manner of working as solely indicative of his humble mediatorial state. John Calvin provides a rather forthright example of this interpretive stance. Calvin regards both the Arian and the orthodox exegesis of Jn 5:19-30 as misguided. According to Calvin, the Arians were wrong to conclude that this text revealed the Son's inferiority to the Father, while the orthodox Fathers were wrong to conclude that this text revealed the Son's distinctive personhood as one who is simultaneously "from the Father" and yet "not deprived of intrinsic power to act." Indeed, the Genevan Reformer considers a properly Trinitarian exegesis of this passage as "harsh and far-fetched." In his judgment, the proper subject matter of Jn 5:19-30 is the Son of God only "so far as he is manifested in the flesh."[40]

Although our text makes undoubted reference to the Son's mediatorial office—he executes judgment "because he is the Son of Man" (5:27), the eschatological agent of God and representative of God's people (cf. Dan. 7:13-14), an interpretation such as Calvin's seems too modest, and that for at least three reasons. First, the language used in the present passage to describe the manner in which the Son follows the Father's initiative, thereby performing the Father's works, is exactly the same as the language used in later passages to describe the manner in which the Spirit follows the initiative of the Father and the Son, thereby performing their works. As the Son can do nothing ἀφ' ἑαυτοῦ, but only what he sees the Father doing (5:19), so the Spirit will not speak ἀφ' ἑαυτοῦ, but only what he hears: drawing forth the truth from the common wellspring of the Father and the Son and distributing it to Jesus's disciples (16:13-15). Because this language cannot be reduced to the Spirit's *forma servi*—he has no *forma servi* (!), so it should not be reduced to the Son's *forma servi*.[41] Second, part of the rationale provided in this passage for the Son's manner of working is that the Son is doing the bidding of the one who "sent" him (5:30; cf. 4:34; 5:36-37; 6:38-39; etc.). And, as Augustine long ago observed, the Son's sending *precedes* his incarnation.[42] The Son is "consecrated and sent *into* the world" (10:36). Thus, the manner in which the Son works in obedience to his Father's commission is not simply indicative of the state in which he assumed the *forma servi* but of his own proper filial relation to the Father, which precedes his assumption of the *forma servi*. Third, and most telling for the present discussion, Jn 5:19-30 follows the pattern of contemplative reflection exhibited in John's Prologue which, as we have seen, grounds the might of the

40. John Calvin, *Commentary on the Gospel according to John*, trans. William Pringle (repr. Grand Rapids, MI: Baker, 1998), vol. 1, 198–207. On Calvin's general reticence toward Trinitarian reflection in his exegesis of classical Trinitarian proof-texts, see Arie Baars, *Om Gods verhevenheid en Zijn nabijheid: De Drie-eenheid bij Calvijn* (Kampen: Kok, 2004), 291–308.
41. Augustine, *The Trinity*, 2.5.
42. Augustine, *The Trinity*, 4.27.

Word's power (1:3) in the Word's existence and nature (1:1). The Son shares the Father's unique and sovereign power to *give life* to those he will (5:21) because he shares the Father's unique and sovereign power to *live*: he has "life in himself." Moreover, both of these powers that the Son shares with the Father are powers that he has received from the Father: "as the Father has life in himself, so he has granted the Son also to have life in himself" (5:26; cf. 10:18). And therefore: Just as it is the Son's proper *modus essendi* to have life in himself and to have it from the Father who begets him, so it is the Son's proper *modus agendi* to raise the dead and to have this power from the Father who sends him.

In light of the preceding discussion, we are in a position to appreciate how the concept of a "proper" act illumines the topic at hand. The fact that the Son does not pursue his own initiative but that of the Father who sends him is not merely a consequence of the human form he assumed in the incarnation. The fact that the Son does not do his own will but the will of the Father who sent him is a consequence of his distinctive *modus agendi*, which follows from his distinctive *modus essendi*. More briefly stated: "'To send' implies authority, and 'to be sent' implies subordination to authority [*subauctoritatis*] *in the order of eternal production in the Godhead*."[43] In this sense, the obedience of the Son to the Father who sends him constitutes the Son's *opus proprium* within the undivided *opera Trinitatis ad extra*.[44]

IV

The present interpretation raises at least three questions, two that would have animated classical theologians (and that continue to animate contemporary

43. Bonaventure, *Breviloquium*, 1.5.5 (italics ours).

44. Based upon his eternal procession from the Father and the Son, should we also speak of the Spirit's "obedience" to the Father and the Son in the economy of salvation? One might take our methodological approach and say that the sending of the Spirit implies that his "proper" identity ought to be spoken of as enacting obedience in the economy or as receptive filiation within the immanent life of the Godhead (the latter effectively introducing two sons within the Godhead). In other words, one might take our approach as potentially undermining our ability to differentiate the proper characteristics of the second and third persons of the Trinity. But this is precisely why the *filioque* is important: the Spirit's movement in both the missions and the processions is similar to the Son's movement, yet the Spirit is sent by and proceeds from the Father *and* the Son whereas the Son is sent by and proceeds from the Father *alone*. Even if one took the proposal that this double procession occurred from the Father through the Son, there would still be a distinction in terms of proper relational characterizations. We do not claim to be expressing everything there is to say about the Son's properties (or for that matter the Spirit's), which exceed his receptive relation to the Father, but we do believe that our approach in no way nullifies the theologian's ability to distinguish Son from Spirit.

theologians working faithfully within the Thomist tradition), the other which animates modern theologians. The first question is: Does such an assertion threaten to divide the common will of the Father and the Son into two separate wills? Thomas Joseph White suggests that this is the primary problem with the obedience of the eternal Son: "It would seem that one must forfeit either the notion of a unity of will in the persons, or reinterpret Barth's notion of a distinction of persons in God derived through obedience."[45] White suggests that the Son's identity as Wisdom—his unique personal nature—manifests his possession of a "unique spiritual Will" that is shared with the Father; indeed, he argues that this is part and parcel with Athanasius's polemics against those "fourth century 'Arian' or anti-Nicene theologians [who] appealed to New Testament examples of the obedience of Christ in order to argue for a preexistent, ontological subordination of the Logos to the Father."[46] In light of White's concern, then, we must ask: Does the obedience of the eternal Son undermine the shared divine will? Aquinas asks and answers this question in his commentary on Jn 5:30:

> But do not the Father and the Son have the same will? I answer that the Father and the Son do have the same will, but the Father does not have his will from another, whereas the Son does have his will from another, i.e., from the Father. Thus the Son accomplishes his own will as from another, i.e., as having it from another; but the Father accomplishes his will as his own, i.e., not having it from another. Thus he says: I am not seeking my own will, that is, such as would be mine if it originated from myself, but my will, as being from another, that is from the Father.[47]

In other words, the Son's obedience to the Father in the work of salvation is not indicative of a *second will* alongside that of the Father but of *the proper mode whereby Jesus shares the Father's will as the only-begotten Son of the Father.*[48]

The second question is similar, though it involves a worry about divine omnipotence rather than the divine will. White suggests that the obedience of the eternal Son "risks to undermine the intelligibility of Barth's own soteriological affirmation that God, in order to save us, must in no way be alienated from his own prerogatives of omnipotence in the Incarnation."[49] White argues that obedience

---

45. White, "Intra-Trinitarian Obedience and Nicene-Chalcedonian Christology," 393.
46. White, "Intra-Trinitarian Obedience and Nicene-Chalcedonian Christology," 389.
47. Aquinas, *Commentary on the Gospel of John*, 294–5; cf. Aquinas, *Summa Theologiae*, 1a.42.6, *ad* 3. For analysis of Aquinas's exegesis of Jn 5:30, see Thomas Joseph White, "The Voluntary Action of the Earthly Christ and the Necessity of a Beatific Vision," *The Thomist* 69 (2005): 497–534.
48. This is not to deny dyothelitism, but to suggest that the Son's obedient human will is determined by and expressive of his obedient divine will, i.e., the proper filial manner in which he executes the undivided divine will *ad extra*. See Aquinas, *Summa Theologiae*, 3a.48.6.
49. White, "Intra-Trinitarian Obedience and Nicene-Chalcedonian Christology," 389.

necessitates a lack of power—so that "one can therefore plausibly suggest that either we must rethink the claim to eternal obedience in the Son, or else qualify in important ways any affirmation of his omnipotence."[50] Are these the only options or is there an excluded middle? It seems at this point that the answer is to go deeper into the Thomist tradition rather than further from it. Indeed, the notion of redoubling/reduplication (*redoublement*) provides the conceptual framework for finding our way to the middle excluded by White's question. The eternal Son exists receptively as one whose self-existence (*autotheos*) and Almightiness are granted to him by the Father.

As noted above, Trinitarian theology requires the use of two forms of attribution: essential characteristics (common terms) and personal characteristics (proper terms). Gilles Emery has employed the term "reduplication" or "redoubling" (*redoublement*) to describe this linguistic rule impelled by the very nature of a Trinitarian metaphysics: "To express the Triune mystery, one must use two words, two formulas, in a reflection that joins the aspect of the unity of the divine substance to that of the distinction of the persons."[51] The Son is divine, yes, but he is also generated eternally from the Father. The first characteristic is common and can be attributed to the Father and Spirit as well; the second trait, however, is proper to the Son and can be attributed to him alone. It is crucial, though, to see that, while different proper terms can be applied only to one or another divine person, some terms must be applied to every divine person. In other words, there is no genuine knowledge of a divine person unless the common (what it means to be the one God) is matched by the proper (what it means to be the one God in this distinctive relation).[52]

Aquinas argues that this redoubling is impelled by biblical language *a la* John 5:

> Hilary calls our attention to the remarkable relationship of the passages so that the errors concerning eternal generation can be refuted. Two heresies have arisen concerning this eternal generation. One was that of Arius, who said that the Son is less than the Father; and this is contrary to their equality and unity. The other was that of Sabellius, who said that there is no distinction of persons in the divinity; and this is contrary to their origin.
>
> So, whenever he mentions the unity and equality, he immediately also adds their distinction as persons according to origin, and conversely. Thus, because he mentions the origin of the persons when he says, "the Son cannot do anything

---

50. White, "Intra-Trinitarian Obedience and Nicene-Chalcedonian Christology," 395.

51. Gilles Emery, *The Trinitarian Theology of St. Thomas Aquinas*, trans. Francesca Aran Murphy (New York: Oxford University Press, 2007), 46.

52. Denial of this point necessarily leads to the view that the divine essence is a fourth person behind the three divine persons, in as much as it requires the divine essence be viewed in an abstract and discrete manner. The divine essence is abstract, if that means shared by the three, but it is always concrete in the person of Father, Son, or Spirit, and never existent in any other way.

of himself, but only what he sees the Father doing" (5:19), then, so we do not think this involves inequality, he at once adds: "for whatever the Father does, the Son does likewise." Conversely, when he states their equality by saying: "For just as the Father raises the dead and grants life, so the Son grants life to those to whom he wishes," then, so that we do not deny that the Son has an origin and is begotten, he adds, "the Father himself judges no one, but he has given all judgment to the Son."[53]

Again, exegesis pressures Aquinas to speak in redoubled language about God: witness about the common life of the Trinity matched by testimony to the proper characteristics of each divine person.

With respect to the issue at hand, the obedience of the eternal Son is not contrasted with his omnipotence; rather the two exist at one and the same time.[54] Steven Boyer shows that this approach was followed by Athanasius in his opposition to the Arians and anti-Nicenes:

> The Son eternally comes from and is eternally dependent upon the Father, yet in a manner that in no way entails the Son's being less than or inferior to the Father. To connect dependence to inferiority is in fact to accept an axiom of Neoplatonism that the fourth-century Fathers who knew Neoplatonism best went out of their way to reject ... And by rejecting this tenet of Platonism, the Fathers paved the way for a full-blooded Trinitarian tradition that speaks over and over not of equality *or* order, but of equality *and* order.[55]

As possessor of the divine nature, the Son is equal in power to the Father; as receptive to the Father's gift of life in himself, the Son is ordered to the Father. There is a personal order in the one true God. Almighty power is possessed by all three divine persons, though it is not possessed in the same way. The Son possesses

---

53. Aquinas, *Commentary on the Gospel of John*, 282.

54. For further analysis of how "redoubling" language of the Trinity affects theological reflection on the economy of salvation, see Gilles Emery, "The Personal Mode of Trinitarian Action in St. Thomas Aquinas," *The Thomist* 69 (2005): 31–77. For reflection on how an eternally generated person can share the one divine essence, see John Duns Scotus, *Lectura* I, d.2, p. 2, q. 3 (no. 148) in *Opera omnia*, vol. 16, (ed. C. Balić et al; Città del Vaticano: Typis Polyglottis Vaticanis, 1960).

55. Boyer, "Articulating Order," 260. While affirming Boyer's substantive point, we will not follow him in employing the terminology of "dependence" to describe the obedience of the eternal Son. We will use the term "receptivity" to remain closer to the biblical language of receiving life in himself as a gift from the Father and, thus, to avoid adding terminology that may unduly distort. Given its widespread usage in psychological and therapeutic contexts, and cognizant of the influence of therapeutic conceptualities in the wider contemporary scene, "dependence" likely brings unhealthy conceptual baggage to the analogical task, baggage not present in use of the less frequently employed term "receptivity."

Almightiness (omnipotence) in a filial way, whereas the Father possesses this same attribute in a paternal manner. Equality cannot be reduced to the opposite of order; rather, equality is the setting for a triune order. So the Son's obedience cannot be construed as a reason to jettison the traditional Christian claim that the Son is omnipotent.[56] Indeed, the wind and the waves hearken to his Almighty power, even as his power is exercised to do the will of the one who sent him.

Briefly it should be noted that the two questions raised by Thomas Joseph White are joined together in a single Johannine text, where the will and power of Christ are yoked with his obedience to his heavenly Father. "For this reason the Father loves me, because I lay down my life that I may take it up again. No one takes it from me, but I lay it down of my own accord. I have authority to lay it down, and I have authority to take it up again. This charge I have received from my Father" (Jn 10:17-18).

Jesus here notes that his cruciform obedience flows from his own will and authority. First, he affirms that he surrenders himself to the forces of death "of my own accord" and not because something "takes it from me." Second, he reminds the disciples that he has authority to lay down his life and then to take it up again. The term employed here, ἐξουσία, refers to authority or power. Jesus reiterates that his willed submission to the forces of death is not powerlessness—it is the very exercise of authoritative power. Aquinas comments:

> In Christ, his own nature and every other nature are subject to his will, just like artifacts are subject to the will of the artisan. Thus, according to the pleasure of his will, he could lay down his life when he willed, and he could take it up again; no mere human being can do this … This explains why the centurion, seeing that Christ did not die by a natural necessity, but by his own [will]—since "Jesus cried again with a loud voice and yielded up his spirit" (Matt. 27:50)— recognized a divine power in him, and said: "Truly, this was the Son of God."
> (Mt. 27:54)[57]

Yet the concluding line pairs the will and power of the incarnate Son with the charge (ἐντολή) received from his Father. The Father commands the Son—there is an economic receptivity here. But the charge and command of the Father does not negate the will and power of the Son—in Trinitarian fashion, they are both not only valid affirmations but necessary aspects of the gospel proclamation. Jesus

---

56. A related worry would be whether or not the obedient Son and his commanding Father can share in the divine simplicity given those distinct personal properties. It is crucial to see that the patristic use of the doctrine of divine simplicity took the form of nuancing its pagan employment to fit this kind of Trinitarian grammar, on which see Andrew Radde-Gallwitz, *Basil of Caesarea, Gregory of Nyssa, and the Transformation of Divine Simplicity* (New York: Oxford University Press, 2009).

57. Aquinas, *Commentary on the Gospel of John, Chapters 6-12*, trans. Fabian Larcher and James Weisheipl (Washington, DC: Catholic University of America Press, 2010), 203.

wills to do this, and he exercises real authoritative power in so doing, and yet his action in this regard is according to his Father's charge.[58] There is a noncompetitive relationship between his powerful will and his submission to the Paternal will.[59] Karl Barth will say of the incarnate Son: "This man wills only to be obedient—obedient to the will of the Father, which is to be done on earth for the redemption of man as it is done in heaven."[60]

The third question, mentioned already in section II, ranges over wider formal territory than the previous two and can be stated as such: Does not all this smack too much of a "substance ontology" or an unevangelized "essentialism"? Once again, we may address this question with the aid of the Fourth Gospel. John's Prologue distinguishes the being of the Word who "was [ἦν]" and "is [ὤν]"[61] with the Father (1:1-2, 18) from the becoming that characterizes the economy of creation and redemption (1:3, 6, 10, 14, 17 [ἐγένετο throughout]).[62] In so doing, the Prologue exhibits "the doctrine of Jews and Christians which preserves the unchangeable and unalterable nature of God" over against the changeable nature of the creature (cf. Ps. 102:25-27).[63] This being of the Word, however, is not that of Aristotle's Unmoved Mover, who remains forever locked in self-enclosed contemplation over against all worldly becoming. This is the being of the Word who lives in eternal active relation to his Father and who temporally extends his active relation to others[64] through his obedient execution of the Father's will: The only-begotten Son "who is at the Father's side" (1:18) came into the world in order to extend to his creatures "the right to become children of God" (1:12).

The distinction between the divine procession (in this case, the eternal generation of the Son) and the divine mission (the obedient journey of the Son) is crucial if the doctrine of the obedience of the eternal Son is to be affirmed within a classical catholic and Reformed Trinitarian metaphysics. However, the purpose for distinguishing the unchanging being of the Word *ad intra* from his temporal

---

58. See Augustine, *Homilies on the Gospel of John, 1-40*, trans. Edmund Hill (Hyde Park, NY: New City, 2009), 31.6. (508–9).

59. Paul N. Anderson refers to John's "dialectical reflection" regarding a number of "Christological tensions" in his "On Guessing Points and Naming Stars: Epistemological Origins of John's Christological Tensions," in *The Gospel of John and Christian Theology* (ed. Richard Bauckham and Carl Mosser; Grand Rapids, MI: Eerdmans, 2008), 311–45.

60. Barth, *CD*, IV/1, 164; cf. Matthew Levering, "Augustine and Aquinas on the Good Shepherd: The Value of an Exegetical Tradition," in *Aquinas the Augustinian* (ed. Michael Dauphinais et al; Washington, DC: Catholic University of America Press, 2007), 237.

61. Jn 1:18 is possibly an allusion to Exod. 3.14 [LXX]. Cf. Rev. 1:8; 4:8; etc., which certainly are.

62. See Barth's exegetical comments on John's Prologue in *Church CD*, I/2, 159–60.

63. Origen, *Contra Celsum*, trans. Henry Chadwick (Cambridge: Cambridge University Press, 1980), 1.21.

64. In a mode suitable to their creaturely natures and which does not elide his singular identity as the Father's μονογενής.

work *ad extra* is not to separate the only-begotten Son from those who become his brothers and sisters but to indicate both the character and the consequence of the mission whereby his Father becomes their Father, and his God becomes their God (cf. 20:17).

With respect to the character of his mission: Distinguishing the Son's eternal generation, which is natural and necessary to his identity, from his saving mission, which is contingent to his identity, preserves the free and gracious character of his mission.[65] Only because the economy "was not motivated by any need of completion in the" being of the Word can it be an act of "incomparable generosity."[66] "The Word became flesh," according to Athanasius, "not for the sake of any addition to the Godhead"—or as he elsewhere states, "not for the Word's own improvement"—"but so that the flesh might rise again."[67] Furthermore, the distinction between eternal generation and economic action preserves not only the free and gracious character of the Son's economic action but also its distinctive filial shape. The counsel to collapse eternal filiation into temporal mission,[68] a counsel designed to secure the real presence of the second hypostasis in history, ironically threatens to rob that history of that which makes it distinctive as the history of the only-begotten. Apart from Jesus's metaphysically prevenient identity as God's beloved Son, we are unable to appreciate that which distinguishes his embassy from the embassy of the Father's other servants (Mk 12:1-12). Apart from his metaphysically prevenient identity as God's own/proper Son, we are unable to appreciate that which distinguishes his gift from the Father's other gifts (Rom. 8:32). To put the point positively, Jesus's identity as God's beloved Son is what characterizes his actions as properly divine filial actions and not simply as actions of an unspecified historical agent.

65. Space forbids unpacking the metaphysical distinction between "natural/necessary" and "contingent." For the sense which we assume, a sense common among Reformed Orthodoxy, see Andreas J. Beck, "Gisbertus Voetius (1589–1676): Basic Features of His Doctrine of God," in *Reformation and Scholasticism: An Ecumenical Enterprise* (ed. W. J. Van Asselt and Eef Dekker; Grand Rapids, MI: Baker Academic, 2001), 205–22; and more extensively J. Martin Bac, *Perfect Will Theology: Divine Agency in Reformed Scholasticism as against Suárez, Episcopius, Descartes, and Spinoza* (Leiden: Brill, 2010).

66. Robert Sokolowski, *The God of Faith and Reason* (Notre Dame, IN: University of Notre Dame Press, 1982), 34.

67. Athanasius, "Letter to Epictetus," 9, in John McGuckin, *Saint Cyril of Alexandria and the Christological Controversy* (Crestwood, NY: St. Vladimir's Seminary Press, 2004), 387. Cf. McGuckin's comments on Cyril of Alexandria's understanding of the incarnational economy: "The Logos had no need whatsoever to appear as man. Two deductions thus followed inevitably about the incarnation: firstly, that it was an entirely free act of divine power, a Charis, or gracious act, of God. Secondly, that it was not for God's benefit but for mankind's" (*Saint Cyril*, 184).

68. Thus recently Robert Jenson, "The Father's Sending and Jesus' Obedience *Are* the Second Hypostasis in God" ("Once more the *Logos asarkos*," *IJST* 13 [2011]: 133).

With respect to the consequence of the Son's mission: Distinguishing eternal generation from economic mission not only preserves the free and gracious character of the economy as an economy of the Father's only-begotten Son, it also helps us appreciate the final cause of the Son's economic mission, which is to communicate to creatures a distinctly creaturely fellowship in the Son's eternal relation to Father through union with him who is the head and firstborn of many brothers and sisters. The fact that the Son's relation to the Father is always fully realized and that our filial relation to the Father is a matter of temporal realization, "an economy for the fullness of time" (Eph 1:10; cf. 1:5), does not mean that the divine and the human offspring of the Father are related to one another as Platonic form to temporal shadow. Rather, the Son's economic obedience is the means whereby other sons and daughters come to share as creatures in his filial relationship to the Father. Economic obedience, the free and gracious overflow of the Son's natural and necessary generation, is the means whereby the Son's prayer is answered: "I desire that they may be with me where I am" (Jn 17:24; cf. 17:5; 1:1, 18). "He put on our flesh," says Calvin, "in order that having become Son of Man he might make us sons of God with him."[69] This "with him" is the final cause of the Son's economic embassy, and the manner in which his perfect filiation comes to perfect ours.

V

We have seen that a Trinitarian account of divine agency must speak by means of redoubling or reduplication. This is not the same as speech by means of appropriation, which tethers particular actions to specific divine persons (normally for reason of emphasis). Rather this is to say that the external works of the Trinity are indivisible (*opera ad extra trinitatis indivisa sunt*), though they are performed by all the persons in their own person-specific, "proper" ways. Dogmatic reasoning aids exegetical reflection in noting the common and proper engagement of each triune person in the various acts of the divine economy. Only in such a context does the obedience of the eternal Son fit within a classical catholic and Reformed Trinitarian metaphysics—such a setting, however, is surely in need of this doctrinal development if it is to remain attentive to the ever-fresh prompting of the living Word.

We have seen that the divine missions do extend the divine processions: the mode of being shapes the mode of acting. The relationship between processions and missions indicates that the divine freedom and self-sufficiency is not to be misinterpreted as divine aloofness; quite the contrary, as Dorner says, "God is not merely distinct from the world, but also distinguishes Himself from it and it from Himself ... and by means of this absolute inalienable Self-mastery of

---

69. I. John Hesselink, *Calvin's First Catechism: A Commentary* (Louisville, KY: Westminster, 1997), 23.

God, this doctrine opens the prospect that God can communicate Himself to the world without detriment."[70] God is not aloof, and the shape of his communicative communion with us is not arbitrary. The three persons act in union with one another—indivisibly—though this union is a harmony of activity drawing on the active manner proper to each person. Thus, the divine missions flow forth and manifest the temporal extension of the divine processions; the relations of origin within the Triune life, then, shape the form of external works performed by the three persons together. One such extension has been considered here: the eternal Son's receptivity in relation to his Father—expressed poignantly in the doctrine of eternal generation—provides the metaphysical and relational grounds for his free enactment of his proper activity in the divine economy, which is time and again characterized as obedience. T. F. Torrance is surely right: "The perfect human life of Jesus in all his words and acts reposes entirely upon the mutual relation of the Son to the Father and the Father to the Son."[71] Yet this "mutual relation" must be clarified in ways appropriate to the canonical witness, which identifies that relation as one of receptivity and obedience on the part of the incarnate Son. Making use of distinctions deep within the classical Trinitarian tradition—hammered out by Thomists and drawn upon by classical Reformed thinkers—we have shown that the obedience of the eternal Son is not only exegetically necessary, but dogmatically coherent with the classical Trinitarian metaphysics of this catholic and Reformed tradition.

70. Isaak A. Dorner, *A System of Christian Doctrine*, trans. Alfred Cave (Edinburgh: T&T Clark, 1885), vol. 1, 338. Cf. the exposition of Richard Sibbes: "God's goodness is a communicative, spreading goodness … If God had not a communicative, spreading goodness, he would never have created the world. The Father, Son and Holy Ghost were happy in themselves and enjoyed one another before the world was. But that God delights to communicate and spread his goodness, there had never been a creation nor a redemption" ("The Successful Seeker," in *Works of Richard Sibbes* [ed. Alexander B. Grosart; Edinburgh: Banner of Truth Trust, 1983], vol. VI, 113).
71. Torrance, *The Incarnation*, 127.

Chapter 9

INTO THE FAMILY OF GOD: COVENANT AND THE GENESIS OF LIFE WITH GOD

On Moral Foundations, Covenant, and the Missionary Work of Systematic Theology

The wise one "built his house on the rock," while the foolish one "built his house on the sand" (Mt. 7:24, 26). Jesus's binary analysis alerts us to the moral foundations of our experience, and Christians throughout the centuries have thus thought about the wise and the foolish, the righteous and the wicked, the children of light and the children of darkness. More recently, the foundations seem to have multiplied. Moral psychologists Jonathan Haidt and Craig Joseph have suggested what they term "moral foundations theory" as a rubric through which one can assess cultural or ideological differences based on the six categories of harm, fairness, liberty, loyalty, authority, and purity.[1] In so doing, they intentionally expand the horizon beyond previous rational-focused theories of moral judgment, looking first to intuitions which prompt rational and affective judgments of different sorts. Ideological opponents or cultural aliens may differ on the fundamental definition of one such foundation, Haidt and Joseph observe; they even differ with respect to which foundational intuitions are in play. In his more recent work, *The Righteous Mind*, Haidt has discussed not merely variable perceptions of purity but opposing valuations of the category itself.[2] If the words of our Savior should have alerted us to the significance of building on solid foundations, then these descriptive studies alert us to the complexity and variability of such labors. To the Psalmist's question "What is man?" (Ps. 8:4), we can find many answers.

Yet foundations must be plotted in the right domain. Even biblical lineaments, to say nothing of divergent takes from wider culture, must be thought together. As Oliver O'Donovan says:

---

1. Jonathan Haidt and Craig Joseph, "Intuitive Ethics: How Innately Prepared Intuitions Generate Culturally Variable Virtues," *Daedalus* 133, no. 4 (2004): 55–66.

2. Jonathan Haidt, *The Righteous Mind: Why Good People Are Divided by Politics and Religion* (New York: Pantheon, 2012).

We will read the Bible seriously only when we use it to guide our thoughts towards a comprehensive moral viewpoint, and not merely to articulate disconnected moral claims. We must look within it not only for moral bricks, but for indications of the order in which the bricks belong together.[3]

Whether it is the task of moral theology or of the doctrine of God and his works more broadly, we quickly find that systematic reflection is prompted by the very nature of the Bible itself. We can say also that systematic or dogmatic theology plays a critical role in the practice of moral reasoning, especially in a setting such as our own in the late modern Western world. In the kind of environment within which we move, described under Charles Taylor's category of expressive individualism,[4] systematic theology plays a uniquely significant missionary role. When men and women come to faith with little to no sense of the broader principles and practices of the Christian way, then the task of looking far and wide, of thinking top to bottom, and of seeking to tie things together becomes all the more important. Systematic theology functions as a set of protocols, then, against narrowing our confession to something less than the "whole counsel of God," of centering or prioritizing our profession on matters of personal predilection or cultural prestige rather than biblical emphasis, of mangling the shared and singular facets of biblical–theological language, and of lapsing into incoherence rather than appreciation of the biblical mystery that "in many times and in various ways" the word attests the one gospel of the incarnate Son (Heb. 1:1).

In each of these ways, systematic theology serves as an aid to more illumined reading of God's word, that we might hear its notes harmoniously, and as a guide to more faithful attestation of the gospel, that we might be a chorus of confession. These analytic moments, then, are a missionary mode of systematic theology. It is significant to speak, as does Nicholas Lash, of theology as a "set of protocols against idolatry" and thus to note its role as a form of intellectual discipleship and the constant interplay between dogmatics and ascetics. Given the formative ways in which we are shaped by life here in Babylon—the powers and principalities at work in our cultural moment—we do well to tend to ourselves and to our language, realizing that we need Jeremiah's word "to pluck up and to break down, to destroy and to overthrow, to build and to plant" (Jer. 1:10). The living and active word of God cuts not only through kingdoms with power but "piercing to the division of soul and of spirit, of joints and of marrow, discerning the thoughts and intentions of the heart" (Heb. 4:12). Systematic theology plays a role in aiding this intellectual discipleship by giving a sense of the scope and sequence of God's word.

3. Oliver O'Donovan, *Resurrection and Moral Order: An Outline of Evangelical Ethics* (Grand Rapids, MI: Eerdmans, 1986), 200.

4. Charles Taylor, *A Secular Age* (Cambridge: Belknap, 2007), esp. 473–95; see also hints in idem, *The Ethics of Authenticity* (Cambridge, MA: Harvard University Press, 1992), 61; idem, *Sources of the Self: The Making of Modern Identity* (Cambridge, MA: Harvard University Press, 1990), 497, 509.

So we come to the "Creation Project," to Genesis, and—let me place my wager on the table—the value in disciplining ourselves to avoid narrowing, misprioritizing, mangling, and going incoherent in tempting false starts, or, to put it in happier terms, the value in reading this portion of Holy Scripture with the grain of the whole text. The book of Genesis sketches the moral foundations not only of human society and creatureliness but also more specifically of the church and Christian worship. To help make sense of both origins and ends, the book draws our attention to the doctrine of the covenant and the pledge that people are drawn "into the family of God." Covenant comes from Genesis, whether in the overt form of divine dealings with Noah and Abram or in the implicit foundations of life in the garden and the deep magic underneath God's providential care to Joseph's kin. Not surprisingly, covenant plays a pivotal role in the sketching of redemptive history, functioning like a hub within which so many pivots of prophetic instruction are rooted. We will follow the basic theological moves of the doctrine of the covenant in this fundamental text, seeking to sketch its implications for a number of theological and anthropological concerns. My concern is not so much to argue for the centrality of covenant here by drawing on either word studies or upon exegetical reasoning of snippets within Genesis as it is to help show how this theological category alerts the reader to the broader patterns of the text. In so doing I seek to provide something of an index by which to draw out the intellectual role played by covenant.

As we begin, we do well to note that instruction on covenant—like that of the doctrine of creation more broadly—carries with it moral and ascetical impulses. The late John Webster spoke of that primal work of God:

> Most of all, it obliges those who consider it to recover the posture of creatures, the dependence and gratitude of derivation and the repudiation of self-subsistence. This is acutely hard for the children of Adam, for we contend against our creaturely nature and calling, from stupidity or pride or fear that unless we snatch at our being and make ourselves authors of its perpetuation and dignity, it will slip away from us. And so we propose to ourselves, sometimes a little guiltily and sometimes with frank confidence, that we constitute a given reality around which all else is arranged. Even God may be so placed, as God "for us," a protagonist whose identity, not wholly unlike our own, is bound to us, and whose presence confirms the limitless importance of the human drama.[5]

As with creation, so with covenant: it calls us out of ourselves and disciplines our thoughts (like our breath) to find sustenance from the outside and to turn singly unto the living and true God. To change our posture so as to bow before our Creator, to kneel before our Judge, and to lift our hands up unto our Redeemer,

---

5. John Webster, "*Non ex aequo*: God's Relation to Creatures," in *God without Measure*, vol. 1 of *God and the Works of God* (London: T&T Clark, 2015), 126.

we will turn to ask now how the doctrine of the covenant casts new light upon the human creature and the wider creation.

In this chapter, I will treat three significant tasks of systematic theology: the ways in which covenant illumines the emphases of God's word, draws out the common and proper forms of communicating the good news, and ties together key strands of biblical instruction in a coherent (even if not comprehensive) fashion.[6]

The Centrality of Fellowship: On Biblical Breadth and Evangelical Emphases

Many things may rightly be confessed of human creatures: embodiment, rationality, sexuality, and so forth. Christian anthropology takes up the task of moral psychology even while tending to our animal nature. Cornel West regularly reminds us that we live between womb and tomb and therefore have to attend to the funky character of our being. Fair enough, and Genesis helps suggest ways in which thinking about God, humanity, and the wider creation dare not get unhelpfully abstract lest we forget the fruit and the foreskins, the ways in which sin and redemption occur amidst our entangled existence. Rusty Reno's meditations on Genesis remind us that here, perhaps as nowhere else, we catch the "scandal of particularity."[7]

As we consider the particularities of divine revelation, systematic theology has a calling to keep us from theological myopia, enlarging our vision to take in the full breadth of God's teaching regarding creation and its many facets. True enough, but attentiveness proves to be crucial also and especially in remaining alert to priorities of the Christian confession. Just as the priority of the "image of God" speaks to the character of the human in a Godward way, so the doctrine of the covenant also attests a distinctly theological anthropology and doctrine of creation more broadly.

Emphases matter, and we dare not assume that our gravest concerns match the scriptural order of love. We begin with an eye to the wider canon. The centrality of fellowship with God can be seen in noting the two dominant strands through which the prophets and apostles highlight this life with God.[8] They employ no metaphors or images so much as those of marriage and of adoption. Perhaps no canonical feature is so startling in this first regard than the inclusion of the Song of Songs in Holy Scripture. Jews and Christians alike have noted that the theological significance of this text is directly related to its symbolic meaning, namely, that it portrays the intimate communion of YHWH and his people in the starkest of terms,

---

6. Due to space, I will not consider a fourth fundamental task of systematic theology, namely, to attend to the breadth of biblical teaching.

7. R. R. Reno, *Genesis* (Grand Rapids, MI: Brazos, 2010), 23, 26–7, and pt. 4.

8. For analysis, see Michael Allen, *Justification and the Gospel: Understanding the Contexts and Controversies* (Grand Rapids, MI: Baker Academic, 2013), 69–70.

that is, those drawn from the realm of conjugal bliss.[9] The prevalence of the Song of Songs in patristic and medieval homiletics and liturgy manifests its remarkable impact upon the Christian imagination, conveying the rich and personal union with God that is to mark the Christian's life. Indeed, Karl Shuve has shown how, far from being an interpretive conundrum, the Song of Songs was used most frequently as a settled text which was used to explain other, more complex exegetical discussions.[10] Modern reading habits have rendered us less capable of sensing the power of that classical focus upon the Song, but that is our loss. Our forebears knew how to read what might seem abstract love songs in light of the particular promise of God's love for Israel.[11]

And the metaphor of adoption and familial love is equally emphasized across the canon, in as much as the love of the Father for the Son takes the form of sharing that beneficence with his many adopted brothers and sisters, who are "fellow heirs" with Christ (so Rom. 8:16–17). Israel had been identified as God's son—the lineage of the beloved son, Isaac—and that language later applies to her Davidic king (2 Sam. 7:14). Eventually, in Jesus Christ, all believers share in this inheritance of Abraham's seed (so Gal. 3:29; Eph. 3:6). What is notable throughout this redemptive-historical development is that the image employed to depict the divine–human relation is one of familial identity and the parent–child bond.[12] The repeated use of these metaphors, and the manner in which adjoining language is so regularly employed in the imaginative and literary structure of the canon, signals the biblical emphasis upon the relational intimacy and personal fellowship between God and his people that is conveyed in its own way by each of these two most prevalent images.

This prevalence flows from the imagery found in Genesis, for the theophanies of Genesis occur with little fanfare. Gen. 12:7 strikes us with its plainness: "Then YHWH appeared to Abram and said, 'To your seed I will give this land.'" William Brown has contrasted the appearance of God in Genesis with the cataclysmic and pyrotechnic manner of divine nearness in either the burning bush (Exodus 3–4) or the terror of Sinai (Exod. 19:16–20; cf. Heb. 12:18–21). Genesis speaks in ordinary tones of God walking in the Garden and of appearing to talk. In so doing, the text commends the telos of human existence: to be with God.[13]

---

9. See especially Jon D. Levenson, *The Love of God: Divine Gift, Human Gratitude, and Mutual Faithfulness in Judaism* (Princeton, NJ: Princeton University Press, 2016), 90–142 (esp. 132, 169).

10. Karl Shuve, *The Song of Songs and the Fashioning of Identity in Early Latin Christianity* (Oxford Early Christian Studies; New York: Oxford University Press, 2016), 3.

11. R. R. Reno, "Beginning with the Ending," in *Genesis and Christian Theology* (ed. Nathan MacDonald et al; Grand Rapids, MI: Eerdmans, 2012), 40.

12. The Westminster Confession of Faith acknowledged the power of this image by including a chapter on adoption (ch. 12).

13. William P. Brown, "Manifest Diversity: The Presence of God in Genesis," in *Genesis and Christian Theology* (ed. Nathan MacDonald et al; Grand Rapids, MI: Eerdmans, 2012), 4–7.

We can see this emphasis upon fellowship in the rendering of Genesis 17, namely, that the promise of progeny in verse 4 and of land in verse 8 climaxes with the encore, "I will be their God" (17:8). But this deep bond does not begin with the patriarch; it goes all the way back into the primeval account. The text of Genesis 1–2 also manifests this concern, for immediately upon creation, the human being is identified as related to God (his image and likeness), as commissioned by God (to exercise dominion), and as present with God ("and he walks with me, and he talks with me"). This last point is worth drawing out. When God concludes his work of creation, it culminates in his dwelling there or "resting" there on the seventh day (Gen. 2:2–3). Indeed, we learn later that it is not unusual for the LORD God to be "walking in the garden" with the "presence of the LORD God among the trees of the garden" (Gen. 3:8). We not only see the intended intimacy between the Creator God and the human creature in these Edenic realities, but we observe them contrasted with the curse executed in Genesis 3. There the immediate result of human sin is death, manifest in the form of dismissal from Eden, from the tree of life, ultimately from this communion with the one true God (Gen. 3:22–24). The climax of the curse matches the climax of nature in the creation account: the presence of God. Whether in the Sabbath gift of the seventh day or the final curse of Genesis 3, we see that human beings are made for life with God. And, by implication, we might say that God is intent on sharing the triune life with us. For this reason, as Jon Levenson and Gordon Wenham have shown, the creation accounts make use of temple imagery to depict their purpose in helping us understand human life as meant for the very presence or space of God.[14]

The Holy Scriptures conclude here as well, for the final portrait of our blessed hope depicts a New Jerusalem. This glorified city is arrayed with all manner of blessing and bling. It is a return to Edenic life, for the tree of life is present therein (Rev 22:2). It is not merely a trip back to an innocent garden; rather, it is a journey forward to a glorified heavens and earth, wherein the glory and perfection of God have spread over the whole span of created reality. The King's promise is nothing less than "behold, I am making all things new" (Rev. 21:5). The central promise, however, is one of divine presence: "Behold, the dwelling place of God is with man. He will dwell with them, and they will be his people, and God himself will be with them as their God" (Rev. 21:3). The absence of a particular place called the temple is shown to be beside the point, in as much as the reality to which that shadow pointed is found in its fullness: God is present and available everywhere in this new and glorified city.

14. Jon R. Levenson, "The Temple and the World," *Journal of Religion* 64 (1984): 275–98; Gordon Wenham, "Sanctuary Symbolism in the Garden of Eden Story," in *I Studied Inscriptions from Before the Flood: Ancient-Near Eastern, Literary, and Linguistic Approaches to Genesis 1–11* (ed. Richard Hess and David Tsumara; Winona Lake, IN: Eisenbrauns, 1994), 399–404. See also Gregory K. Beale, *The Temple and the Church's Mission: A Biblical Theology of the Dwelling Place of God* (New Studies in Biblical Theology; Downers Grove, IL: InterVarsity Press, 2004).

And divine presence is not only the alpha and omega of biblical teaching. This fellowship between the triune God and his people serves also as the focal point of the canon's central episode. Jesus is Immanuel ("God with us"), and his gospel involves the claim that the "Word became flesh and dwelt among us" (Jn 1:14). The language of tabernacling points to this reality: the personal presence of the one true God in the face of Jesus. This centrality finds expression most powerfully, of course, in the transfiguration account (Mt. 17:1-8; Mk 9:2-8; Lk. 9:28-36). As Peter observes this powerful divine presence (with all its verbal cues pointing to something along the lines of the pyrotechnic displays which Moses beheld atop Mt. Sinai in Exodus 34), he notes that they need to cover Jesus and his friends up ("If you wish, I will make three tents here," using the term *skenás* for tabernacles). This disciple clearly interprets this event along the lines of divine glory coming near. The answer from the heavens does not reverse or downgrade that interpretation; by the time the heavens have replied, the disciples have fallen on their faces and are terrified (Mt. 17:6). Yet Jesus comes to touch them and to say "rise and have no fear" (Mt. 17:7). Surely this event points to the way in which the gospel economy makes possible the transition from Genesis 3 and Exodus 34, wherein sinners cannot enjoy the unmediated presence of God, to Revelations 21–22, wherein we are promised a world full of that glorious divine dwelling. With this turn, those who cannot see are even touched, and those in peril are told to have no fear, their God is near. Covenant will be the instrument through which this kind of fellowship becomes possible, the order in which that sort of presence attains reality. As it orders this relation, covenant gives shape to the thread right at the heart of the Bible and of human life.

The Form of the Covenant: On Biblical Borrowing and Doctrinal Distinctiveness

Another task of systematic reflection in its missionary mindset relates to borrowing and modifying, to the common and the proper. Scriptural language comes from and returns unto a wider world of communication, so we work with words that can wield shared meaning or may take notable redefinition. We fix our attention on images which are common but also commandeered to a unique cause, and we linger with questions that are anthropologically basic but addressed by the singular God of Israel and of Jesus. We do well then to assess the ways in which the biblical instruction of prophets and apostles—in this case, of Genesis—is and is not distinctive with respect to other forms of communication and confession. As we speak of covenant, we are in the thick of it. If ever it were clear that we trade in koine and not in some specially devised lingo of the Holy Ghost (whether Greek or otherwise), it is here. Covenant is the language of the prince and the polis, of the marriage and the market.

Decades ago, archaeology helped shed light on some comparative resources, and William Moran, Moshe Weinfeld, and Dennis McCarthy showed the light cast upon Pentateuchal texts by reading them over against ancient Near Eastern references to covenants of varying sorts.[15] More recent years have only brought further analysis as Gary Knoppers and Jon Levenson have continued to explore parallels.[16] Observing parallels, of course, does not equate to interpreting meaning.

Covenant comes as common lingo, but it is put toward the most particular ends here in Genesis. God's pledge to Abram will have global significance (Gen. 12:3) though it takes the form of attention to progeny and, much later, to a particular dynasty. Genealogy tells many things, I suppose, most of which I'm probably too much of an amateur to note. But central among them must be the significance of election for covenant. In his Kantzer Lectures delivered ten years ago now, John Webster addressed this tie-in, saying "like creation, election is a divine fiat, *ex nihilo* ... covenant means election, and election is uncaused origination."[17] It must be noted that prevenience is not a distinctive mark of biblical covenants; agreements are proferred and suggested all the time, initiated by one party or another. The unique character of this covenant concerns its ex nihilo fashion, namely, that God elects Israel when, strictly speaking, Israel does not exist. Abram has much: wife and wealth, kin and a company. But he has no son, no heir, yet God summons him that his progeny might cover the earth with blessing, to be as numerous as the stars of the heavens, and to bless the very nations who, unlike his line, already exist aplenty (Gen. 12:1–3).[18]

---

15. William L. Moran, "The Ancient Near Eastern Background of the Love of God in Deuteronomy," *CBQ* 25 (1963): 77–87; Moshe Weinfeld, "The Loyalty Oath in the Ancient Near East," *UF* 8 (1976): 379–414; idem, "The Covenant of Grant in the Old Testament and in the Ancient Near East," *JAOS* 90 (1970): 184–203; Dennis J. McCarthy, *Treaty and Covenant* (AnBib 21A; 2nd ed.; Rome: Biblical Institute Press, 1978). Similar analyzes were offered by George Mendenhall and Meredith Kline, drawing widespread attention from many evangelicals.

16. Gary Knoppers, "Ancient Near Eastern Royal Grants and the Davidic Covenant: A Parallel?" *JAOS* 116, no. 4 (October–December 1996): 670–97; Jon Levenson, *The Love of God: Divine Gift, Human Gratitude, and Mutual Faithfulness in Judaism* (Princeton, NJ: Princeton University Press, 2015), esp. ch. 1.

17. John Webster, "God Is Everywhere, But Not Only Everywhere" (Kantzer Lecture, no. 3, delivered at Trinity Evangelical Divinity School, 2007), 20.

18. For reading of Gen. 12:3a and the verb *nibrĕkû* in a canonical lens and a missionary trajectory, see Jo Bailey Wells, *God's Holy People: A Theme in Biblical Theology* (SJOTSS 305; London: T&T Clark, 2000), ch. 6; cf. the concessive reading proposed by R. W. L. Moberly, *The Theology of the Book of Genesis* (Old Testament Theology; Cambridge: Cambridge University Press, 2009), 141–61. The state of the debate regarding the verbal form probably does not solve anything in and of itself, demanding argument from nearer or further context of one sort or another, as evident by reading Keith Grüneberg, *Abraham, Blessing, and the Nations: A Philological and Exegetical Study of Genesis 12:3 in Its Narrative Context* (BZAW 332; New York: de Gruyter, 2003).

Divine election defines the unique nature of this covenant. As Paul will later put it, God is "not served by human hands, as though he needed anything" (Acts 17:25). This divine sufficiency or fullness was expressed long before in the identifying or naming of God to his servant Moses. Before he was "the LORD, the God of your fathers, the God of Abraham, of Isaac, and of Jacob" (Exod. 3:15), he was already "I AM WHO I AM" (Exod. 3:14).[19] Whereas ancient grants and loyalty oaths of varying sorts invariably concerned benefit and blessing, necessity and diplomacy, we see that God's action cuts against the grain of covenant cutting. Here we have a Lord making a pact without any potential or desired addition to his storehouse or extension of his kingdom. The language of aseity tinges the testimony of divine covenant. As with creation, so with covenant; election is apart from merit or fitness and without concern for provision or progress on the part of God.

The Bible intentionally conveys the shape of divine fellowship through the admittedly common lens of covenant, but the Scriptures shape that confession in a way that comports with the singular being of God. This God can choose the void and the infertile, the weak and the lowly. When the promise to Abram seems to finally be within sight, Moses must attest the counterintuitive nature of God's election to covenant with Israel:

> The LORD your God has chosen you to be a people for his treasured possession, out of all the peoples who are on the face of the earth. It was not because you were more in number than any other people that the LORD set his love on you and chose you, for you were the fewest of all peoples, but it is because the LORD loves you and is keeping the oath that he swore to your fathers, that the LORD has brought you out with a mighty hand and redeemed you from the house of slavery, from the hand of Pharaoh.
>
> (Deut. 7:7–8)

Eventually Peter will speak of the elect people of God who are a "chosen race, a royal priesthood, a holy nation, a people for his own possession," and he will attest that "once you were not a people, but now you are God's people; once you had not received mercy, but now you have received mercy." This he attributes to the action of God from nothing, alluding to Genesis 1 in his claim that this God "called you out of darkness into his marvelous light" (1 Pet. 2:9, 10). Prophet and apostle alike

---

19. See Michael Allen, "Exodus 3," in *Theological Commentary: Evangelical Perspectives* (ed. Michael Allen; London: T&T Clark, 2011), 25–40, repr. as Chapter 3 in this volume; idem, "Exodus 3 after the Hellenization Thesis," *Journal of Theological Interpretation* 3, no. 2 (2009): 179–96, repr. as Chapter 2 in this volume; and Andrea Saner, *"Too Much to Grasp": Exodus 3:13–15 and the Reality of God* (JTI SuppSeries 11; Winona Lake, IN: Eisenbrauns, 2015).

see the basis of covenant ultimately not in the aptitude or quantity of the people but solely in the divine mercy.[20]

Biblical covenants ought not be shoehorned into some extra-biblical form. Gary Knoppers has suggested what others are busy working out in greater detail, namely, that we have good reason to question the older archaeological analysis of ancient Near Eastern covenants falling into either the conditional or unconditional type. Jon Levenson and others have shown, more fundamental for our purposes, that these categories prove less than illumining in reading the accounts of Genesis.[21] The Abrahamic Covenant cannot be likened unconditional in as much as Abraham's faith commends him (Gen. 15:6; cf. Rom. 4:3). We do have good reason to catch the way in which Paul construes the Abraham cycle differently from other Jewish interpreters who would read Abraham much like Phinehas as a man of zeal and obedience whose final willingness to sacrifice Isaac prompted God to say "Now I see that you fear God" (Gen. 22:12, following R. W. L. Moberly's interpretation). But Paul not only locates justification prior to the binding of Isaac in Genesis 22 but also prior to the relatively miniscule sacrifice of his foreskin in Genesis 17; such is the plain argument of Rom. 4:9–11.[22] Faith is brought into stark relief in this telling of Father Abraham's story.[23]

Faith, not works, sayeth the apostle. Faith is a unique sort of condition and is not new with Abraham (more on these points to come), but it must not be missed that faith serves as a condition. Abraham pleases God (Heb. 11:6) and is declared righteous (Rom. 4:3) with his trust (Gen. 15:6). The apostolic analysis refines and does not reject the causality of the covenant. Scholastic theologians and Protestant confessions would later speak poignantly of the instrumental causality of faith in this covenant. Westminster Larger Catechism 73 is standard here:

> How doth faith justify a sinner in the sight of God? A. Faith justifies a sinner in the sight of God, not because of those other graces which do always accompany it, or of good works that are the fruits of it; nor as if the grace of faith, or any act thereof, were imputed to him for justification; but only as it is an instrument, by which he receiveth and applieth Christ and his righteousness. (See also Heidelberg Catechism 61).

20. Rom. 9:6-13 reads two stories of Genesis (the births of Isaac and of Jacob) through the lens stated more bluntly in 9:16, namely, that "so then it depends not on human will or exertion, but on God, who has mercy." We dare say, in light of this exegesis, that Paul reads Abraham in light of his son and grandson, that is, as similarly elected for covenant apart from fitness and thus in an incongruous sort of grace.

21. Levenson, *The Love of God*, ch. 1.

22. Moberly, *The Theology of the Book of Genesis*, ch. 10.

23. I am following Francis Watson, *Paul and the Hermeneutics of Faith* (London: T&T Clark, 2004), ch. 4; John Barclay, *Paul and the Gift* (Grand Rapids, MI: Eerdmans, 2015), 484n94; Jonathan Linebaugh, *God, Grace, and Righteousness in Wisdom of Solomon and Paul's Letter to the Romans: Texts in Conversation* (NovTSupp 152; Leiden: Brill, 2013), ch. 7.

This scholastic concern to distinguish the causal character of faith only makes sense if faith is in fact construed as a condition and a cause, raising the relevant questions "of what sort?" and "in what way?"

To consider the conditional character of even the Abrahamic covenant serves as but one entryway by which the familiar distinction between grants and oaths ought to be refined radically or even replaced. Whether such a schema helpfully sorts the varying covenantal options in the ancient Near Eastern world, it does not elucidate the specific character of the covenants in Genesis. We can say that the divine covenants relate to a global itch, namely, to be bound to others for the sake of one's good. Yet this global phenomenon takes a particular form which does prove to be rather scandalous.

The Fittingness of Faith for Humans: On Theological Coherence

Finally, we do well to explore the ways in which covenant helps show significant coherence amongst various prongs of biblical instruction. In Genesis itself, covenant helps tie together certain strands of scriptural communication. And later texts, ranging from Hos. 6:7 to Isa. 24:5, speak of the "everlasting covenant" in ways which seem to trace it back beyond even its explicit attestation in Genesis. Such texts have suggested to interpreters that covenant proves basic to biblical anthropology, and that we are authorized "by good and necessary consequence" then to speak of a covenant of creation (often called the covenant of works, as in the WCF 7.2, or the covenant of nature).

Within the Reformed tradition, the most common approach to describing this relational order and vocational *telos* of human existence before God has been to describe not only covenant with God, but specifically the covenant of works instituted by God. The Westminster Confession of Faith articulates this doctrine in its discussion of the covenant: "The first covenant made with man was a covenant of works, wherein life was promised to Adam, and in him to his posterity, upon condition of perfect and personal obedience."[24] The covenant of works involves a goal: life for Adam and all his posterity. It also involves a condition or requirement: "perfect and personal obedience" to God's commands. While the covenant of works was initiated unilaterally by the Lord, maintenance of life in God's favor and enjoyment of his final bestowal of life forevermore requires human responsive action.[25] Thus the provision of grace—not only life itself, but also divine presence and divine proclamation—leads to and calls forth human action.

We have considered ways in which the doctrine of the covenant alerts us to a fundamentally theological construal of creation and of human creatures especially. We should conclude by reflecting on how the doctrine of the covenant of works

24. "Westminster Confession of Faith," in *Book of Confessions*, 180 (VII.2).
25. Levenson, *The Love of God*, 61–2.

informs our understanding of holiness and sanctification. This covenant of creation was instituted in a period of human innocence and marks human life in the natural order. Thus, it is not an intervention into human ills or a response to moral failure; it is original and basic, thereby showing God's fundamental expectations for how his fellowship with human creatures may and will play out in days ahead.

The particular mode of this covenant of works also reveals much about the course of creaturely holiness.[26] We can note two angles quickly, and then turn to reflect on two more at greater length with regard to the way in which this primal covenant displays the coherence—better, the fittingness—of faith as the definitive human posture before our heavenly Father.

First, this primal covenant, as with all others, tells us of God, not merely of creatures. God chooses to be with us and not apart from us. God enters freely and apart from need or lack within and prompting or pressure without. Nonetheless, God does enter into this pact with our ancestors, and this—like every word of the gospel to come—tells us something profound first and foremost of the triune God. Not that God can be reduced or framed fully by the works of the divine economy and the glorious news of merciful action for our good, but that God is revealed herein. Father, Son, and Spirit are shown to take their fellowship toward others in an inclusive manner, that their glory and life might be shared. In so doing, the triune love comes to be common (i.e., communicated) in an ordered mode which is appropriately signaled by the language of covenant, that is, of ordered relationship. We do not have access to the Godhead willy-nilly but through the Son and by his Spirit. Covenant cutting from the very beginning tells us not only about the common characteristic of God's fullness that proceeds outward but even about its proper form through the ministrations of Son and Spirit. "Great are the works of the LORD, studied by all who delight in them," for "full of splendor and majesty is his work" (Ps. 111:2, 3). I would love to linger here regarding the theological significance of the fact that covenant proves to be basic to God's ways in his external works, but my immediate charge is to reflect more fully on the anthropological and creational implications.[27] So we press on.

26. In both the sixteenth and seventeenth centuries, when the federal theology was being developed, and today as well, debates swirl regarding the precise character of the covenant of works. The specific provisions and demands are argued in various theological contexts: Was the tree of life a lingering promise or a gift already being enjoyed? Was the Decalogue revealed to Adam and Eve, even though this giving of a natural law is not explicitly mentioned? Why was the partaking of the tree of the knowledge of good and evil somehow so problematic? These and other questions continue to be debated, but they need not detain us from making some more fundamental observations.

27. The two cannot be separated, of course, as I have attempted to draw out elsewhere: "Toward Theological Anthropology: Tracing the Anthropological Principles of John Webster," *International Journal of Systematic Theology* 19, no. 1 (2017): 6–29. See also John Calvin, *Institutes*, I.i.1.

Second, the covenant of works witnesses to God's universal designs for communion with his human creatures. In the ancient world the phraseology of the image of God could be restricted regularly to positions of prestige (e.g., the emperor or king), but Genesis 1 identifies the male and the female—indeed the entirety of the human species—as made after God's likeness and in his image. Still further, we learn that Adam represents us all in this covenant of works, such that his actions have implications for all men and women. The apostle Paul insisted to the Romans that all were in Adam and suffering the effect of his failed work in this covenant (see Rom. 5:12–21). We may say, then, that the covenant of works bound all humans at its time of inception to approach fellowship with God in this particular way, and we should confess still further that the covenant of works continues to bind all men and women to relate to God in this specific manner.[28]

Third, the covenant of works shows that communion with God is bounded by the commands of God. A moral order governs relational proximity. "My eyes are upon the faithful in the land, that they may dwell with me" (Ps. 101:6). Not only must we see the moral shape to this fellowship, but we observe that the Creator God is the Covenantal Lord and, thus, the one who determines the order of fellowship. God initiates life together. God sketches its contours. God gives commandments and sets expectations. There is no room for negotiation.

Who shall ascend the hill of the LORD? And who shall stand in his holy place? He who has clean hands and a pure heart, who does not lift up his soul to what is false and does not swear deceitfully. He will receive blessing from the LORD and righteousness from the God of his salvation. (Ps. 24:3–5)[29]

These formed obligations are not arbitrary either: "For the LORD is righteous; he loves righteous deeds; the upright shall behold his face" (Ps. 11:7).

We turn from fellowship generally to covenant more specifically. At the most basic level, a covenant is a relationship that has been ordered so as to have a particular form. Humans cross paths and encounter others in happenstance encounters day after day; such nebulous connections can and should be contrasted, however, with the kind of committed and defined relations marked by a political, economic, or theological covenant. We learn in Genesis that God grants that order and reveals that shape. Of the various theophanies that occur in this text, it is the

---

28. Note, however, that some reformed theologians have argued for the idea of the abrogation of the covenant of works. For analysis, see W. J. Van Asselt, "The Doctrine of the Abrogations in the Federal Theology of Johannes Cocceius (1603–1669)," *CTJ* 29 (1994): 101–16.

29. Hans Boersma points to the cross-canonical (or figural) reading of Psalm 24 that took shape immediately in Christian circles, via the teaching that the heavenly throne-room is original and the earthly is but a copy (so Heb. 8:5 and 9:23–24), in "Going Up the Hill (Psalm 24)," in *Sacramental Preaching: Sermons on the Hidden Presence of Christ* (Grand Rapids, MI: Baker Academic, 2016), 81–93.

covenant dream of Gen. 15:7–21 that includes the "smoking fire pot" and "flaming torch" and thus appears more similar to the later appearances of Exodus (13:21–22; 19:18; cf. Deut. 4:11–12).[30] Only when covenant appears as the defined and deepened theophanic presence does the cataclysmic imagery set in.

We oftentimes chafe at order being bestowed upon us from the outside and without our election. Milton's *Paradise Lost* portrays Lucifer with the message: "I know none before me; I am self-begot." Oliver O'Donovan diagnosed this condition three decades ago:

> When every activity is understood as making, then every situation into which we act is seen as raw material, waiting to have something made out of it. If there is no category in thought for an action which is not artifactual, then there is no restraint in action which can preserve phenomena which are not artificial. This imperils not only, or even primarily, the "environment" (as we patronizingly describe the world of things which are not human); it imperils what it is to be human, for it deprives human existence itself of certain spontaneities of being and doing, spontaneities which depend upon the reality of a world which we have not made or imagined, but which simply confronts us to evoke our love, fear, and worship. Human life, then, becomes mechanized because we cannot comprehend what it means that some human activity is "natural."[31]

Creation attests a life that comes to us apart from our choosing, by what the prophets and apostles call the will of God. And we do well to note that the metaphysical agency of the Creator finds its match in the moral legislation of the Maker. Fundamental to owning one's nature as creature, then, must be holding a posture that is dependent and receptive. We do well to note the basic human commitments signaled by Jon Levenson in this regard: "Discovering ourselves to be in relationships that we never chose is a key component in the process of having responsible adults."[32] If we identify such commitments from weak fathers and mothers and siblings and the like, how much more the covenantal order of the family of God?

Fellowship with God takes particular shape and form, then, in both catholic and reformed theology. John Webster has noted the order that relational life with God takes:

> Further, to be a creature is to have a particular shape, to exist as a particular configuration. Formed by God, creaturely being has a given nature. Nature is not, of course, to be construed in crudely necessitarian terms as ineluctable fate; it is the bestowal of and summons to life in a particular direction, with a particular

30. Brown, "Manifest Diversity," 18–19.

31. Oliver O'Donovan, *Begotten or Made? Human Procreation and Medical Technique* (Oxford: Oxford University Press, 1984), 3.

32. Levenson, *The Love of God*, 56.

bearing. In this nature, the creature *lives*, that is, the creature is characterized by spontaneity and agency. This is above all because in its nature the creature is ordered to fellowship with God. It is of the nature of creatures both to be given and to act out what they are, to be determined for life not only *from* and *under* but also *for* and *with* the creator.[33]

Webster notes that creation by God, an act that is free and generous, is matched by design and instruction by God, a provision that is equally sovereign and gracious. The same God who calls all things into being of his own power and goodness also calls them to a particular form and vocation, in so doing ordering their life before him and with one another.

It is perhaps helpful to think about the link between the beginning (protology) and the end (eschatology). The very same God who made the heavens and the earth and all things therein also destines them to a particular glory and perfection. Again Webster is helpful:

> This means that to be a creature is to be appointed by God the creator to a specific destiny or end. As the creature receives its being at the loving hands of God, and is formed to be a particular being, so also the creature is pointed to a particular perfection, namely full fellowship with God. Creatures are not merely caused; they are summoned to fulfill their nature over time, to realize themselves according to the form bestowed upon them.[34]

The central focus of the human vocation will be "full fellowship with God," and this relational reality takes "specific" and "particular" form befitting human "nature" and the "form bestowed upon them." Webster is highlighting the common calling of all humans by their Creator and Lord. In the catholic tradition others have articulated this order by pointing to the doctrine of the image of God. Similarly others, Webster included, have discussed the doctrine of human nature, arguing that biblical teaching disallows us from shirking the idea of a human substance or nature that binds us all together in a common beginning and a desired end.

Fourth, the covenant of works involves the basic demand that humans entrust themselves to their Creator God. "As the creature has itself in being with respect to God, so also it ought to have itself in working, for the mode of working follows the mode of being."[35] Notice that central to the covenant here is the calling to eat and, thus, to receive sustenance in the right way. Christians are committed to the

---

33. John Webster, "The Dignity of Creatures," in *God without Measure*, vol. 2 *Intellect and Virtue* (London: T&T Clark, 2015), 34.

34. Webster, "The Dignity of Creatures," 34–5.

35. Francis Turretin, *Institutes of Elenctic Theology*, vol. 1 (Phillipsburg, NJ: Presbyterian & Reformed, 1992), 503 (VI.iv.9).

doctrine of *creatio ex nihilo*, precisely to signal the free work of a God who gives and does not take life.[36] All the way down goes God's grace. As Oswald Bayer says:

> Creation and new creation are both categorical gift. The first Word to the human being is a gifting Word: "You may freely eat of every tree!" (Gen. 2:16)—renewed in the gifting Word of the Lord's Supper: "Take and eat. This is my body, given for you!"[37]

The inverse, of course, is that human being is gift all the way down and straight through history—we began with the fruit of the garden, we end with the feast of the city to come; always we are fed by another's generous provision.

But the question arises: Where and how will one eat? How will life be procured? By God's design and directive or by one's own or another's intuition and wisdom? Fundamental to that moral quandary is the matter of one's trust, whether placed in oneself or in another. The deepest calling of the covenant of works is the summons to consistent and perfect, unceasing and constant trust in the God who created, who promised, and who gives again and again. That it is termed by many to be a covenant of works in no way means that it does not involve at its heart the call to trust.[38] This covenant does include other commands—what to eat and what not to eat, how to exercise dominion, the Sabbath command, and, as many argue, the

36. On the revolutionary nature of the doctrine of creation from nothing, see Janet Martin Soskice, "Athens and Jerusalem, Alexandria and Edessa: Is There a Metaphysics of Scripture?," *International Journal of Systematic Theology* 8, no. 2 (April 2006): 149–62. Luther applies the doctrine of justification free from any merit within us and fully in Christ at just this point (as a gift ex nihilo) in his "Small Catechism," in *The Book of Concord: The Confessions of the Evangelical Lutheran Church* (ed. Robert Kolb and Timothy Wengert; Minneapolis, MN: Fortress, 2000), 354–5: "I believe in God the Father almighty, Creator of heaven and earth. What is this? Answer: I believe that God created me and all that exists, and that he gave me my body and soul, eyes, ears and all my members, my mind and all my abilities. And I believe that God still preserves me by richly and daily providing clothing and shoes, food and drink, house and home, spouse and children, land, cattle, and all I own, and all I need to keep my body and life. God also preserves me by defending me against all danger, guarding and protecting me from all evil. All this God does only because he is my good and merciful Father in heaven, and not because I have earned or deserved it. For all this I ought to thank and praise, to serve and obey him. This is most certainly true."

37. Oswald Bayer, "Creation: Establishment and Preservation of Community," in *Martin Luther's Theology: A Contemporary Interpretation* (trans. Thomas H. Trapp; Grand Rapids, MI: Eerdmans, 2008), 98–9; see similar moves made by Ian McFarland, *From Nothing: A Theology of Creation* (Louisville, KY: Westminster John Knox, 2014), ch. 4.

38. Indeed, some suggest that it is better to refer to it as a covenant of creation for this and other reasons; see, e.g., Henri Blocher, "Old Covenant, New Covenant," in *Always Reforming: Explorations in Systematic Theology* (ed. A. T. B. McGowan; Leicester: Apollos, 2006), 255.

entirety of the Decalogue—yet we do well to note that the heart of its call is a matter of trust.[39]

Here we can return to our earlier comments on faith in the Abrahamic covenant: a condition, to be sure, but a condition of a certain sort. We read Genesis at this point with the guidance of the apostle, for we can see the way that Paul interprets Abraham's story and draws out teaching on justification; pausing to consider the prepositions helps us see something of the unique posture of faith. In Paul, the instrumentality of faith is expressed in various forms. We are justified "through faith" (*dia pisteos*) (Rom. 3:22), "by faith" (*ek pisteos*) (Rom. 3:30), and "by faith" (the dative *pistei*) (Rom. 3:28).[40] Interestingly, never are we said to be justified "on account of faith" (*kata pistin*) or "on the basis of faith" (*dia pistin*; see the one exception in Phil. 3:9 qualified immediately as *epi tei pistei*). Faith uniquely amongst the many actions performed by human creatures points away from the power of the one believing and fully stands or falls upon the trustworthiness of its object. Not surprisingly, then, faith marks the beginning and the end of creaturely action, for it so fittingly expresses the metaphysical and covenantal character of our being.

To the typical assumptions about the contents of the book of Genesis, John Calvin appended another and final end: that we see that "the holy Fathers, one after another, having by faith embraced the offered promise, were collected together into the family of God, in order that they might have a common life in Christ." Indeed, several ends are found therein: "that we may know what is the society of the true Church, and what the communion of faith among the children of God"; "that they might seek the certainty of this adoption from the Covenant which the Lord had ratified with their fathers"; and that they "might know that there was no other God, and no other right faith." Assurance of different sorts is found therein. "But it was also his will to testify to all ages, that whosoever desired to worship God aright, and to be deemed members of the church, must pursue no other course than that which is here prescribed."[41]

Our admittedly piecemeal sketch of the doctrine of the covenant and, in particular, of the covenant of works reveals much about the shape of human holiness and the project of instilling moral foundations. Humans were created for fellowship with the triune God. The Lord's original design centered upon this communion and took the form of moral and relational guidance fit to bring them

---

39. The call to faith within the covenant of works is illustrated so well by its identification of the Sabbath as holy such that humans stop and rest on the Sabbath, on which see Gen. 2:3, Heb. 3:12, 19 and 4:1–11, which, when read together, show that Sabbath and belief are integrally related.

40. See J. M. G. Barclay, "'By the Grace of God I Am What I Am': Grace and Agency in Philo and Paul," in *Divine and Human Agency in Paul and His Cultural Environment* (LNTS 335; ed. J. M. G. Barclay and Simon J. Gathercole; London: T&T Clark, 2006), 153.

41. John Calvin, "Argument," in *Commentaries on the Book of Genesis*, vol. 1 (trans. John King; Grand Rapids, MI: Eerdmans, 1948), 65–6.

unto this social and spiritual reality. Many details might be traced further—and are by others throughout the tradition—yet we have reflected broadly enough to see the ways in which this initial covenant relationship relates to the definition of and path toward human holiness, indeed the very notion of taking on the character of one's heavenly Father as in the covenant relations of the divine family. In so doing the covenant draws a number of notes together into a harmony. It helps also to alert us to the melody line of Genesis, so that we might hear God's insistent call to fellowship with him with an abruptness and resolve that we might otherwise miss amidst the tragedy and deliverance, the primal mystery and the cosmic scope. While the text itself gestures toward the significance of the term, the concept of covenant helps alert us as we go back to the text to do so with a distinctly Christian span of attention, sequence of priorities, shape of commonality amidst distinctiveness, and sense of unity.

Chapter 10

SOURCES OF THE SELF: THE DISTINCT MAKINGS OF
THE CHRISTIAN IDENTITY

Introduction

"This is my Bible. I am what it says I am. I have what it says I have. I can do what it says I can do. Today I will be taught the word of God. I boldly confess my mind is alert, my heart is receptive; I'll never be the same. In Jesus' name." These words speak a blunt and beautiful word, namely, that the Bible reveals who we are, what we have, and what we can do; that this revelation deserves alertness and receptivity; and that all these things change us in Jesus's name. It's best said—I have to say—with a big, implacable grin. That is right. This confession comes from the lips of Joel Osteen, which perhaps reveals that committed attentiveness to biblical teaching about the self is no straightforward and simple matter. Who does the Bible say I am? How does it do so? To what effect? These questions warrant our attention. Today I want to draw your attention to the sources of the self or, more specifically, the distinct makings of the Christian identity as we learn from Holy Scripture.

My analysis will proceed by attending to four aspects of Christian anthropology.[1] First, the created self will be considered, so that the original design for human nature might be appreciated as a fundamental and continuing baseline for human existence, a backdrop for human pain and lament, and a map for any human reorientation. Second, the crooked self will be described, so that we can discern the shape of sinful being and the ways in which sin disfigures the dignity of created human nature and depraves every nook and cranny of our being today. Third, the resurrected self will be brought forward for reflection, in order that the gift of new life in Jesus Christ and its consequences for human selfhood may be seen in their brilliance. Fourth, the transfigured self finally warrants attention, that the God of the gospel's ultimate purposes in transforming, sanctifying, and eventually glorifying redeemed humanity will have their sway over the definition of human nature.

---

1. Cf. Charles Taylor, *Sources of the Self: The Making of Modern Identity* (Cambridge, MA: Harvard University Press, 1989). See also J. B. Schneewind, *The Invention of Autonomy: A History of Modern Moral Philosophy* (Cambridge: Cambridge University Press, 1998); Larry Siedentop, *Inventing the Individual: The Origins of Western Liberalism* (Cambridge: Belknap, 2014).

In so doing I am presenting what may appear to be a contemporary variant of an approach that goes back to Augustine himself and that has had a prestige throughout the tradition, namely, the fourfold state of humanity.[2] And yet this is not simply a narrative sketch of redemptive historical moments *à la* the fourfold state—creation, fall, redemption, and final restoration—but a fourfold attentiveness to aspects of anthropological teaching that are pertinent here and now. Whereas the traditional fourfold nomenclature serves to describe epochal history in its movements, here aspects of present reality are explored in nonreductive ways that involve tending to varied, irreducible depictions of the human and Christian self. In each case I gesture to a range of scripturally pertinent passages but linger over one text at greater length.

The following exposition is admittedly schematic and should surely be expanded in a number of ways.[3] Nonetheless, the point in turning to four aspects of Christian teaching regarding the self is to prompt breadth and range in our self-perception. We are prone to meander toward myopia, taking up one aspect of biblical anthropology (whether its created integrity or its sinful depravity or perhaps its Christological redefinition) as if that sufficed. Just as some might complain of putting God in a box, so we can put the human self in a box by tidily and narrowly suggesting that some element of biblical teaching suffices to describe the whole terrain. In the face of such temptations, Oliver O'Donovan has suggested the metaphor of "wakefulness" to describe this recurring call to attentiveness that is given the church.[4] Theology commits itself to that wakeful attentiveness to the

2. See, e.g., Augustine, *Treatise on Rebuke and Grace*; Bernard of Clairvaux, *Grace and Free Choice*; Peter Lombard, *Sentences*, II.distinction 25; Girolamo Zanchi, *Dei operibus Dei intra spatium sex dierum creatis*, lib. III, cap. 3, in *Omnia opera theologica*, tom. Tertius, col. 704; Anthonius Thysius, "Disputation 17: On Free Choice," in *Synopsis Purioris Theologiae, (1625)*, vol. 1: *Disputations 1-23* (Studies in Medieval and Reformation Traditions 187; ed. Dolf te Velde; trans. Riemer A. Faber; Leiden: Brill, 2015), 429–30; Francis Turretin, *Institutes of Elenctic Theology*, VIII.2.ix; Thomas Boston, *Human Nature in Its Fourfold State* (London: Banner of Truth Trust, 1964). For contemporary analysis of its Augustinian form, see Han-Luen Kantzer-Komline, *Augustine on the Will: A Theological Account* (Oxford Studies in Historical Theology; Oxford: Oxford University Press, 2019).

3. David Kelsey has suggested a threefold way in which humanity is presented in Christian theology (via creation, reconciliation, and eschatology), though I believe that more can be said regarding their connections than he suggests; see Kelsey, *Eccentric Existence: A Theological Anthropology*, vols. 1-2 (Louisville, KY: Westminster John Knox, 2009). Taylor describes three sources of emerging modern selfhood (inwardness, affirmation of ordinary life, and an expressivist notion of nature as a moral source) which impinge upon one another, to which a fourfold Christian reply ought to be offered.

4. Oliver O'Donovan, *Self, World, and Time: Ethics as Theology*, vol. 1: *An Induction* (Grand Rapids, MI: Eerdmans, 2013), 9. For earlier reflections on this "attentiveness," see Oliver O'Donovan, *Resurrection and Moral Order: An Outline for Evangelical Ethics* (2nd ed; Grand Rapids, MI: Eerdmans, 1994), 110.

breadth of God's Word and its interconnections, cognizant that we are all prone to myopia of one sort or another. To be alert to the totality of biblical teaching about the self—not just the self in other eras yet to come or long past, but the self here and now—we must pay attention to these four aspects of Christian anthropology.

The First Aspect: The Created Self (Genesis 1)

Christian anthropology begins with creatureliness. We are created by the triune God, the maker of heaven and earth. He speaks, and humans exist. He declares them to be very good, and they persist. "In him we live and move and have our being" (Acts 17:28). A design for dependence shapes the very logic of creatureliness which Johann Georg Hamann expressed in this way: "Woe to us if we should be found to be our own creator, inventor, and author of our own future well-being. The first command in the Bible says: 'Eat!' and the final one says: 'Come, all is ready.'"[5]

No text has so shaped Christian imagination regarding the created self as Genesis 1. The signal verses address the sixth day of creation:

> Then God said, "Let us make man in our image, after our likeness. And let them have dominion over the fish of the sea and over the birds of the heavens and over the livestock and over all the earth and over every creeping thing that creeps on the earth." So God created man in his own image, in the image of God he created him; male and female he created them. And God blessed them.
>
> (Gen. 1:26-28)

Some have argued that image of God language has dominated anthropology more than is warranted; for instance, the late John Webster found this to be an instance of misproportioned theological discussion. They are right to observe that the Scriptures speak of the self and of human existence in many ways other than use of image language, but they overreact if they do not also acknowledge the canonical primacy of Genesis 1 as an entryway and, therefore, as a focal image for discerning humanity in a scriptural shape. Image language is not the whole, but it does persist rightly as a crucial reference point.

Committing to beginning with the image is not the same as grasping the meaning of that commitment, however, and four approaches have dominated Christian reflection through the centuries. First, classical Christians tended overwhelmingly to identify the image with that faculty that most closely resembles God and most notably differentiates humans from animals, speaking either of the intellect or of the soul. Like Aristotle, then, they speak of the image identifying human creatures as rational animals. Second, Luther and others have agreed that the image bespeaks closeness to God and differentiation from all other animals,

---

5. J. G. Hamann, Letter to F. H. Jacobi (December 5, 1784), in *Briefwechsel,* vol. 5 (ed. A. Henkel; Wiesenbaden:Insel-Verlag, 1965), 275 lines 26-8.

but they viewed it as pertaining to moral agency and holy character. Here humans are moral animals. In the last century, two more views have largely routed the field of interpretation. The third view focuses upon the proximity of image language to the commission given (in v. 26 and again in v. 28: "be fruitful and multiply and fill the earth and subdue it and have dominion over the fish of the sea and over the birds of the heavens and over every living thing that moves on the earth"). Humans image God by ruling creatively on his behalf as a sort of ambassador; this third view treats human images of God as political or creative animals. Fourth, Karl Barth and then Karol Wojtyla found verse 27 to be most definitive: sexual differentiation and unity marks out the relational being that mirrors the inter-Trinitarian life that God enjoys from all eternity. Sexual relations typify most powerfully what is true more broadly: humans are relational animals in this approach.

Each of these views can offer arguments, some strong. And each emphasis connects with something valid about human existence: humans are intellectual, moral, political, and relational, and each of these facets of human being and action are of theological significance. Yet none of that need imply that these as a whole or in part represent what the language of image is meant to connote. It may well be that these are valid doctrines drawn wrongly from this particular biblical imagery. They might be probed for their textual validity: for instance, does the proximity of image language and the commission or mandate necessarily mean they are equated? They might be probed for the way they seem to suggest that these emphases differentiate humans from other animals: Are other animals really lacking each of these facets of life (say, relationality)? They must also be probed for the way in which each one parses humanity and fixes itself upon a sliver of the self as image of God, whereas Genesis 1 seems to speak of the whole human as God's own image and likeness.

What might we conclude? Anna Williams says that "one of the definitive features of Christian anthropology is that it declines to define humanity in solely human terms."[6] What does she mean? More importantly, what's the significance of such a refusal to be so defined? If humans are first named as an image, then they are always and ever defined by reference to someone else. They are an echo, never existent and never understandable apart from their originary source. To be the image of God, first and foremost, ought to evoke a sense of dependence in human beings. The image is not the original; the image is a copy or likeness of that source (whether it is a priceless portrait being imaged on a cheap postcard *or* it is an eternally self-existent God being imaged by a created being like a man or woman). When we speak of image and likeness, then, we ought to begin with the distinction between God and human creatures, and we do well to focus on how we live rightly before God as those who are not themselves God.

Rowan Williams has argued that Augustine pointed in similar directions regarding human selfhood:

6. A. N. Williams, *The Divine Sense: The Intellect in Patristic Theology* (Cambridge: Cambridge University Press, 2007), 6.

Growing into the image of God, then, is not a matter of perfecting our possession of certain qualities held in common with God ... We come to "image" God by grasping that our reality exists solely within his activity of imparting ... The image of God in us might be said to entail a movement into our createdness, because that is a movement into God's own life as turned "outwards."[7]

Eric Johnson has spoken of "active receptivity" in this regard, and David Kelsey has lauded the call to "eccentric existence."[8] Expressed variously, as images we live before God in a manner that reflects something of him via our dependence upon him.

The Second Aspect: The Crooked Self (Numbers 14)

We begin with the famous words of Virginia Woolf: "On or about December 1910 human character changed." She referred to Roger Fry's exhibition "Manet and the Post-Impressionists" at the Grafton Galleries in London, a controversial exhibit that opened that November and represented a new world bereft of the old class system, the old economy, and the old sense of manners and customs. That exhibit represented something decisive to Woolf's imagination (at least in a symbolic fashion). December 1910 aside, Christians do believe that particular dates do lead to changes in human character; thus, we speak of the state of humanity in Adam (e.g., Rom. 5:12-21). The fall into sin that is retold in Gen. 3:1-7 decisively alters the human condition.

How might this crooked self be understood? A range of texts present themselves as viable pathways: Gen. 3:16-19 presents the curse; Genesis 4-11 widen the cosmic range of sin's consequence; Exod. 32:1-6 recounts the golden calf incident which will be employed later as a paradigm for Israel's sin (e.g., Deut. 9:8-29); Psalm 14 laments the worldwide condition of depravity; Psalm 51 poignantly presents the Psalmist's confession of his own sin and need for redemption; Rom. 3:9-20 (and really 1:18-3:20 as a whole) condemns all, Gentiles and Jews alike, as unrighteous before God's law.

The apostles repeatedly turn to the wilderness generation, however, in shaping the Christian imagination. 1 Cor. 10:1-22 speaks of those who knew God's liberating love but were eventually "overthrown in the wilderness" (10:5). Heb.

---

7. Rowan Williams, "Sapientia: Wisdom and the Trinitarian Relations," in *On Augustine* (London: Bloomsbury, 2016), 175; see also: "We image the divine wisdom to the extent that our self-perception is a perception of our own absolute dependence on the self-giving of that wisdom: to the extent that we see when we look at ourselves is freely generative grace," and "the image is a 'movement into our createdness'" (181).

8. Eric Johnson, *God and Soul Care: The Therapeutic Resources of the Christian Faith* (Downers Grove, IL: IVP Academic, 2017), 88–9. Some similar gestures are found in Kelsey, *Eccentric Existence*.

3:7-19 builds on earlier teaching that Jesus excels Moses by reminding the Hebrew Christians of those who were "unable to enter his rest" (3:18). Christians are to be just and faithful pilgrims, and the wilderness generation serves as an emblem of sinfulness of which we ought to be wary.

Where do we learn about this wilderness generation's sin? Every Pentateuchal book speaks of sin, from the golden calf in Exodus 32 to the Nadab and Abihu episode in Leviticus 10. The book of Numbers, however, offers a lengthy, organized portrayal of human sin. Here the exodus generation dies, and their children are born for entrance into the promised land; Dennis Olson refers to its movement as the "death of the old and the birth of the new." This transition does not merely happen, however, but is explained and necessitated by a sequence of failures on the part of Israelites.[9] David Stubbs has observed the way in which Numbers presents these ten failures by fixing on seven instances. Whereas seven days of creation bring order and blessing the world in Gen. 1:1-2:4, here seven episodes of sin instance devolution and the movement to disorder in the middle section of Numbers (from 10:11-25:18).[10] Further, the seven episodes of sin appear in the form of a chiasm: the first and seventh pertain to varied misfortunes (11:1-3 and 21:4-9), the second and sixth relate to the absence of food and water (11:4-34 and 20:2-13), the third and fifth address the leadership of Moses (and later Aaron) (11:35-12:16 and 16:1-17:11), and the fourth sits there alone at the center as a sin regarding the call to enter the promised land (13:1-14:45).[11]

Numbers 14 represents the very center of that wayward generation's wandering from God. Stubbs observes: "This fourth rebellion is the crux of Israel's rebellions in the wilderness. It forms the center of the sevenfold pattern of Israel's unfaithfulness toward God in Numbers, it is the longest of the rebellions, and it is the most serious, both in terms of the offense against God and the punishment given in response to it."[12]

God tells Moses that twelve spies ought to be sent into Canaan, the land which "I am giving to the people of Israel" (13:1). The spies were selected and commissioned, and they returned after forty days in that promised land (13:25). They returned to Moses, Aaron, and all the congregation with a report—two really. The majority report of ten spies affirmed the fruitfulness and appeal of the land but observed the size and fortifications of its occupants (13:27-29); when Caleb called the people to go and occupy the land, the majority report warned against such

9. Dennis T. Olson, *The Death of the Old and the Birth of the New: The Framework of the Book of Numbers and the Pentateuch* (Brown Judaic Studies 71; Chico, CA: Scholars, 1996).

10. David Stubbs, *Numbers* (Brazos Theological Commentary on the Bible; Grand Rapids, MI: Brazos, 2009), 22–3. Stubbs also observes that the first section of Numbers (1:1-10:10) twice employs the phrase "at the command of the Lord" seven times (in chs. 3–4 and again in ch. 9) thus "underscoring Israel's obedience" and contrasting with the later rebellions (25).

11. Stubbs, *Numbers*, 113.

12. Stubbs, *Numbers*, 126.

action: "We are not able to go up against the people, for they are stronger than we are" (13:31). The congregation cried out and wept and "grumbled against Moses and Aaron," calling for a new leader and a return to Egypt (14:1).

Moses and Aaron fell at such words. At this point Joshua and Caleb presented the minority report from the spy expedition, affirming the goodness of the land, acknowledging the size of its occupants, and articulating reasons for hope: "If the Lord delights in us, he will bring us into this land and give it to us" (14:8). Their reason for this hope is singularly theological: "the Lord is with us; do not fear them" (14:9). The people went to stone Joshua and Caleb, at which point God intervenes. God chastises the people and calls for their destruction (14:11-12). Moses intervenes with prayer, however, and calls for God's forbearance (14:13-19). The Lord promises pardon and yet pledges that this generation will die in the wilderness and their children alone will be given the promised land (14:20-38). Moses gave this report to the congregation, who "mourned greatly" (14:39). They then insisted, even against Moses's warning, to go up the next morning and attack the Amalekites and Canaanites. Though Moses told them that the Ark and he would not go with them, they went and were roundly defeated (14:45).

Chapter 14 seems to tell of two sins. The first sin appears in the people's refusal to go up and take the land and further their insistence that they better appoint new leaders to guide their return to Egypt. Their justification is offered: "Why is the Lord bringing us into this land, to fall by the sword? Our wives and our little ones will become a prey. Would it not be better for us to go back to Egypt?" (14:3-4) Their punishment will bring poetic justice in that only those "little ones" will eventually be brought into the land. And why are they judged? They sin by omission, refusing to obey God's call. Caleb and Joshua identified the root issue in their failed warning: "Only do not rebel against the Lord. And do not fear the people of the land" (14:9).

The second sin could not appear more different, as it marks a sin of commission. Having received news of God's judgment and their fate, the people initially "mourned greatly" (14:39). That initially promising move was following by their assertive action. They rise early, they go up to the heights, and they declare "here we are. We will go up" (14:40). Even when Moses warns that "the Lord will not be with you" (14:43), "they presumed to go up" (14:44). Here they sin by commission, doing that which they have been warned not to do. And here the issue is identified as presumption or overconfidence, an arrogant swagger that leads them into a futile overexertion.

While there are two distinct sins that appear divergent, other texts look back and find a common root. Deuteronomy 1 recounts the episode (1:19-46) and fixes upon the issue of trust: "in spite of this word you did not believe the Lord your God" (1:32). Hebrews 3 employs this generation as a warning (3:7-19) and identifies the reason for their failure: "So we see that they were unable to enter because of unbelief" (3:19). Both texts point to belief or trust as the central issue. They do so because trust is written right into the assessment of Numbers 14 itself. When God gloriously intervenes, he says: "How long will this people despise me? And how long will they not believe in me, in spite of all the signs that I have done among them?" (14:11) Though God's mighty works have shown him to be trustworthy, they do not trust him. And this is not merely true of the first error but also definitive of the second sin, for their response reveals a misperception of God's rebuke. They have received his judgment as though the problem was an underdeveloped sense of self-esteem. Whereas God's convicting words pertain to how they despise and disbelieve him, they nowise evince any concern for or awareness of his importance to them. They do not imagine his presence to be definitive; they gauge their prospects solely on their own strength, whether it leads them to despairing hesitation or prompts them to presumptive overexertion.[13]

What have we gleaned about sin and crookedness? Dennis Olson says: "In the end, the issue is not competing estimates about the human strength of the Israelite army versus the Canaanites. The question is not who is taller or who has larger fortifications or who has more weapons. Ultimately, all such reliance on human power and estimates is irrelevant. The issue is trusting in the power of Israel's God."[14] Augustine of Hippo helps here to remind us of a truth that is easily missed: "All those who wander far away and set themselves up against you are imitating you, but in a perverse way; yet by this very mimicry they proclaim that you are the Creator of the whole of nature and that in consequence there is no place whatever where we can hide from your presence."[15] Genesis referred to humans as the image of God after the fall (5:3; 9:6), but this continued reality does not mean that humans continue to be a good or valid image. By refusing to lean into God trustingly, humans image God poorly. "Whether in pride or despair, the old wilderness generation failed to learn the fundamental lesson of the first commandment—to fear, love, and trust God above anything else."[16] With their self-enclosed estimation of future prospects, both small and great, they portray or reflect an image of God that is inept or disengaged. Hence the image of Augustine and later Luther that the self here is bent crooked and becomes curved in upon itself, incapable and frankly disinterested in looking outward for direction and sustenance.[17] Sin varies, as the distinct moments of Numbers 14 signal, but it always somehow mangles that way we are made for "active receptivity."

---

13. This self-definition also masks honesty about dependence on others or minimizes its value; see such an argument presented powerfully in Jean-Jacques Rousseau, *Reveries of the Solitary Walker* (trans. Peter France; New York: Penguin, 2004), 104.

14. Dennis T. Olson, *Numbers* (Interpretation; Louisville, KY: Westminster John Knox, 1996), 80 (also 86).

15. Augustine, *Confessions*, Book 2, Section 14.

16. Olson, *Numbers*, 89.

17. See the analysis of Matt Jenson, *The Gravity of Sin: Augustine, Luther and Barth on Homo Incurvatus in Se* (London: T&T Clark, 2006); Kelsey, 1:432.

The Third Aspect: The Resurrected Self (Galatians 2)

The story of humanity does not end with enmity. God intervenes.

> And you were dead in the trespasses and sins in which you once walked, following the course of this world, following the prince of the power of the air, the spirit that is now at work in the sons of disobedience—among whom we all once lived in the passions of our flesh, carrying out the desires of the body and the mind, and were by nature children of wrath, like the rest of mankind. But God, being with in mercy, because of the great love with which he loved us, even when we were dead in our trespasses, made us alive together with Christ.
>
> (Eph. 2:1-5)

Life and resurrection come from God's generous, omnipotent hand. The Adamic self is followed by the Christian self.

A host of texts depict the Christian self, that is, the self that is united to Jesus Christ: Mt. 5:2-11 portrays the one whose character marks them out as a child of God (5:9), while Jn 15:1-11 speaks of the way in which fruitfulness, love, and joy are experienced only in abiding in Christ; Hebrews will reflect at length in chapters 5-10 on access, even boldness and confidence, that can be had in and through Jesus; and Paul repeatedly takes up the language of union with Christ in a variety of prepositional constructions.[18]

If we want to grasp the strange logic of the gospel, however, perhaps no text focuses attention upon the transformative impact of union with Christ and widens one's grasp of its cosmic implications as Gal. 2:15-20.

> We ourselves are Jews by birth and not Gentile sinners; yet we know that a person is not justified by works of the law but through faith in Jesus Christ, so we also have believed in Christ Jesus, in order to be justified by faith in Christ and not by works of the law, because by works of the law no one will be justified. But if, in our endeavor to be justified in Christ, we too were found to be sinners, is Christ then a servant of sin? Certainly not! For if I rebuild what I tore down, I prove myself to be a transgressor. For through the law I died to the law, so that I might live to God. I have been crucified with Christ. It is no longer I who live, but Christ who lives in me. And the life I now live in the flesh I live by faith in the Son of God, who loved me and gave himself for me.

The context must be observed. Paul has told of the Antioch Incident where the apostle Peter recoiled from table fellowship with Gentile believers when a party appeared from Jerusalem (2:12). His example was followed by "the rest of the

---

18. The recent literature is voluminous. On the issues involved, I especially recommend Grant Macaskill, *Union with Christ in the New Testament* (Oxford: Oxford University Press, 2013).

Jews ... even Barnabus" (2:13). Interestingly, Paul repeatedly terms this behavior "hypocrisy," for it is a public relapse that veers from the normal practice of Peter, Barnabus, and the Jews who typically shared a table with these Gentiles (2x in 2:13). Paul will turn to more fundamental issues to address this cafeteria dispute, but it is in fact the cafeteria dispute that he addresses. The matter involves identity and belonging: are these Gentile converts one with the Jews like Peter? More fundamentally, though, it is a Christological question: is union with Jesus Christ enough to make a way to unite these diverse persons and to overturn those social and cultic divides?

Paul invokes language of justification, the declaration of justice before God, to address those matters of identity. But he also turns emphatically to Christology which is the root of justification anyways; solus Christus ("Christ alone") is always the root of sola fide ("by faith alone") in Protestant theology. And what does he say of Christ and his pertinence for human beings? 2:19-20 fixes attention upon the transforming consequence of life in Christ in two ways: displacing our dying self, and resurrecting our Christian self. First, Paul employs repeated language of displacement: "through the law I died to the law" (2:19); "I have been crucified with Christ" (2:20); and, finally, "it is no longer I who live" (2:20). Law leads to death—we share accursed death with Christ (as his own death—not some metaphor or analogous experience—is our own), so that, in the end, the "I" who lives is no longer "I." Second, Paul uses repetitive statements of agency and action: "so that I might live to God" (2:19); "it is ... Christ who lives in me" (2:20); and "the life I now live in the flesh I live by faith in the Son of God" (2:20).[19] Jonathan Linebaugh emphasizes the relational character of displacement and reorientation, that is, of death and resurrection, by observing the movement from dative syntax to the employment of personal terms and prepositions:

> According to Paul's grammar, death and life are not abstract or absolute concepts, they are relative—or better: relational. In Galatians 2:19, life and death are first defined with the dative: death is death to the law and life is life to God. As the confession continues, prepositions color in these relations christologically: Christ died for me (*hyper emou*), which is itself the concrete gift (Gal 2:21) that grounds and includes my having been crucified with (*syn*) Christ and on the far side of which "Christ lives in me (en emoi)."[20]

---

19. See Jonathan Linebaugh, "The Christo-Centrism of Faith in Christ: Martin Luther's Reading of Galatians 2:16, 19–20," *New Testament Studies* 59, no. 4 (2013): 535–44; as well as "'The Speech of the Dead': Identifying the No Longer and Now Living 'I' of Galatians 2.20," *New Testament Studies* 66, no. 1 (2020): 87–105; and Michael Allen, "'It Is No Longer I Who Live': Christ's Faith and Christian Faith," *Journal of Reformed Theology* (2013): 3–26.

20. Linebaugh, "The Speech of the Dead," 95–96; see also Susan Eastman, *Paul and the Person: Reframing Paul's Anthropology* (Grand Rapids, MI: Eerdmans, 2017), 160.

The setting shows the subversive impact of that union upon all other realities. How many other identity-defining matters could be added to the ones in play here? Leaving to the side more grotesque variants such as racism or sexism, more insidious demands can subtly seep into church potlucks. Use of the right Bible translation, keeping of the right liturgical calendar or Sabbath-keeping regimen, "getting the gospel," expressing some particular demeanor (whether of simple reverence or of celebratory jubilation) in worship, being appropriately gospel-centered, etc. Galatians will later speak of the relativizing impact of Christ Jesus:

> In Christ Jesus you are all sons of God, through faith. For as many of you as were baptized into Christ have put on Christ. There is neither Jew nor Greek, there is neither slave nor free, there is no male and female, for you are all one in Christ Jesus. And if you are Christ's, then you are Abraham's offspring, heirs according to promise.
>
> (Gal. 3:26-29)

The experiential distinctions between male and female and slave and free are significant. But that first distinction stands singularly at the head: "neither Jew nor Greek." It not only leads the litany of 3:28 but also represents the key example in 2:11-21. What so significant? Misogyny or patriarchy shifts male power in ways detrimental to women, and slave economies powerfully lead to the exploitation of the many by the few. But neither misogyny nor slavery is mandated by God. The Jew–Gentile distinction, however, was a divinely mandated distinction rooted in God's electing call (Gen. 12:1) and God's covenantal promise (Gen. 17:8; see the exposition in Gal. 4:21-31 of the Sarah and Hagar story in Genesis). God made a distinction, electing some and passing over others, thereby predestining some to life and consigning others to death. The reason the Jew–Gentile distinction lingers throughout so many New Testaments texts as a matter for judgment and prudence is that it is a social divide of divine origin. It is not happenstance or mere cultural preference. While it could be clouded by pride or sin, it is not itself birthed of or sustained by sinfulness.

And yet God relativizes or, better, fulfills it in Jesus Christ. The culinary regimen of Moses and the hygienic rituals of Abraham no longer mark out those in and out. Why? Because we share in Christ by faith, in his death we die and in his life we live. In his death all our identities—success and failure, spirituality and social markers—are crucified. In his life all our person—righteousness and blessing, belonging and purpose—is birthed anew. There is substitution here (see especially Gal. 3:10-12), but there is also incorporative union.

Many things might and should be said of resurrected life in Christ, but we have focused upon the fundamental way in which union with Christ reorients the human to life extrinsically. So is the Christian self the same self from creation? Is there continuity or utter disjunction? Linebaugh concludes:

> No: death and life divide the no longer and now living I and the life of the latter is gifted, ex-centric, and in Christ. But also yes: though I no longer live, there is

a me that is ever and always loved. To speak "the speech of the dead," is seems, is to talk twice: life and death and death and life separate the self. And yet, in and across the passages of creation, sin, grace, and glory there is a me that was and is and will be loved. To combine the confession: I am—outside myself, by grace, and in Christ a me whom God did, does, and will ever love.[21]

Augustine and Martin Luther employed the image of the human who had been curved in on itself in sin now being drawn outward again.[22] The self here has been not only directed to but connected with the death and life and, therefore, the blessing of Jesus.

The Fourth Aspect: The Transfigured Self (Song of Songs 4 and 7)

We might be inclined to think that closing with Christ concludes the sequence. In all sorts of ways, of course, it does, and yet other Scriptures will speak in ways that go beyond the displacing and reorienting language of Galatians 2. Jesus foretells of the commendation given the Lord's own in the words of a parable: the master declaring "well done, good and faithful servant" eventually prompts his eschatological prophecy that the King will invite those "blessed of my Father" to "inherit the kingdom prepared for you" and will extol their generosity and self-forgetful care for the least among them (Mt. 25:23 and 31-40); not surprisingly in his sojourn on earth, Jesus himself would prize the generosity of the widow giving her mite (Mk 12:21-24; Lk. 21:1-4) or the faith of the centurion (Lk. 7:9) or the confession of Peter (Mt. 16:17) or the single-mindedness of Mary (Lk.10:42). The particular character and specific actions of humans are cause for praise, from the lips of God on the throne and God incarnate in his earthly sojourn.

Delight and celebration in Song of Songs perhaps press this notion further than any other text. Before considering particular passages in the Song, its broader place in the canon deserves mention. The Song of Songs is titled in such a way to evoke the wonder that this is the greatest of all such songs (just as "holy of holies" is the holiest place, so "song of songs" means that this song is better still than the Psalms and all the rest of scriptural hymnody). Through the ages, Jews and Christians have been able to say that with a straight face only because they believed this tale of lover, her beloved, and their varied friends or townsfolk ultimately figures the love of the people of God and God himself or, more specifically, of the bride of Christ

---

21. Linebaugh, "The Speech of the Dead," 105.

22. On the relationship of the two figures, see especially Jenson, *The Gravity of Sin*, 95-7; *contra* Anders Nygren, *Agape and Eros* (trans. Philip S. Watson; New York: Harper & Row, 1969), 48, 108, 210, 235–6, 253, and 264; and Philip Cary, *The Meaning of Protestant Theology: Luther, Augustine, and the Gospel That Gives Us Christ* (Grand Rapids, MI: Baker Academic, 2019), *passim*.

and Christ himself. Various other texts employ this marital and erotic imagery in negative ways (see Hosea) and positive evocations (see Eph. 5:32). The Song of Songs works with this marital and sexual figure at great length.

In that frame, then, it is not surprising that the lover speaks of her beloved and his beauty. At points it may seem foreign or lead the reader to blush, but it makes all the sense in the world that the figure of the church should praise her Lord and redeemer. But that's not all that the Song includes. The Song also recounts twice the delight that the Christ figure takes in the bride (Song 4:1-16; 6:13-7:10). Again modern ears may be thrown by the comparisons ("your teeth are like a flock of shorn ewes" [4:2] or "your belly is a heap of wheat, encircled with lilies" [7:2]), but many may be more startled at the very acclamation itself. It is one needful thing to say "I am my beloved's and he is mine" (6:3; also 2:16), but a sufficient reading must also confess "I am my beloved's, and *his desire* is for me" (7:10). He desires the bride, and he recounts with brilliant detail what draws him to her in her particularity and specificity. God does not merely graciously agree to tolerate humans but delights in their created forms.

That divine delight startles, so we need to be changed to receive it as wise and appropriate. In his treatise *On Loving God*, Bernard of Clairvaux spoke of the love of God as involving four stages or degrees of growth and maturation.[23] First, one loves oneself for one's own sake. Second, one loves God for one's own sake; here God is loved, but instrumentally or for the purpose of something—oneself— that one deems higher. With the third degree, Bernard speaks of the sweetness of salvation in that one can now love God for his own sake, not for his utility in scratching some other itch. God is here viewed as the prize and the treasured possession. And yet this is not where Bernard stops, but he goes on to speak of that final degree of the love of God wherein one loves oneself for God's own sake. Here the fear of the Lord not only redirects our religious life or the way we view our relationship to God, but it comes to have primacy in all areas of life (most especially one's self-image or self-perception). Whatever my own love of myself may be, it ought to always be for God's sake or not at all.[24] But, viewed inversely, for God's sake I'm meant to have an appreciative and thankful delight for who I have been made and re-made to be.

"Although, therefore, Christ offers us in the gospel a present fullness of spiritual benefits, the enjoyment thereof ever lies hidden under the guardianship of hope, until, having put off corruptible flesh, we be transfigured in the glory of him who goes before us."[25] Those words come from John Calvin, not from a desert father. Note that the Genevan reformer turns to the language of transfiguration here,

---

23. Bernard of Clairvaux, *On Loving God*, trans. Jean Leclerq and Henri Rochais (Kalamazoo, MI: Cistercian Publications, 1973).

24. Bernard here takes up a tradition from Peter Lombard (on signs and things) that goes all the way back to Augustine of Hippo, first in *On Christian Teaching* and then in *City of God*.

25. John Calvin, *Institutes of the Christian Religion*, II.ix.3 (1:426).

not that of transubstantiation, as he describes the fullness of blessing that is ours now. God's presence yoked to the Christian self involves its radiant indwelling and transfiguring illumination, not its transfer to some other category of being. As with transfiguration, the substance of the human remains definitively human—the image of God, human nature, natural law, each of these tent-posts of definitive human shape remain intact. Unlike transubstantiation, the human form does not mask something miraculously other and divergent or heterogeneous in its character; while the soul is invisible, the sanctified soul does not morph into anything other than a human soul. As with transfiguration, the human bears witness to the presence of something greater than itself, the very indwelling of God's own Holy Spirit conforming the human unto the creaturely image of God's own Son. Unlike transubstantiation, "Christ in you, the hope of glory" does not entail mixture with the divine or ontological exchange of any sort. Personal union—the stuff of covenant and of communion—marks the sanctified life, and here we see that, adapting the words of the Psalmist, grace and nature meet, the indwelling of God and the definitive shape of human nature (first in Adam and then eventually in Jesus himself) kiss each other.[26]

Concluding Implications for Further Reflection

From where have we have come? To where might we be going? Each of these four aspects has bearing on the present experience of Christians today, a point with which we ought to conclude. Each plays a role in identifying who we are, albeit in distinct ways. We do well not to shoehorn identity language into only one of these, whether that's toward creational or Christological aspects. To identify a self with its textured specificity will require all of these elements, if it is to be whole. That said, noting the importance of breadth is merely a prompt for further exploration about how to relate to each aspect. Other questions arise only when we appreciate the biblical and theological breadth by which the self is identified and described—when is one aspect pertinent? how do they relate? while it is helpful to identify all four aspects, in what ways do we relate to each of them? in what situations is someone out of tune or unaware of one or another aspect in particular?—and warrant our consideration. Christian reflection on the self needs to continue, as it has for centuries now. In conclusion, I suggest two implications.

First, we ought to be wary of supposed Augustinian anthropology gone reductive. There is a narrowed Augustinianism that views the human simply through the prism of sin and misses that other element: created goodness. Against the Pelagians, Augustine did confess that every nook and cranny of our selves has

---

26. These last sentences are taken from Michael Allen, "Grace and Nature," in *Sanctification* (New Studies in Dogmatics; Grand Rapids, MI: Zondervan Academic, 2017), 225.

been depraved or disordered by sin and death. Sin cannot be confined, and its spread cannot be segmented and regimented.

Augustine also spoke of sin as a privation precisely because he wanted to avoid lapsing into Manichean dualism. He insisted that we remain creatures of the living God. Depravity and disorder do not unwind or reverse the results of God's kind action, however much they turn it sideways. Some take this privative approach to sin to lack existential bite, but it is precisely the existence of the good disordered that actually makes sin so heinous (i.e., the abusive parent is so jarring because parents are such a good and, in this case, so mangled). We dare not reduce Augustinian anthropology to a misanthropic word. Augustine affirms the goodness of creation in the present tense alongside the extensiveness of sin, and our current reflections on the self must be alert to both duties.

Augustinian teaching on goodness without his anti-Pelagian reflection about depravity leads to a vapid affirmation and an inability to challenge the status quo or appreciate our need for salvation. But Augustinian hamartiology without a corresponding appreciation of the beauty and regnant goodness of creation now actually undermines the shrill nature of sin and death and refuses to offer thanks and praise to God for his good gifts to which even our most sinful efforts cannot give defeat.

<u>Second</u>, we need be equally concerned about reductive views of Christology that treat the redemptive change wrought in Christ wholly through its justifying or substitutionary aspects. Indeed, there is a need for a wider grasp of new creation as well, wherein our identity is wholly caught up in union with Christ and our life, peace, and power are drawn entirely from his self, yes, but also where our created and natural specificity is transfigured in him to be worthy of praise (even from God's own lips). We cannot confess any less than both the justifying words of Christological union from Galatians 2 as well as the divine delight in his bride as found in Song of Songs 4 and 7.

The church has a mission to offer care to souls, those already inside and those presently outside, by speaking words of life and comfort and peace in Christ alone. Systematic theology helps us to discern how we might do so without removing Christ from the wider scriptural context (taking creation and sin into account as well) or delimiting Christ by failing to see all that he is and does (attending not only to justification but also to that other gospel gift: transformation unto glory). Christ assumes our plight, walks our path, dies our cursed death, and rises for our glory and blessing. He is substitute and our most defining characteristic, so that we not only enjoy his riches but also bear his very name. And yet he also sings over us in the particularities that he, with his Father and Spirit, created and then recreated by his gracious power. We boast only in him, but he does take delight in regaling the glories of his work in us (not just that which binds us together as one, but also that which marks off our distinct and particular histories and intricacies).

Created giftedness is no antique epoch. Sinfulness is pervasive, to be sure, but not the sum total of our anthropology. Christological definition is in fact definitive, but it opens the way to divine delight in our created, transformed, and someday transfigured particularities. To sum up: we dare not homogenize humanity or reductively confess the gracious work of Christ. If we are going to diagnose and care well for souls, we need to know their various aspects. To appreciate how Christian identity is made, we need attentiveness to the distinct, biblical sources of the Christian self.

Chapter 11

THE CHURCH AND THE CHURCHES:
A DOGMATIC ESSAY ON ECCLESIAL INVISIBILITY

Toward a Dogmatic Ecclesiology
of Ecumenical Expectations

Contemporary discussions of ecclesiology and ecumenism have integrated a variety of disciplinary concerns, suggesting the importance of sociohistorical, politico-ideological, even economic methods of investigation.[1] At their most influential moments, recent ecumenical discussions have lingered graciously in careful thought over matters of ecclesial practice and, in particular, liturgical formation amongst the varied ecclesiastical communions. Thus documents like the World Council of Churches' Faith and Order Commission's justifiably well-noted "Baptism, Eucharist, and Ministry" have tailored the ecumenical enterprise along cultural–linguistic lines. Following theorists like Alasdair MacIntyre and George Lindbeck, Ludwig Wittgenstein, and Clifford Geertz, the commonalities and differences of practice within varied denominations and churches have been the focus of relatively traditional ecumenical efforts.

In a different vein, however, have been the ideological pursuits of radical inclusivity within the mainline denominations and amongst minority factions of other communions. In these situations, ecumenism has followed the path of broader cultural engagement: relativism and tolerance have been brandished as moral commonplaces for the embrace and encouragement of a bevy of sociocultural and indeed ecclesiastical practices and professions. Oftentimes the inclusivist agenda has been (sub)merged within the aesthetics, or even the participatory ontology, of the (to all appearances) traditional ecumenical concerns noted above. Whether couched in terms of sacramental and ministerial praxis or in the incarnational extension of the *assumptio carnis*, to contemporary ecclesiastical embrace of varied sexualities and liturgical pluralisms, ecumenical theory has been driven toward visible points of contact. These tangible commonplaces may be inherently ecclesiastical (liturgical) or generically cultural (tolerance, inclusivism), yet they

1. Many thanks to Prof. Henri Blocher for his gracious comments.

pursue the conversational task of ecumenical reflection (oftentimes strictly) with reference to the visible actions of the churches.[2]

A dogmatic theology of the Church involves an approach befitting its object of study: investigation of the particular shape which the community of those gathered by and around the Word of God takes in the economy of triune grace.[3] That this investigation limits itself to consideration of the people of the Word (rather than some phenomenological category) further implies that dogmatic ecclesiology will critically appropriate the confessional understanding of Scripture for the sake of testifying to the Church which the Gospel creates. My task, then, will be to sketch a dogmatic account of the Church and the churches. This sketch will focus on the question of Christian unity in light of the observable splintering of the institutions and contexts tied to Christendom. In so doing, four *foci* will be considered: the doctrine of God, the economy of salvation, eschatology, and the relation of true and false churches to the Church. My goal will be to suggest the dogmatic necessity of the invisible Church within ecclesiology and note the effects of such a doctrine for assessing denominational divisions and the place of ecumenism within the salvific economy. The present chapter will proceed from the confessional texts of the post-Reformation Reformed tradition, thereby sketching what ecumenical expectations might be dogmatically appropriate within this particular confessional context.

The Church of the Transcendent and Triune God

The Church lives in the space provided by God. That God makes space for the Church's life entails the distinction of God and Church. Just as God and world must be distinguished by the doctrine of *creatio ex nihilo*,[4] so also the Church and the triune God are differentiated by the doctrines of calling, vocation, and election (Eph. 2.10). The Church's life and the divine life cannot be identified or merged.[5] The life of God freely precedes and exists independently of the causal activities of the people of God.[6] The unceasing freedom of the Lord finds ultimate expression

2. For an excellent survey of recent literature on the integration of sociological analysis (particularly of the communitarian style) and contemporary ecclesiology, see Stanley J. Grenz, "Ecclesiology," in *The Cambridge Companion to Postmodern Theology* (Cambridge Companions to Religion; ed. Kevin J. Vanhoozer; Cambridge: Cambridge University Press, 2003), 252–68.

3. John Webster, "On Evangelical Ecclesiology," in *Confessing God: Essays in Christian Dogmatics II* (London: T&T Clark, 2005), 153–4.

4. Janet Martin Soskice, "Athens and Jerusalem, Alexandria and Edessa: Is there a Metaphysics of Scripture?" *IJST* 8, no. 2 (2006): 153.

5. *contra* Henri De Lubac, *Catholicism: Christ and the Common Destiny of Man* (trans. Lancelot Sheppard and Elizabeth Englund; San Francisco, CA: Ignatius, 1988), 53, 73, 82, 88, 127, 196.

6. Webster, "On Evangelical Ecclesiology," 156–8.

in the claim that the incarnate Son of God did not circumscribe the life of the second person of the Trinity.[7] Even more so, the "body of Christ" does not directly, nor extensively, represent the Son's identity.[8]

The Church does live, however, and this must be attributed solely to the determination of God's Word to shape this community.[9] Therefore, the life of the Church and the divine life must be asymmetrically ordered as speaker and listener.[10] That the Word precedes and provides in no way violates the freedom of the Church as a communal agent (e.g., reader and preacher of God's Word; celebrant of Eucharistic feast). Rather, the transcendence of God qualitatively distinguishes the action of God and this God's people such that ontological competition cannot occur.[11] The Spirit mediates the Word through these graced activities: mortifying and vivifying in exegesis and proclamation, sanctifying the common elements for union with Christ in the sacraments. As David Willis puts it, "Holiness is not the opposite of creatureliness, but is the right use of creatureliness."[12] God makes the Church holy, thereby perfecting her concrete life as uniquely formed for fellowship in Christ.

A dogmatic account of the Church's life, therefore, must attend to the ontological shape of the creaturely life of God's people, given by the transcendent Lord of grace. Such metaphysical clarification follows from the logic intrinsic to the Scriptural accounts of the triune God's self-revelation (Exod. 3.14; Isa. 46.5, 9-10).[13] The implicit ontological judgments necessitated by such texts must precede and qualify later considerations of ecclesiology, lest the Church somehow occlude the place of Christ himself.[14]

7. E. David Willis, *Calvin's Catholic Christology: The Function of the So-Called* Extra Calvinisticum *in Calvin's Theology* (Studies in Medieval and Reformation Thought 2; Leiden: E. J. Brill, 1966), 26–60.

8. Ian A. McFarland, "The Body of Christ: Rethinking a Classic Ecclesiological Model," *IJST* 7, no. 3 (2005): 244–5. cf. Karl Barth, *Church Dogmatics* IV/1: 667–8 (hereafter *CD*).

9. Webster, "On Evangelical Ecclesiology," 154.

10. John Webster, "Christ, Church, and Reconciliation," in *Word and Church: Essays in Christian Dogmatics* (Edinburgh: T&T Clark, 2001), 228; Christoph Schwöbel, "The Creature of the Word: Recovering the Ecclesiology of the Reformers," in *On Being the Church: Essays on the Christian Community* (ed. Colin E. Gunton and Daniel W. Hardy; Edinburgh: T&T Clark, 1989), 122; Martin Luther, *WA* 8:491.

11. Kathryn Tanner, *Jesus, Humanity, and the Trinity: A Brief Systematic Theology* (Minneapolis, MN: Fortress, 2001), 2–4.

12. David Willis, *Notes on the Holiness of God* (Grand Rapids, MI: Eerdmans, 2002), 48.

13. Matthew Levering, *Scripture and Metaphysics: Aquinas and the Renewal of Trinitarian Theology* (Challenges in Contemporary Theology; Oxford: Blackwell, 2004), 47–74; Brevard S. Childs, *Exodus: A Critical, Theological Commentary* (OTL; Louisville, KY: Westminster, 1974), 83; *pace* R. Kendall Soulen, "ʏʜᴡʜ the Triune God," *Modern Theology* 15 (1999): 34.

14. Tanner, *Jesus, Humanity, and the Trinity*, 20–1; Webster, "On Evangelical Ecclesiology," 179; Douglas Farrow, *Ascension and Ecclesia: On the Significance of the Doctrine of the Ascension for Ecclesiology and Christian Cosmology* (Grand Rapids, MI: Eerdmans, 1999), 259; *pace* de Lubac, *Catholicism*, 53 (but see 363).

The Church of the Electing God

That the Church is distinct from the world follows only from the freedom of God's election unto fellowship with sinners through the Word (Jn 17.14). Her common elements are sanctified by God's actualizing call, wherein the divine declaration sets apart that which is culturally and historically natural for distinctly supernatural ends.[15] That the Church participates in the economy of salvation, therefore, involves the Church in the covenantal relation of Lord and servant, as well as the eschatological sublimation of nature in the beginning by grace at the end. Grace neither destroys, nor merely perfects nature; rather, grace perfects nature through a disruptive event which must be classified as mortification and vivification.[16] Not only ecclesiology more broadly, but the churchly fellowship considered under the rubric of ecumenism remains tethered to God's sanctification of a people. The unity of the Church beckoned forth by Jesus in prayer (Jn 17.21-22) follows the pursuit of ecclesial sanctification (Jn 17.17, 19). However this unity is to be considered must be tied to the manner in which Jesus's sanctification involves that of his people.

Dogmatic ecclesiology, therefore, requires that the Church be considered not only subsequent to Trinitarian orthodoxy (in the vein of Nicaea), but soteriological orthodoxy (as clarified in the Protestant confessions). Differences between Roman Catholicism, Eastern Orthodoxy, liberal *Kulturprotestantismus*, and confessional evangelicalism flow through the doctrine of salvation (e.g., justification) to the nature of mediation in the Church (e.g., sacraments, authority).[17] The shape of soteriology, then, affects the concrete life of the Church and suggests the manner by which communal existence will form around the Word. A Reformed soteriology which emphasizes the continuing integrity of humanity and created nature, even in the *hypostatic* union, will restrict speech about the Church's life in nature-appropriate ways (*finitum non capax infiniti*).[18]

---

15. Karl Barth, "The Real Church," *SJT* 3, no. 3 (1950): 341–2.

16. George Hunsinger, "Baptized into Christ's Death: Karl Barth and the Future of Roman Catholic Theology," in *Disruptive Grace: Studies in the Theology of Karl Barth* (Grand Rapids, MI: Eerdmans, 2000), 269–70; Colin E. Gunton, "Creation: (2) The Spirit Moved Over the Face of the Waters. The Holy Spirit and the Created Order," in *Father, Son, and Holy Spirit: Essays toward a Fully Trinitarian Theology* (London: T&T Clark, 2003), 109–110, 112, 118; *pace* de Lubac, *Catholicism*, 283–4.

17. Willis, *Notes on the Holiness of God*, 94: For example, Roman Catholic doctrine supplants the true humanity of the sacramental elements and, similarly, the Church by their participation in the divine movement (deification or *theopoeisis*). In this way, neither transubstantiation nor papal infallibility takes the creaturely nature of the *communio sanctorum* seriously enough; *contra* de Lubac, *Catholicism*, 286.

18. Adrienne Dengerinck Chaplin, "The Invisible and the Sublime: From Participation to Reconciliation," in *Radical Orthodoxy and the Reformed Tradition: Creation, Covenant, and Participation* (ed. James K. A. Smith and James H. Olthuis; Grand Rapids, MI: Baker Academic, 2005), 90–1, 104; *pace* de Lubac, *Catholicism*, 211.

The Church will not be burdened with divine tasks, nor will the sanctifying calling out of these people be withdrawn from its broader redemptive–historical context.[19] The Church exists as people elected for service, marked only by God's mortifying and vivifying speech, *simul iustus et peccator*. The creaturely being of the redeemed people has been assumed in Christ and glorified in his raising; the inclusion of the saints in this vicarious identity grounds the self-effacing nature of the Church's Gospel, as well as her attestation. The Church in the economy of divine grace finds justification *solus Christus*, thereby mandating an extension of the material principle of the Reformation into extensive ecclesiological qualification and restraint.[20]

The Wandering Church

The Church wanders from bondage in sin and death to the awaited city of God.[21] That her life is marked by pilgrim expectations, *simul iustus et peccator*, suggests that her constitution may be particularly difficult to discern in concrete history. The battle for assurance of personal salvation may be paralleled by the quest for discernment of the Church's true visible unity; true fellowship is "hid with Christ in God" (Col. 3.3).[22] Such epistemological caution is not in vogue within the recent ecumenical and ecclesiological literature. In fact, the distinction between the visible and invisible Church has been lambasted as of late, by Roman Catholic and mainline ecclesiologies which have proposed a patently visible Church or none at all.[23] From Bonhoeffer's worries during the Nazi era, to the pleas of narrative theologians of hope during the tumultuous Sixties, to the bold anti-secular posturing of the Radical Orthodoxy movement, the invisibility of the Church has been denounced as a flight from responsibility and reality to sectarianism

---

19. Westminster Confession of Faith xxviii.3; see Michael Horton, "Participation and Covenant," in *Radical Orthodoxy and the Reformed Tradition*, 129–32; George Hunsinger, "Fides Christo Formata: Luther, Barth, and the Joint Declaration," in *The Gospel of Justification in Christ: Where Does the Church Stand Today?* (ed. Wayne C. Stumme; Grand Rapids, MI: Eerdmans, 2006), 77–8.

20. Suggestions of this in Calvin, *Institutes*, IV.i.21, 27. Calvin helpfully notes the fittingness of confessing "forgiveness of sins" immediately after confession of the "communion of saints." See Gerhard O. Forde, "The Word That Kills and Makes Alive," in *Marks of the Body of Christ* (ed. Carl E. Braaten and Robert W. Jenson; Grand Rapids, MI: Eerdmans, 1999), 1; *pace* de Lubac, *Catholicism*, 226.

21. First Helvetic Confession xi; see Augustine, *City of God*, I.35.

22. G. C. Berkouwer, *The Church* (Studies in Dogmatics; trans. James E. Davison; Grand Rapids, MI: Eerdmans, 1976), 178–82.

23. de Lubac remains a notable exception (to some extent); see *Catholicism*, 72, 273, 292, 363 (but see 53).

and fantasy.[24] Rather than recede into some idyllic realm of ecclesial remove, the Church's concrete practices have been the ontological and pastoral focus of recent ecumenical efforts.[25]

Yet the Church of the Word cannot accept such terms and allow ecclesial definition to proceed in an immanent fashion, for the Word which makes alive must first kill.[26] That the Spirit continually inspires the life of the Church around the Word in no way minimizes the need for the Spirit's illumination of proper acknowledgment of the Church and Word. The visibility of the Church, therefore, involves what John Webster has called a "spiritual visibility."[27] That is, her true manifestation cannot be considered an universally perceptible truth available to all.[28] Quite to the contrary, the Nicene marks of the Church confess *belief*, not observation, of the Church's life as one, holy, catholic, and apostolic. The Spirit alone makes known the Church's veiled glory.

The invisible Church lives as a concrete people veiled by the flesh and made visible in the Spirit. That is, the Church's invisibility is an epistemological limitation.[29] Is it merely an epistemological principle? The Westminster Larger Catechism defines the invisible Church as "the whole number of the elect, that have been, are, or shall be gathered into one under Christ the head."[30] This definition distinguishes these elect members of Christ ontologically—as those gathered to live united in Christ—privileging the ontic over the noetic.[31] The actual number composing the Church visibly and invisibly differs, because the visible Church as mixed multitude includes the elect and those who profess faith, but already have or yet will fail to persevere in faithfulness. At this point the argument for invisibility by Barth falls short, insofar as he fails to ground adequately the epistemic invisibility in an ontic reality under the rubric of divine election/predestination. The provisional communion of the reprobate within the *communio sanctorum* marks the primary need for a doctrine of the invisible Church—the elect only to be revealed in definitive fashion at the eschatological judgment—which Barth shies from, apart

24. Dietrich Bonhoeffer, *Discipleship* (Minneapolis, MN: Fortress, 2001), 113; Robert Jenson, *Systematic Theology* (2 vols.; New York: Oxford University Press, 1997–1999), 1:205–6; 2:211–227; John Milbank, *The Word Made Strange: Theology, Language, Culture* (Oxford: Blackwell, 1997), 159–65.

25. See, e.g., James J. Buckley and David S. Yeago, eds., *Knowing the Triune God: The Work of the Spirit in the Practices of the Church* (Grand Rapids, MI: Eerdmans, 2001), 8; see the recent criticisms by Nicholas Healy, "Practices and the New Ecclesiology: Misplaced Concreteness?" *IJST* 5 (2003): 287–308.

26. Forde, "The Word That Kills and Makes Alive," 11–12.

27. Webster, "On Evangelical Ecclesiology," 175, 179; Barth, *CD* IV/1: 654.

28. Barth, "The Real Church," 338–40; idem, *CD* IV/1: 654.

29. Webster, "On Evangelical Ecclesiology," 181–2.

30. Westminster Larger Catechism 64.

31. *pace* John Murray, "The Church: Its Definition in Terms of 'Visible' and 'Invisible' Invalid," in *Collected Writings of John Murray*, vol. 1: *The Claims of Truth* (Edinburgh: Banner of Truth Trust, 1976), 231.

from relatively reticent admissions of divine providence. Only secondarily does the invisibility of the Church serve to highlight the sinful-yet-justified nature of the Church's witness, wherein even the truly redeemed are less than patently obedient in their attestation. Care in distinguishing these two uses of the doctrine—as well as maintenance of both—will be necessary in addressing the quest for true unity.

Invisibility marks the life of the Church due to her eschatological placement (Jn 17.11).[32] That the triune God has made space for her being in the wake of Christ's passion and with anticipation for his glorious return marks her life with unfulfilled expectation. Christ's vindication has been distinguished as "first fruits" from the long-awaited resurrection of those in Christ (1 Cor. 15.23).[33] Thus the New Covenant promises have yet to be enacted in their fullness, leaving the makeup of the Church mixed rather than a strictly regenerated membership.[34] This eschatological context leads G. C. Berkower to claim that "the continuity of the Church becomes visible in hope."[35] The eschatological invisibility of the Church, therefore, extends ecclesiology along the principle of *sola fide*.

Yet the invisible Church resides in the visible Church, partaking of the ordinary "means of grace" found in her consecrated ministry of the Word.[36] Ontological passivity—dependence upon the life-giving Spirit—cannot be likened to phenomenological laxity, nor can it facilitate a docetic ecclesiology which spiritualizes the material by abolishing it.[37] The spiritual character of the Church works through creaturely mediation, attestations which hearken in human voice and symbolic testimony. Even champions of the invisibility of the Church affirm the mandate to vigorously work for the purification of the visible churches.[38]

Her concrete life, however, can never be ascribed metaphysical necessity, for her life follows from God's election. That is, the Nicene Creed confesses *credo ecclesium*: "I believe the Church," rather than "I believe *in* the Church."[39] This

---

32. Forde, "The Word That Kills and Makes Alive," 2; Douglas Farrow, "Eucharist, Eschatology, and Ethics," in *The Future as God's Gift: Explorations in Christian Eschatology* (ed. David Fergusson and Marcel Sarot; Edinburgh: T&T Clark, 2000), 205, 214; idem, *Ascension and Ecclesia*, 3.

33. Colin E. Gunton, "The Church and the Lord's Supper: 'Until He Comes.' Towards an Eschatology of Church Membership," in *Father, Son, and Holy Spirit*, 224.

34. Calvin, *Institutes of the Christian Religion*, IV.i.13; on the partial fulfillment of the "new covenant" promises of Jeremiah 31, see Richard L. Pratt, Jr., "Infant Baptism in the New Covenant," in *The Case for Covenantal Infant Baptism* (ed. Gregg Strawbridge; Phillipsburg, NJ: Presbyterian & Reformed, 2003), 168-9; *pace* Henri Blocher, "Old Covenant, New Covenant," in *Always Reforming: Explorations in Systematic Theology* (ed. A. T. B. McGowan; Leicester: Apollos, 2006), 247-8.

35. Berkouwer, *The Church*, 194.

36. Westminster Shorter Catechism 88; Westminster Larger Catechism 35, 153-4; Westminster Confession of Faith xxvii.3; Calvin, *Institutes*, IV.i.4-5.

37. Tanner, *Jesus, Humanity, and the Trinity*, 71-3.

38. Belgic Confession, xxviii; Barth, *CD* IV/1: 653-4; Calvin, *Institutes*, IV.i.7.

39. Berkouwer, *The Church*, 10; Calvin, *Institutes*, IV.i.2.

dogmatic point simply affirms the sanctification of this creaturely company for divine use in the ministry of reconciliation (2 Cor. 5.18ff.). As with the spiritual presence of Christ in the visible words of washing and feasting, so the ecclesial life will be only spiritually discerned because eschatologically limited: as Christ is absent from the table physically (because ascended physically), so the Church will fail to evidence concrete obedience in any perfect or unceasing measure.[40]

The Invisible Church, True Church, and False Churches

The Church enlivened by the Spirit of the Word transgresses all sociocultural boundaries (Gal. 3.28; Eph. 2.11-22). Communion enjoyed by those gathered around the pulpit, table, and font involves fellowship with fellow saints across the globe and through the centuries (the *communio sanctorum*). Yet the typical observer will see anything but joyful fellowship among those within the churches of the twenty-first century. Denominations abound; proselytism continues; anathemas remain. A theology of the Church must address the concrete plethora of churches.

The invisibility of the Church does not directly solve the dilemma of relating at institutional levels, for the invisibility applies primarily to individuals within churches.[41] Contrary to some Lutheran renditions of the invisibility doctrine, its purpose is primarily to note the presence of a mixed multitude within the people of God and only secondarily to distinguish the just activities of the Church amidst the enduring sinfulness of the as-yet-not-fully-redeemed saints.[42] Yet the invisibility of the Church does affect the life of the churches and therefore dogmatically precedes consideration of the true Church and the false churches. That there are churches does not necessarily reflect sinful failure to maintain unity, except when such multiplicity reflects differences other than geographical diversity.[43] Disunity for reasons of petty difference, scandal, or (worse yet) theological division reflect failures to appropriately maintain Christian communion. Thus the Reformers and their confessional heirs sought to note the marks which characterize the life of a true, though perhaps less than ideal, Church in hopes of identifying the churches with which one ought to fellowship.

The true marks of the Church are the preaching and reception of the pure Word of God and the right administration of the two sacraments.[44] Later confessional

---

40. Barth, *CD* IV/1: 662.

41. Scots Confession xvi.

42. Calvin, *Institutes*, IV.i.7; Westminster Confession of Faith xx.1; First Helvetic Confession xvii; *pace* I. U. Dalferth, "The Visible and the Invisible: Luther's Legacy of a Theological Theology," in *England and Germany: Studies in Theological Diplomacy* (Studies in the Intercultural History of Christianity; ed. S. W. Sykes; Bern: Peter Lang, 1982), 33–7.

43. Barth, *CD* IV/1: 671; see Second Helvetic Confession xvii.

44. Second Helvetic Confession xvii; Westminster Confession of Faith xxvii.4.

documents and orthodox dogmatics included the appropriate exercise of church discipline as a third mark; however, this was likely included within the Word and sacraments in earlier formulations and ought be seen as an expansion for clarification, rather than addition of an alien principle.[45] Nevertheless, these marks do not remove the invisibility of the Church. Rather, they are touchstones by which the visible Church might be tested and found acceptable as an instrument and witness of the Gospel.[46]

Thus the invisibility of the Church must be adequately acknowledged— not removed—in each of its two manifestations, albeit differently.[47] Regarding individual hypocrisy, church discipline can and must be enacted faithfully; yet such efforts, no matter how well-intentioned, will never remove all hypocrisy from the Church.[48] Only the eschatological judge, Jesus Christ, will decisively separate the righteous from the unrighteous (Mt. 13.24-30, 47-58).[49] Similarly, regarding ecclesial sinfulness amidst the life of even the righteous, hidden behind facades of flesh and failure, the Church can and must listen to the Word and allow her witness—in Word and sacrament—to be tested by the Gospel (*semper reformanda*). False churches will be shunned, such that the Church may be unified gradually, imperfectly, but concretely in some fashion through the varied lives of the true churches. That is, the division of churches into true and false may incrementally aid the quest for unity by making explicit the grounds for true fellowship, adequate witness to the Gospel. The most difficult decisions will undoubtedly involve the provisional judgments about varying degrees of faithfulness to the Word and different levels of failure to rightly administer the sacraments.[50] Such witness will certainly remain "daily advancing," though imperfect and visible only to the eyes of faith, and in so doing be on the pilgrim path of holiness.[51]

45. Heinrich Heppe, *Reformed Dogmatics* (ed. E. T. Bizer; trans. G. T. Thomson; London: Wakeman Trust, nd), 668–70; see also Scots Confession xviii; Belgic Confession xxix.

46. "Touchstone" (*ad Lydium lapidem*) comes from Calvin, *Institutes*, IV.i.11.

47. For careful response to both individual hypocrisy and institutional apostasy, see Belgic Confession xxix.

48. Heppe, *Reformed Dogmatics*, 666–7.

49. Calvin, *Institutes*, IV.i.13.

50. On the notion of such degrees, see Westminster Confession of Faith xxvii.4–5; Calvin, *Institutes*, IV.ii.8.

51. Calvin, *Institutes*, IV.i.17.

Chapter 12

THE GOSPEL AND THE CATHOLIC CHURCH RECONSIDERED

Introduction

"We find ourselves in a situation so fundamentally shaped by modernity and its doctrine of the free individual that the individual subject now stands even at the center of what passes for ecclesiology."[1] If these words by Gary Badcock seem plausible, albeit depressing, we do well to ask how we might move the needle regarding an ecclesiology that is a bit more extroverted or centered-outside oneself. We should specifically ask: How might we think church as an element of the gospel? Michael Ramsey influentially related the church to the mystery of the gospel and, in so doing, made a series of notable claims about its catholicity.[2] Most bluntly, "The fact of Christ includes the fact of the Church. And this is not a novel speculation added to the original Gospel; it springs from that Gospel."[3] Indeed, "The history of the Church and the lives of the saints are acts of the biography of the Messiah."[4] Similarly, E. L. Mascall sought to identify the church with the ongoing implications of the incarnation of the Son of God, thereby relating the vocation and identity of the church with that of the Christ himself.

Prompted by the chapter "The Spirit and the Bride" in Michael Horton's recent volume, *Rediscovering the Holy Spirit*, this chapter examines ways in which the accounts of Ramsey and Mascall need to be filled out further: (1) according to a more variegated or broad account of the gospel economy that rightly moves from incarnation to ascension and Pentecost as well and (2) with attention to the economic and exegetical particularity through which Christ and church are coordinated and united. In this regard Horton's concerns can and should be heard alongside that of Robert Sherman and John Webster as we seek a dogmatic

---

1. Gary Badcock, *The House Where God Lives: Renewing the Doctrine of the Church for Today* (Grand Rapids, MI: Eerdmans, 2009), 291.

2. Michael Ramsey, *The Gospel and the Catholic Church* (London: Longmans, Green, and Co., 1936; repr. Peabody, MA: Hendrickson, 2009).

3. Ramsey, *Gospel and the Catholic Church*, 30.

4. Ramsey, *Gospel and the Catholic Church*, 31.

approach that honors the watchwords of breadth and particularity in seeking to think the relationship of the gospel and the Catholic Church anew.[5]

Michael Ramsey: The Gospel and the Catholic Church

The former archbishop of Canterbury Michael Ramsey sought to relate the church's life and order to the gospel itself, more specifically, tying order and episcopacy to the death and resurrection of the Messiah. By examining the first several chapters in his startling book *The Gospel and the Catholic Church*, we can see how he located the church Christologically and even messianically.

How is this link established? Not from afar. Ramsey begins:

> The death and the Church—the one has sprung from the other. Yet the connection is closer still. For it seems not only that Christ creates the Church by dying and rising again, but that within Him and especially within His death and resurrection the Church is actually present. We must search for the fact of the Church not beyond Calvary or Easter but within them.[6]

He will shortly thereafter speak of the Cross in two startling ways. First, death means "death to the self qua self, first in Christ and then in the disciples," and this "is the ground and essence of the Church."[7] Second, "the Cross is to him not a

---

5. Significant ecclesiological accounts from Reformed theologians since the work of Ramsey and Mascall would prominently include G. C. Berkouwer, *The Church* (trans. James E. Davison; Grand Rapids, MI: Eerdmans, 1976); J. A. Van Den Ven, *Ecclesiology in Context* (Grand Rapids, MI: Eerdmans, 1996); Paul Avis, *The Church in the Theology of the Reformers* (London: Marshall, Morgan, & Scott, 1981); Christoph Schwöbel, "The Creature of the Word: Recovering the Ecclesiology of the Reformers," in *On Being the Church: Essays on the Christian Community* (ed. Colin Gunton and Dan Hardy; Edinburgh: T&T Clark, 1989), 110–55; John Webster, "The Self-Organizing Power of the Gospel of Christ: Episcopacy and Community Formation," and "Christ, Church, and Reconciliation," in *Word and Church: Essays in Christian Dogmatics* (Edinburgh: T&T Clark, 2001), 191–210 and 211–32; John Webster, "On Evangelical Ecclesiology," in *Confessing God: Essays in Christian Dogmatics II* (London: T&T Clark, 2005), 153–94; John Webster, "In the Society of God: Some Principles of Ecclesiology," in *God without Measure: Working Papers in Christian Theology*, vol. 1: *God and the Works of God* (London: T&T Clark, 2015), 177–94; Michael Horton, *People and Place: A Covenant Ecclesiology* (Louisville, KY: Westminster John Knox, 2008); Hans-Peter Großhans, *Die Kirche—irdische Raum der Wahrheit des Evangeliums* (Leipzig: Evangelische Verlagsanstalt, 2003); Gary Badcock, *The House Where God Lives*; Robert Sherman, *Covenant, Community, and the Spirit: A Trinitarian Theology of Church* (Grand Rapids, MI; Baker Academic, 2015).

6. Ramsey, *Gospel and the Catholic Church*, 17.

7. Ramsey, *Gospel and the Catholic Church*, 22.

defeat needing the resurrection to reverse it, but rather a victory so decisive that the resurrection follows quickly to seal it."[8] He expounds this cruciform victory as "exalting on the cross" which matches and can "hardly seem separate" from the "exalting to heaven."[9]

Ramsey will turn then to language of indwelling and of Pentecost and thereby of how "the death is still an event *outside* them; it is yet to become a happening *within* them."[10] By faith—that is, by conscious self-abegnation—Christ is "inclusive head and center of a new humanity."[11] Positively, Ramsey will speak of personal union and of participation in the Christ. Negatively, he will retort that Christianity "is never solitary" and that "individualism therefore has no place in Christianity, and Christianity verily means in extinction."[12] Stranger still, however, he claims that in extinguishing individualism, Christianity delivers the individual unto himself and that the singular Christian knows herself beloved of God in fresh and new ways. "Thus the losing and the finding are equally real. While the claim that individualism must die is unrelenting, and while Paul, Apollos, and Cephas are 'nothing,' beyond Resurrection and in the one Body they are known once more and their singleness is seen."[13]

Ramsey returns to the notion of "death to self"—which you'll remember was his gloss on the concept of Death—and will espouse the claim that "to 'believe one holy Catholic and Apostolic Church' is to die to self."[14] Odd, yes? And yet powerful, in as much as he expresses the link of faith (believing this church) to issues of apostolicity and other Nicene marks; believing the church—believing *this sort of* church—involves true death to self in Christ Jesus, further appropriating one's inclusion within his victorious death. He will then move on to discuss global unity represented everywhere by local unity, tying this to exegesis of the language of ecclesia or the "assembly."[15] This unity he expounds in the inclusive reality of the Messiah himself, in the historical events of his death and resurrection, and ultimately in the eternal will of the one God. Indeed "unity is God's alone, and in Him alone can anything on earth be said to be united."[16] Ramsey expounds this participation in God's own unity Christologically and, even more specifically, messianically in the inclusive events of Death and Resurrection.

"The outward order of the Church therefore is no indifferent matter; it is, on the contrary, of supreme importance since it is found to be related to the Church's

---

8. Ramsey, *Gospel and the Catholic Church*, 22–3; Jn 12:23 and 13:31 identify the cross with Christ's glorification, but this likely does not prompt an identification of it with his victory.

9. Ramsey, *Gospel and the Catholic Church*, 23.

10. Ramsey, *Gospel and the Catholic Church*, 26.

11. Ramsey, *Gospel and the Catholic Church*, 28, 29.

12. Ramsey, *Gospel and the Catholic Church*, 32, 33.

13. Ramsey, *Gospel and the Catholic Church*, 33.

14. Ramsey, *Gospel and the Catholic Church*, 38.

15. Ramsey, *Gospel and the Catholic Church*, 40-1.

16. Ramsey, *Gospel and the Catholic Church*, 42.

inner meaning and to the Gospel of God itself."[17] Indeed, "Every part of the Church's true order will bear witness to the one universal family of God and will point to the historic events of the Word-made-flesh."[18] Ramsey identifies three such "parts" of ecclesial order: Baptism, Eucharist, and the Apostle(s). He will then turn to further examination of liturgy, of truth and authority, and of historical survey, but it is in these first few chapters that we have seen his messianic molding of ecclesiastical order and unity. Perhaps the most interesting facet of this later exposition is his identification of the gnostic threat not merely to theology writ large but to ecclesiology in particular—what he will call the spiritual threat or the temptation of solitary Christianity—and his pressing two remedies as essential by way of reply: first, "the historical facts of Christianity" and, second, "the structure of the one Body that claims continuity with those facts."[19] Here he gestures toward a fourfold structure of Sacraments, Episcopacy, Scriptures, and Creeds, eventually espoused in the Chicago Lambeth Quadrilateral of 1886 and 1888.[20]

Ramsey's account of the church—her self lost and regained and gifted anew with unity, order, and structures—is located not merely Christologically but messianically. The focus is upon death and resurrection for Jesus Christ and all those enfolded within him. Yet one might wonder if the Christological account is broad enough: Does it fix its sights too much upon death and resurrection with rather little to speak of preexistence or of Pentecost, of life and teaching or of ascension on high? While Ramsey hints ever so briefly at moments like Pentecost, his account does narrow upon the messianic passion, indeed even at times seeming to conflate death and resurrection into a singular event of victory. Might we press further his Christological commitment without falling foul of our duty to honor its canonical range?

E. L. Mascall: Christ, Church, and the Incarnation

A contemporary of Ramsey, E. L Mascall, moves in a similarly Christological direction to describe the being of the Christian and the church.[21] Yet his account of church and her relationship to Jesus turns in a much broader direction, perhaps offering a corrective or supplement to that offered by Ramsey.

What is the key thread in this study? "The thread that unites them all is the doctrine of the permanence of the manhood of the glorified and ascended

17. Ramsey, *Gospel and the Catholic Church*, 43.

18. Ramsey, *Gospel and the Catholic Church*, 43.

19. Ramsey, *Gospel and the Catholic Church*, 48.

20. Ramsey, *Gospel and the Catholic Church*, 49; for the Chicago-Lambert Quadrilaterial, see The Episcopal Church, *The Book of Common Prayer, and Administration of the Sacraments and Other Rites and Ceremonies of the Church, Together with the Psalter or Psalms of David* (New York: Church Publishing Inc., 1979), 876–7.

21. E. L. Mascall, *Christ, the Christian, and the Church: A Study of the Incarnation and Its Consequences* (London: Longmans, Green, & Co., 1946).

Christ."[22] This theme of the permanent humanity of the heavenly Christ functions "to get beneath" common binaries in search of a synthesis; all this from the author of another notable study entitled *Via Media*.[23] Amid other pairings, such as imputation and impartation, Mascall turns to the doctrine of "incorporation into Christ," addressing its nature and its effects.[24] The Christian is adopted into Christ and thereby participates in God on High. This double incorporation sits amid a greater matrix of three unions: "The first of these is a union of persons in one substance, the second is a union of natures in one Person, the third is a union of personal beings through union of their natures."[25] Though these three unions are "altogether different in their characters," only in their interplay does incorporation into Christ mean not merely adoption into his own persona but also participation in the whole Godhead in and through him.

The Christian is incorporated, however, not only into the permanent humanity of the risen Christ but also into the realistic body of his church. "Becoming a Christian and becoming a member of the Church are synonymous; faith and baptism are conjoined."[26] Thus we turn to Paul's teaching on the church as the Body of Christ. The language sometimes situates Christ as Head over against the body, while it elsewhere identifies Christ as the body in whom members are individuals.[27] Both adoption and participation have an "analogue in the sphere of the Church," according to Mascall, such that there is not merely a set of attributes possessed by the church in Christ but also a web of relationships into which she is enfolded Christologically within the Triune being of God.[28]

How does the ascension pair with the incorporation of the church into Christ's own body? Mascall gestures in two seemingly contradictory directions. First, he affirms a strong sense in which the fullness of the church is essential not only for the inclusion of individuals but even for Christ; startlingly, he says of Christ that while "in one sense he is perfect without us; in another, he needs us for his perfection."[29] He turns to the Augustinian language of the *totus Christus* here and

22. Mascall, *Christ, the Christian, and the Church*, v.
23. E. L. Mascall, *Via Media: An Essay in Theological Synthesis* (London: Longmans, Green, & Co., 1956).
24. Mascall, *Christ, the Christian, and the Church*, 77–91 (on nature) and 92–108 (on effects).
25. Mascall, *Christ, the Christian, and the Church*, 93.
26. Mascall, *Christ, the Christian, and the Church*, 109.
27. Mascall, *Christ, the Christian, and the Church*, 110–11.
28. Mascall, *Christ, the Christian, and the Church*, 128. Engagement of debates regarding nature and grace and the shape of participation are taken up afresh on 223–7; see also E. L. Mascall, *Nature and Supernature* (London: Darton, Longman, & Todd, 1976).
29. Mascall, *Christ, the Christian, and the Church*, 120. Note the context (preceding the quote on 120): Mascall locates the imperfection within the framing of body language to speak of Christ as Body-and-Head of the body (which is still being built up), and he frames the perfection as applying specifically to Christ as Head alone of the Body (who is complete and actual in and of himself).

specifies the way in which Christ's mission is brought to completion only with the inclusion of all his brothers and sisters into his body. But this jarring word of necessity and togetherness is not the only attestation. Second, Mascall shifts to acknowledge next that "in the New Testament, side by side with the conception of the Church as Christ's Body there appears the conception of the Church as his Bride."[30] In a lengthy digression to address the character of this metaphor across Scripture, he outlines its nature as highlighting the over againstness or relational differentiation involved in linking Christ and Church not merely as soul and body but also as Bridegroom and Bride.[31]

Presumably Mascall does not mean to suggest that these emphases conflict or compete, but that they are both impelled by the biblical and theological materials (e.g., by Pauline teaching on the *soma* on the one hand and the Song of Songs and Eph. 5:23-32 on the other hand). The Christian and the Church are incorporated into Christ, thereby receiving his blessing and his triune life by grace and as creaturely and bridal counterparts to him. Hence Mascall then has to address the nature of unity further and the Eucharistic gift and symbolism of a unity not yet fully achieved.[32] Indeed his account of perfection and imperfection returns with his argument for a sacramental—even Eucharistic—piety. "The Sacramental Body is, in a quite definite sense, perfect, while the Mystical Body is not";[33] hence, feeding upon the perfect *Corpus* enables one to more fully embody him in the mystical *Corpus*.

Mascall's account does not suffer quite the strictures of Ramsey's *Gospel and the Catholic Church*. Here there is a universal concern for locating all reality to the Christ, not merely in his messianic role or his Passion but to his whole person and the full range of his works in preexistence, existence on earth, and postexistence, indeed emphasizing this risen and ascended postexistence of the still human Son in his triune glory. And yet one can still wonder if in so doing Mascall has himself loosened the Christological account from the kind of economic and exegetical specificity that, over a limited range, was the great strength of Ramsey's account? Have we sacrificed particularity for universality or at least breadth here? He has sought to affirm the Creator–creature distinction even amid a vigorous account of adoption and participation. But he has matched Ramsey's sacramental and Eucharistic piety in a directly Anglo-Catholic vein. Is that a necessary by-product of an account to think church within the gospel of Christ and incorporation therein? In light of these two vigorous accounts of relating gospel and church, we shall turn to yet another such attempt.

---

30. Mascall, *Christ, the Christian, and the Church*, 124.

31. To draw on terms from much later in his book, the first emphasis calls us to be Christocentric while the second reminds us not to thereby fall into being christoterminal (Mascall, *Christ, the Christian, and the Church*, 227).

32. Mascall, *Christ, the Christian, and the Church*, 135–7 (on unity) and 158–200 (on Eucharist).

33. Mascall, *Christ, the Christian, and the Church*, 163.

Michael Horton: "The Spirit and the Bride"

Where a churchly gospel is, must there be Anglo-Catholicism? For church to be related to the gospel of Jesus Christ, must we look to death and resurrection particularly or to incarnation generally, or might we also focus especially on the events of ascension and Pentecost? Is there a way forward that is no less Christological than these accounts but does so in a tack that honors the demands of Christological and canonical breadth on the one hand and of economic and exegetical particularity on the other hand?

Michael Horton's *Reconsidering the Holy Spirit* presents something that might be called a third-article theology.[34] In seeking to reply to those who might appropriate a strong pneumatology but thereby "failed to entail a robust ecclesiology," he first considers accounts that falsely conflate "Christ with the Spirit (and both with the church)."[35] In *la nouvelle théologie*, in Anglo-Catholicism, or even in the psychological–romanticist ecclesiology of Schleiermacher and his heirs, the Spirit is displaced because the Ascended Christ returns as the Church.[36] He then turns to radical Protestants and their pursuit of immediate individual access of the triune God: "an unmediated encounter within the individual."[37] Whether in Barth's extremism or that of the Spiritualists, "many Protestant ecclesiological assumptions today are closer to the radical than to the magisterial Reformation in spirit and substance."[38]

What intervention might help? "Once more the importance of recognizing the intersection of ascension and Pentecost becomes self-evident. Lacking pneumatological mediation, proposals such as these spiritualize Jesus, transforming the human person into a cosmic ecclesial personality."[39] But such malnourished approaches turn the spiritual experience into transubstantiation, whereby the creature is changed into the divine, rather than transfiguration, whereby the creature might be glorified as a creature incorporated into or indwelt by the divine.[40]

Horton concludes by charting a path to recovering more fully Augustine's idea of the *totus Christus*.[41] "Augustine's notion of *totus Christus* is simply another way of expressing the doctrine of union with Christ and in *De Trinitate* the Spirit is seen as essential in bringing about this union."[42] The *totus Christus* concept must be plotted

---

34. Michael Horton, "The Spirit and the Bride," in *Rediscovering the Holy Spirit: God's Perfecting Presence in Creation, Redemption, and Everyday Life* (Grand Rapids, MI: Zondervan Academic, 2017), 289–321.

35. Horton, "The Spirit and the Bride," 290.

36. Horton, "The Spirit and the Bride," 291–5.

37. Horton, "The Spirit and the Bride," 303.

38. Horton, "The Spirit and the Bride," 303.

39. Horton, "The Spirit and the Bride," 296.

40. Horton, "The Spirit and the Bride," 304.

41. Horton, "The Spirit and the Bride," 305; he offers an anatomy of modern renditions of the concept on 290–8.

42. Horton, "The Spirit and the Bride," 305.

not merely metaphysically, though Horton does affirm this, but primarily on an eschatological map.[43] Appreciating the events of ascension, Pentecost, heavenly session, and future return in glory helps to highlight the eschatological tension of life in the mystical body as well as the covenantal communication of agency and of gifts in the interim. As Horton concludes his chapter, we are reminded that "at present, the church is the bride, not yet the spouse, and as it grows it longs for the bridegroom's arrival to escort his betrothed to the wedding feast."[44]

If Reformed Protestants (and near neighbors) are going to present an argument for an ecclesiology that is not merely strategic but substantive, then they will need to locate that church within the gospel of Jesus Christ. And if they are to locate the church within the gifts of the gospel of Jesus Christ, they will need to present an account that is just as broad and equally particular as the accounts of Mascall and Ramsey, respectively. And if they wish to do so while remaining evangelical without tilting into Anglo-Catholic conflation of risen Christ and his Eucharistic Church, then they will need to frame a churchly metaphysics with a rich eschatological foundation that attends not merely to the death and resurrection but also the resurrection and postexistence of Jesus Christ, not merely his ascension and session on high but also his giving of the Spirit, not merely the sending of the church but also his personal, future return in glory from on high. Perhaps such an account might, as Horton suggests in the conclusion to his chapter, accent how "the Spirit creates an extroverted church" that not only leads away from the rank individualism of our day but beckons us into identification as nothing less than the body of the incarnate, risen, ascended, reigning, and soon to return Lord.[45]

43. Horton, "The Spirit and the Bride," 306. For my own approach to the *totus Christus* concept, see Chapter 13 in the present volume.

44. Horton, "The Spirit and the Bride," 320. Might it be that such a Reformed account of the church amidst the full economy of God's works and the eschatological path of redemptive history will give greater texture to the often pliable focus of recent decades on church as *communio*? For survey and support of that trend, see especially Robert W. Jenson, "The Church as *Communio*," in *The Catholicity of the Reformation* (ed. Carl E. Braaten and Robert W. Jenson; Grand Rapids, MI; Eerdmans, 1996), 1–12.

45. Horton, "The Spirit and the Bride," 318.

Chapter 13

TOTUS CHRISTUS AND PRAYING THE PSALMS

David Moser has sought to reclaim an Augustinian tenet for those of us who wave the banner of Reformed catholicity.[1] Even though several luminaries in the Reformed theological world have cast a suspicious eye upon the *totus Christus*, he argued that we do well to search again and reexamine whether we have grounds to shirk or subvert what may well be a biblical and genuinely catholic doctrine. Moser considers the Augustinian development of the doctrine, five most common objections from Reformed theologians, and then offers responses to each and every objection. As a Reformed catholic, I'm in broad agreement with his proposal, which isn't to say I agree with his every interpretive move. I tend to read Barth a bit differently and, therefore, to agree more with Moser's constructive point against some of what I take to be Barth's instincts. Yet I do share his instinct that recent polemical concerns regarding bloated versions of the doctrine (whether in Milbankian or Jensonian iterations) ought not reduce Reformed confession to a simple "Nein!" Moser rightly returns us to Augustine and, more specifically, to the ways in which the *totus* serves as an instrument to prompt exegetical alertness (e.g., to texts such as Acts 9:4). He is also intuiting something appropriate, I think, when suggesting that the "'mystical body' and *Totus Christus* have a common lineage with overlapping meanings," thereby showing how there's at least resonance with the concept (if not explicit attestation of it) in Reformed confessions.

In what remains, though, I want to think sideways from Moser's argument. I want to practice a classical principle—*lex orandi, lex credendi*—by inquiring how the law of devotion might help govern the law of theology. Doing so is not severed, though, from the exegetical and dogmatic elements of Moser's argument, because the liturgical element considered here is the Reformed prioritization of praying the Psalms. This practice is obviously not the unique possession of the Reformed tradition, though it has been a defining hallmark of that tradition's piety. In what remains, I will explore the hermeneutical implications of the *totus Christus* for our reading and praying of the Psalms. I will argue that the necessarily twofold character of inhabiting the voice of the Psalmist demands the concept of the *totus Christus*. To consider the topic in this vein, then, hopefully shows that the concept

---

1. David Moser, "*Totus Christus*: A Proposal for Protestant Christology and Ecclesiology," *Pro Ecclesia* 29, no. 1 (2020): 3–30.

of the *totus* serves as a crucial prompt for prayer, exegesis, and a doctrine of Christ and, perhaps especially of note, that the concept can help alert us to potential dangers or foreshortenings that can shape praying the Psalms in a less than robust manner.

The totus Christus *and Praying the Psalms*

What is the *totus Christus*? And what might be its scriptural and hermeneutical implications? Craig Carter provides an argument that can be delineated in a sequence of two discrete but related steps when he turns to the concept in what he deems the climactic chapter of his recent book *Interpreting Scripture with the Great Tradition*:

> First, "[i]f the preexistent Son can really and did really inspire David, and if David could and did really speak as a prophet of both himself and of more and better than he knew, then it is not inappropriate to see Christ in the text and to hear Christ speaking through the text."
>
> Second, "[a]nd if Christ really has in history become the head of his body the church, it cannot be impossible that the speaking head speaks for the entire body, which after all is exactly what heads normally do. And if what is said is true of the body as a whole, then it is also true for each individual who makes up a part of that body."[2]

These two steps together make up the hermeneutics of *totus Christus* in Carter's book, both rooted in the work of Augustine of Hippo. One of Augustine's longer and more significant discussions of the *totus Christus* appears in his second exposition of Psalm 30. He wrestles with Christ praying fearfully before the Father and asks how the incarnate Son might be afraid in such a way. The most telling statement is: "The Head was crying out on behalf of the members, and the Head was transfiguring the members into himself."[3] Here is language of representation and of transformation, of a priest mediating for us and a prophet challenging us. The twofold directionality of language in prayer and worship requires elaboration.

The first language leads to a sense that Christ speaks of his own experience that is singular. His way is notable enough—unique even—so as to warrant such proleptic or prophetic witness. The second way of speaking adds the way in which Christ speaks of his own experience that is owned by means of his headship of a body.

2. Craig Carter, *Interpreting Scripture with the Great Tradition: Recovering the Genius of Premodern Exegesis* (Grand Rapids, MI: Baker Academic, 2018), 208.

3. Augustine, *Expositions on the Psalms*, vol. 1: Psalms 1-32 (Works of St. Augustine for the 21st Century III/15; ed. John Rotelle; trans. Maria Boulding; Hyde Park, NY: New City, 2000), 323 (see the wider section 322–5).

He bears the cries of his body before God. Interestingly, both are prompted by learning hermeneutically from the example of Paul. The prosopological approach of Paul has been much discussed in recent years (especially in the work of Matthew Bates and Fred Sanders), but it is also noteworthy that Augustine repeatedly references Acts 9:4 in his *Expositions of the Psalms* as a prompt for Christ speaking of his body's pain as his own ("Saul, why are you persecuting *me*?").[4] They both depend upon a number of other elements which warrant mention here.

First, the *totus Christus* works retrospectively, as it were, so that prophetic precursors spoke and are speaking proleptically of the incarnational mission. Here the doctrines of preexistence and of inspiration are of signal importance. The Son exists prior to his incarnation—indeed, the Son exists prior to his announcement or prophecy. Not only does the Son exist prior to these events, however, but the Son exists eternally outside such synchronic temporality such that he acts communicatively to announce his arrival with transcendent force. Thus, the second lynchpin here is the doctrine of scriptural inspiration by the superintending work of the Holy Spirit of Christ, one significant instance of the broader work of divine providence. If he is the first and the last and the everlasting one and as he speaks personally and authoritatively through his emissaries, then David's prophecy can be his own self-bestowing presence that points beyond the immediate historical circumstance to figure a later and greater fulfillment.

Second, the *totus Christus* works participatively as well, inasmuch as the head takes up the cries of the body, even those that would not be proper to him apart from that body (to whatever extent such can be imagined). Here the doctrines of union with Christ and of priestly mediation are of greatest weight. Christ binds himself to his human subjects in assuming our flesh, form, and nature. Further, Christ takes upon himself that anointed function of ministering our prayers into the very sanctuary of God, having entered there by means of his atoning blood and serving there as our intercessor and great high priest.[5] If he is one with us in our humanity and if he has taken our griefs upon himself, then human lament and confession can be his own to bear into the ear of the Almighty.

If such is the case, then perhaps we are left with a sequence of hermeneutical prompts. First, we always ask: In what ways does this text speak prophetically and, when doing so, does it extend beyond the lifetime of David himself? Here we are asking how God speaks unto his people of what shall be, whether through outright prophecy ("Thus says the Lord") or by way of proverbial colloquialism and poetic trope. These questions are not answered in every text in the same way, though the

4. Rowan Williams has observed fourteen such references to Acts 9:4 as a principle in his Psalms expositions ("Augustine's Christology," in *On Augustine* [London: Bloomsbury, 2016], 146). I would add that his exposition of Psalm 30 introduces the text from Acts as a clarifying lens for reading that Psalm's language.

5. Jason Byassee speaks of this function as "representational" or "perhaps more strongly and biblically, mediatorial" (*Praise Seeking Understanding: Reading the Psalms with Augustine* [Radical Traditions; Grand Rapids, MI: Eerdmans, 2007], 73).

questions should be asked of every text. Second, we inquire where the voice of the psalmist speaks unto God—whether in praise or protest, lament or love—and consider further how that speech has been taken before God by Jesus himself as our great high priest and our forerunner in the heavenly places and, in doing so, how it redirects or transfigures our presumed words that we would otherwise take to God. We must read by asking both how Christ speaks from God of himself to us and how Christ speaks us unto God—both manifest mystical union and sound out the *totus Christus*.

The Theological Discipline of totus Christus

How might this go haywire and what concerns might be kept to the fore in thinking upon the *totus Christus*? The ecumenical adoption of the language has been initiated by mid-century Roman Catholic *ressourcement* in the work of *la nouvelle théologie*; that renewal project within the Roman Communion has rippled further, however, and has impacted the work of John Milbank and Radical Orthodoxy more broadly. It has also been furthered in Faith and Order discussions and memorialized in *Baptism, Eucharist, and Ministry* to some extent. More recent patristic studies have only bolstered this tendency. Over against such momentum, Reformed voices such as John Webster did express concern about the doctrine in some of its most frequent formulations, querying its ability to maintain the singularity of the incarnate Son and the operative function of the Creator-creature distinction (particularly as he saw it expressed in the project of Milbank).[6]

---

6. See a string of critical essays: John Webster, "The Self-Organizing Power of the Gospel of Christ: Episcopacy and Community Formation," in *Word and Church: Essays in Christian Dogmatics* (Edinburgh: T&T Clark, 2001), 191–210; idem, "Christ, Church and Reconciliation," in *Word and Church*, 211–31; idem, "On Evangelical Ecclesiology," in *Confessing God: Essays in Christian Dogmatics II* (London: T&T Clark, 2005), 153–94; idem, "In the Society of God': Some Principles of Ecclesiology," in *God without Measure: Working Papers in Christian Theology*, vol. 1: *God and the Works of God* (London: T&T Clark, 2015), 177–94. Other Reformed theologians writing since the rise of ecumenical ecclesiology in its recently dominant form include G. C. Berkouwer, *The Church* (trans. James E. Davison; Grand Rapids, MI: Eerdmans, 1976); J. A. Van Den Ven, *Ecclesiology in Context* (Grand Rapids, MI: Eerdmans, 1996); Paul Avis, *The Church in the Theology of the Reformers* (London: Marshall, Morgan, & Scott, 1981); Christoph Schwöbel, "The Creature of the Word: Recovering the Ecclesiology of the Reformers," in *On Being the Church: Essays on the Christian Community* (ed. Colin Gunton and Dan Hardy; Edinburgh: T&T Clark, 1989), 110–55; Michael Horton, *People and Place: A Covenant Ecclesiology* (Louisville, KY: Westminster John Knox, 2008); Hans-Peter Großhans, *Die Kirche – irdische Raum der Wahrheit des Evangeliums* (Leipzig: Evangelische Verlagsanstalt, 2003); Gary Badcock, *The House Where God Lives: Renewing the Doctrine of the Church for Today* (Grand Rapids, MI: Eerdmans, 2009); Robert Sherman, *Covenant, Community, and the Spirit: A Trinitarian Theology of Church* (Grand Rapids, MI; Baker Academic, 2015).

David Moser has helpfully itemized objections to the doctrine by recent Reformed theologians in a fivefold manner.

Yet Webster and the Reformed have not been the only ones to express such concerns, and it may be clarifying to reflect on one hesitation expressed by another observer. In his 1982 book *Resurrection: Interpreting the Easter Gospel*, Rowan Williams raised the language of the "body of Christ" at a couple junctures. In a chapter entitled "Talking to a Stranger," Williams says: "The Church is not the assembly of the disciples as a 'continuation' of Jesus but the continuing group of those engaged in dialogue with Jesus, those compelled to renew again and again their confrontation with a person who judges and calls and recreates." If that demurral sounds excessive, he then locates it amidst language of the *corpus*: "The Church may be Christ's 'Body,' the place of his presence; but it is entered precisely by the ritual encounter with his death and resurrection, by the 'turning around' which stops us struggling to interpret *his* story in the light of *ours* and presses us to interpret ourselves in the light of the Easter event." No doubt other paths come to mind, but Williams soon mentions one way in which telling one's own story can go awry if not interpreted via Christ's story: "There is a fundamental level at which I have to say, almost nonsensically, that I do not and cannot know what I want."[7]

So both the *totus Christus* and the *corpus* must be viewed in a wider frame: "The 'Body' image is one of many. We need to be cautious about any tendency to see the Church as a simple 'undialectical' extension of Christ; and … the Eucharist enshrines the dialectic by both confronting us with our victim and identifying us with him."[8] More must be said here, not less. "Christ is with the believer and beyond the believer at the same time."[9] In so doing Williams gestures at a danger in versions of the *corpus* or *totus Christus* doctrine, that is, that it simply subsumes Christ's agency into our own. The Christological account underneath such concern warrants further analysis. The critique does not foreclose development or use of the concept in Williams's Christology, but it does serve to draw out a lingering thread that warrants our attention. The *totus Christus* is meant to highlight the union of Christ and church, to be sure, without thereby undercutting the ordered differentiation ingredient in that union.

The Christology of the totus Christus *Hermeneutic: Back to Augustine for a Doctrinal Sketch*

These critical judgments are no small matter and, perhaps, they turn us back to Augustine himself to examine the underlying Christology. He wrote much but

---

7. Rowan Williams, *Resurrection: Interpreting the Easter Gospel* (Cleveland, OH: Pilgrim, 2002), 77.

8. Williams, *Resurrection*, 76. This dialectic need not and should not be restricted to the Eucharist either; the ministry of the Word and of prayer also enshrines it in spiritual practice.

9. Williams, *Resurrection*, 76.

left us no Christological treatise per se; indeed, to find further help in grasping the Christology in play throughout the *totus Christus* hermeneutics, perhaps a sideways glance at adjacent concerns will prove most helpful. Because Moser considers his reflections on the Psalms especially (appropriate given the central role *totus Christus* plays in that cycle of expositions), I will consider a rather different text wherein similar Christological material may be found. In the year 413, Augustine wrote a small work entitled *On Faith and Works* (*De fide et operibus*). He responded to some men who "think that it is wrong and even absurd that one should first be taught how to live a Christian life and then be baptized. They think rather that the sacrament of baptism should come first: the teaching concerning morals and the life of a Christian should follow afterwards."[10] As he responds to their objections, he ultimately leads us to consider not a Christian struggle but a Christological reality that draws us to the *totus Christus* and the *corpus Christi*.

Augustine begins by considering his anti-Donatist theology and arguing that this does not exclude the importance of church discipline. He realizes that his arguments about the mixed nature of the church—nominal and real congregants therein—might lead some to assume that discipline matters not. Nonetheless, "let no man interpret the passages of Holy Scripture which speak of the present or future existence of good and bad in the Church as meaning that the discipline or vigilance of the Church ought to be relaxed or dispensed with."[11] Augustine calls discipline a "merciful severity," and he insists that Jesus and the apostles were examples of pastors who disciplined their flock well.[12]

He then considers what sort of formation and instruction matters. More particularly, are morals to be taught prior to baptism or should a call to repentance be delayed until after conversion. Augustine argues that the Pentecost sermon of Peter includes a call for repentance, and that this cannot be limited to repentance from unbelief alone.[13] "Both are necessary, morals and faith, for they are mutually connected."[14] Augustine presses still further to speak of how 1 Cor. 3:11-15 and other texts shape our thinking about unrepentant sinners and their eternal fate.[15] And what of baptizing the unrepentant? "It is not we who keep them from coming to Christ: rather, we prove to them from their own lips that it is they who do not wish to come to Christ. We do not forbid them to believe in Christ, but we show them that it is they who do not want to believe in Christ."[16]

So far, perhaps so interesting as a treatise on ethics, repentance, and discipleship; however, how is this discussion relevant to the *totus Christus*? Tellingly, Augustine

---

10. Augustine, *On Faith and Works* (Ancient Christian Writers 48; trans. Gregory Lombardo; New York: Newman, 1988), 7 (I.1).

11. Augustine, *On Faith and Works*, 8 (II.3) 54 (XXVII.49).

12. Augustine, *On Faith and Works*, 9-10 (III.3-4).

13. Augustine, *On Faith and Works*, 18 (VIII.13).

14. Augustine, *On Faith and Works*, 27 (XIII.20).

15. Augustine, *On Faith and Works*, 40 (XVII.32).

16. Augustine, *On Faith and Works*, 38 (XVII.31).

says that Christology is the ultimate foundation for Christian consideration of these questions:

> This is to preach Christ: to say not only what one must believe about Christ but also how one must live who wishes to be joined to the body of Christ; to say, in fact, everything that one must believe about Christ, not only whose Son He is, from whom He takes His divinity, from whom His humanity, what things He has suffered and why, what His resurrection means to us, what is the gift of the Spirit which He has promised and given to believers, but also what kind of members, of whom He is the head, He desires, he forms, loves, sets free, and leads to eternal life and glory.[17]

Augustine applies the *totus Christus* here to proclamation. The body of Christ really is part of Christ's identity, even if not hypostatically. Why? Because as head, "He desires, he forms, loves, sets free, and leads to eternal life and glory." That the ecclesial life is part of the gospel news does not owe to human or even Christian agency in isolation, but by Christ's indwelling power this life of the ecclesiastical body does mark the identity, work, and narrative of the whole Christ. While Augustine in no way reduces Christ to the churchly body, he also insists that we reduce the church's being to her union with her Head and Redeemer.

The Corpus *and the* Totus: *toward a Conclusion*

How does this shape our embrace of the voice of Christ—the whole Christ (*totus Christus*)—in the Psalms? If Augustine has applied the doctrine of Christ and the *totus Christus* to proclamation, how might it also shape our prayer of the Psalms? The whole Christ works not only outside us but also within us by his Spirit. The whole Christ, therefore, transforms our wills and words, and the psalter's testimony to the human condition expresses just such a transfigured cry. Not all of our words can be assumed to be Christ's own as such, for we each lapse into misperceived sorrow and misdirected pleas. Yet all of our concerns can be transformed and taken up by Christ as our head, one capable not only of carrying our burden but helping to clarify its true nature (which often as not involves heightening our sense of its severity). So a thick account of words and an equally full account of the body are needed. Jason Byassee addresses the range of words here: "Christ speaks and acts *representationally*, so that later readers and followers will notice themselves in the story and will pray and confess accordingly. And ... Christ speaks and acts *transfiguratively*, so that those who speak these words and imitate these actions will themselves be changed into Christ."[18] The Psalms are our words taken by Christ to God, and they are Christ's words by which our own—those we offer

---

17. Augustine, *On Faith and Works*, 20 (IX.14).
18. Byassee, *Praise Seeking Understanding*, 75.

apart from him—are transfigured and judged. The *corpus* and *totus Christus* also require full attention that is not limited to either Christ in us or to Christ facing us. As Williams later says, "The Church is where Jesus is met, where bodily, historical grace and reconciliation are now shown, it is the 'body' of Jesus' presence; but the Church still meets Jesus as an other, a stranger; it never absorbs him into itself so that he ceases to be its lover and its judge."[19] In so doing, an Augustinian Christology helps us affirm the hermeneutical functions both of the *totus Christus* alongside the rightful worries of the Reformed and of Rowan Williams about the ascended Christ remaining a judge over our speech, not merely an emissary to take that speech before God just as it is. Such a Christological sketch of the *totus Christus* alongside the *corpus Christi* helps us to see how the principle helps guide a hallmark of catholic and of Reformed piety in a distinctly Christ-centered key.

19. Williams, *Resurrection*, 95. Augustine does emphasize the way in which the *totus Christus* conveys the benefits of salvation already—hence he shifts the verb tense of transfiguration from Paul's future to the perfect tense (Phil. 3:21)—yet this does not negate the fact that we also continue as pilgrims awaiting the "passing" to full conformity of our selves and our cries with God's own in Christ (see Kimberly F. Baker, "*Transfiguravit in se*: The Sacramentality of Augustine's Doctrine of the *Totus Christus*," in *Studia Patristica LXX*, vol. 18 St. Augustine and His Opponents [ed. Markus Vinzent; Leuven: Peeters, 2013], 559–67).

ACKNOWLEDGMENTS

Chapter 1 appeared previously as "The Central Dogma: Order and Principles for Reformed Catholicity," *Reformed Faith & Practice* 3, no. 3 (December 2018): 4–20.

Chapter 2 appeared previously as "Exodus 3 after the Hellenization Thesis," *Journal of Theological Interpretation* 3, no. 2 (2009): 179–96.

Chapter 3 appeared previously as "Exodus 3," in Michael Allen (ed.), *Theological Commentary: Evangelical Perspectives* (London: T&T Clark, 2011), 25–40.

Chapter 4 appeared previously as "Divine Fullness: A Dogmatic Sketch," *Reformed Faith and Practice* 1, no. 1 (May 2016): 5–18.

Chapter 5 appeared previously as "The Triune God," in Douglas Sweeney and Daniel Treier (eds.), *Hearing and Doing the Word: The Drama of Evangelical Hermeneutics* (London: T&T Clark, 2021).

Chapter 6 appeared previously as "Eternal Generation after Barth," in Fred Sanders and Scott Swain (eds.), *Retrieving Eternal Generation* (Grand Rapids, MI: Zondervan Academic, 2017), 226–40.

Chapter 7 appeared previously as "Christ," in Keith Johnson and David Lauber (eds.), *T&T Clark Companion to the Doctrine of Sin* (London: T&T Clark, 2016), 451–66.

Chapter 8, co-authored with Scott R. Swain, appeared previously as "The Obedience of the Eternal Son," *International Journal of Systematic Theology* 15, no. 2 (2013): 114–34.

Chapter 9 appeared previously as "Into the Family of God: Creation, Covenant, and the Genesis of Life with God," *Trinity Journal* 39NS (2018): 181–98.

Chapter 10 appeared previously as "Sources of the Self: The Distinct Makings of the Christian Identity," *Reformed Faith & Practice* 5, no. 1 (2020): 19–36.

Chapter 11 appeared previously as "The Church and the Churches: A Dogmatic Essay on Ecclesial Invisibility," *European Journal of Theology* 16, no. 2 (2007): 113–19.

Chapter 13 appeared previously as "*Totus Christus* and Praying the Psalms," *Pro Ecclesia* 29, no. 1 (2020): 45–52.

Thanks to the various publishers, journals, and editors for help and for permission to reprint.

INDEX

external cognitive principle (*principium
    cognoscendi externum*) 9–10
extra Calvinisticum 99n5

faith, causal character of 140–1, 147
faithfulness 59
fall into sin 153
false churches 172, 173
familial love 135
fear of the Lord 161
federal theology 92
fellowship with God 134, 137, 144–5
feminist theology 75–6
Feuerbach, Ludwig 19
Fiddes, Paul 69
filiation 92
filioque 121n44
finitum non capax infiniti 168
Fishbane, Michael 32
fittingness 96–7, 107
Ford, David 63n63
forgiveness of sins 169n20
forma Dei 110
forma servi 110, 120
freedom, leads to worship 50
Fry, Roger 153
fullness 52
fullness before God 53, 59–60
fullness by God 53, 57–9
fullness from God 53, 55–7
fullness in God 53–5

Gaffin, Richard B. Jr 11n23
Gavrilyuk, Paul 18–19
Geertz, Clifford 165
general revelation 114n20
Genesis, moral foundations in 133
Gilson, Etienne 17, 20–1, 44
glory of God 5, 95
glory through suffering 96
God
    aseity of 6–7, 54–5
    fullness of 8–9, 13–14, 51–62
    glory of 95–6
    holiness of ix
    and human history 39
    immutability of 24, 25n27
    incomprehensibility of 26
    life in himself 54, 66, 68

as love 68
nearness of 44, 50
as rich in mercy 55, 58
simplicity of 25, 44
sovereignty of 11
transcendence of 40, 44–5, 46, 50
God-centered focus viii, 4
Gorman, Michael 11
Gospel of John 113, 116
Gospel of Mark 113
Gowan, Donald 32, 43, 47
grace upon grace 56–7
Gregory of Nazianzus 110
Gregory of Nyssa 17, 75, 89n19, 93
Grenz, Stanley 73
Gunton, Colin 21, 67

Haidt, Jonathan 131
Harnack, Adolf von 20, 83
Hays, Richard 91
Hegel, G. F. W. 39
Heidegger, Martin 17
Hellenization thesis 17–22, 31–3, 51, 69
Hilary 123
historical retrieval vii
historicist Trinitarianisms x
holiness 49–50, 142, 147–8
Holy Spirit
    creates extroverted church 182
    movement in missions and processions
        121n44
Horton, Michael x, 175, 181–2
humanity, fourfold state of 150
Hunsinger, George 109n2
hypocrisy 173
hypostatic union 99, 107

I AM WHO I AM 7, 39, 42, 139
identity ix
identity politics 76
illumination 12
image of God 136, 151–3, 156
immaculate conception of Mary 105n21
immanent Trinity 66–7, 114
incarnation viii–ix, 12, 108n24
incorporation into Christ 179
individualism 177, 182
internal cognitive principle (*principium
    cognoscendi internum*) 10

CPSIA information can be obtained
at www.ICGtesting.com
Printed in the USA
LVHW040140240223
740259LV00012B/1221